Business Strategy

An Introduction

David Campbell

Senior Lecturer in Strategic Management

George Stonehouse

Principal Lecturer in Strategic Management

Bill Houston

Senior Lecturer in Strategic Management

Contributing authors
Harry Robinson (Principal Lecturer in Marketing)
Alex Appleby (Senior Lecturer in Operations Management)
Dr H. C. Andersen (Senior Lecturer in Marketing)
Sharon Mavin (Senior Lecturer in Human Resource Management and Development)

Newcastle Business School
The University of Northumbria at Newcastle
Newcastle upon Tyne, UK

BUTTERWORTH HEINEMANN

OXFORD AUCKLAND BOSTON JOHANNESBURG MELBOURNE NEW DELHI

Butterworth-Heinemann
Linacre House, Jordan Hill, Oxford OX2 8DP
225 Wildwood Avenue, Woburn, MA 01801-2041
A division of Reed Educational and Professional Publishing Ltd

R A member of the Reed Elsevier plc group

First published 1999
Reprinted 2000, 2001

British Library Cataloguing in Publication Data
Campbell, David
  Business Strategy: An introduction
  1. Business planning 2. Strategic planning
  I. Title II. Stonehouse, George III. Houston, Bill, *1928–*
  658.4'012

ISBN 0 7506 4207 6

For information on all Butterworth-Heinemann publications
visit our website at www.bh.com

Typeset by Avocet Typeset, Brill, Aylesbury, Bucks
Printed and bound in Great Britain

FOR EVERY TITLE THAT WE PUBLISH, BUTTERWORTH-HEINEMANN
WILL PAY FOR BTCV TO PLANT AND CARE FOR A TREE.

Contents

Key concept index

Acknowledgements

The authors would like to thank those colleagues who have generously contributed material to this text. All are faculty members at Newcastle Business School:

Harry Robinson – Case: Cardiff Car Components Ltd and Chapter 5;
Alex Appleby – Chapter 12;
Dr H. C. Andersen – Case: Dansk Tyggegummi Fabrik A/S;
Sharon Mavin – Case: Homebase.

Part I

An introduction to the strategic process

Why do we refer to business strategy as a *process*? The answer is that it is never a once and for all event – it goes on and on. There is a need to continually review strategic objectives because the environment is always changing. The purpose of strategy is to make a business fit into its environment. By achieving this, the probability that it will survive and prosper is enhanced.

Furthermore, strategy is a process because it contains distinct 'stages' – three in all:

1 Strategic analysis
2 Strategic selection
3 Strategic implementation and management.

Strategic analysis

The purpose of strategic analysis is to gather information. None of us would be wise to make an important decision about anything in life without adequate and relevant information, and neither would a business.

There are two main stages in strategic analysis. Firstly, strategic analysis involves an examination of an organization's internal environment (*internal analysis*). This takes the form of a thorough analysis of the internal processes and structures of a business in much the same way as a doctor might carry out a thorough medical examination on a person. The purpose

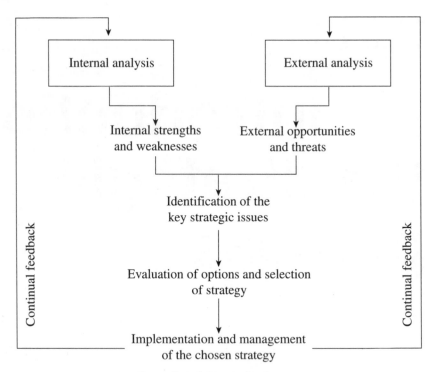

A schematic of the strategic process

of internal analysis is to establish what the organization is good at (its strengths) and what it is not so good at (its weaknesses). We discuss the internal environment in Part II of this book.

The second stage in strategic analysis is an examination of the organization's external environment (*external analysis*). This takes the form of a thorough analysis of two 'layers' of external environment – the micro or 'near' environment, and the macro or 'far' environment. We will encounter the external environment in Part III of the book.

The microenvironment comprises the industry in which the business competes. The organization is usually affected by the factors in this environment often and it may be able to have an influence upon it. We sometimes refer to the microenvironment as the competitive environment because it is within this sphere that an organization competes, both for resource inputs and to sell its product outputs. We discuss this in Chapter 7.

The macroenvironment contains a range of influences that affect not only an organization in an industry, but also the whole industry itself. It follows that a single organization is usually unable to affect the factors in the macroenvironment – successful strategy usually involves learning to cope and adapt to changes. Most textbooks – and this one is no exception – explain the macroenvironment in terms of four main areas of influence –

political, economic, socio-demographic and technological influences. We discuss this in Chapter 6.

From the information gathered from the external analysis, we seek to establish which influences represent opportunities, and which are, or might develop into, threats.

Once we have established the organization's internal strengths and weaknesses, and its external opportunities and threats, the challenge becomes to select a strategy that will address the weaknesses and threats, whilst at the same time will build upon its strengths and exploit its opportunities. The process sometimes involves an additional stage of condensing the strengths, weaknesses, opportunities and threats (SWOT) into a survey of the 'key issues'. These are the most pressing or most important elements of the SWOT statement – those which require the most urgent action or which the strategy should be particularly designed to address.

Strategic selection

The second stage in the strategic process involves taking the important information gathered from the strategic analysis and using it to make an intelligent and informed selection of the most appropriate course of action for the future.

It is at this stage that we come to appreciate the importance of the strategic analysis. If we have gained insufficient or flawed information from the analysis, then we cannot be sure that the strategy selection we make will be the right one.

Selection therefore begins with an examination of the strategic analysis. Once we are acquainted with it, we normally generate a list of the options open to the organization, paying particular attention to how each option will address the key issues. After this, we evaluate each option using a number of criteria. Finally, the most appropriate strategic option is selected. We discuss this matter in Chapter 9.

Strategic implementation and management

The third stage in the strategic process involves taking the selected strategic option and actually putting it into practice. We discuss this stage in Part IV of the book.

This is a rather more complex process than either analysis or selection. It involves *doing* the strategy and this brings into focus a number of other managerial issues. There are a number of areas of which we need to be aware in order to implement a business strategy effectively. Implementation typically involves taking into account the following:

- the adequacy of the organization's resource base (Chapter 10);
- the readiness of the organization's culture and structure to undertake the proposed strategy (Chapter 10);
- the management of any changes that are needed to implement the strategy (Chapter 10);
- deciding which, if any, growth or development paths to pursue (Chapter 11);
- the readiness of the organization's operations function to pursue the proposed strategy and any quality issues that this discussion might throw up (Chapter 12);
- the extent to which the organization positions itself in respect to its geographic coverage and international presence (Chapter 13);
- the impact that the strategy may have upon an organization's internal or external stakeholders and a discussion (if appropriate) of the strategy's implications for the organization's relationship with society (Chapter 14).

Chapter 1

Strategy and strategic objectives

Introduction

Strategic thinking and strategic management are the most important activities undertaken by any business or public sector organization. How skilfully these activities are carried out will determine the eventual long-term success or failure of the organization. In this chapter, we introduce the most basic concepts in the study of these activities. The various definitions of the word *strategy* are discussed and then we explore the levels of decision-making in successful strategic management (at the strategic and operational levels). These are defined and the links between the levels are discussed. Finally, we discuss the nature of strategic objectives – who is responsible for setting them and what they are essentially about.

Objectives

After studying this chapter, students should be able to:

- define the word *strategy* using Mintzberg's five Ps framework;
- distinguish between deliberate (prescriptive) and emergent strategy;
- explain what strategy contains in practice;
- describe what is meant by *strategic* and *operational* decisions;
- explain what is meant by *hierarchical congruence* and why it is important;
- employ the stakeholder model to explain how strategic decisions are arrived at;
- explain the most typical types of objectives that are sought through strategic management.

What is strategy?

At the beginning of a book on business strategy, the question, 'What is strategy?' seems to be the most obvious starting point. The answer to the question is rather more complicated than it might at first appear.

This is because we use the word *strategy* in many ways. You may have heard people talk about a strategy for a business, a strategy for a football match, a strategy for a military campaign or a strategy for revising for a set of exams. It was this multiplicity of uses of the term that led Henry Mintzberg at the McGill University in Montreal (Mintzberg, 1987) to propose his 'five Ps' of strategy.

Mintzberg's five Ps

Mintzberg suggested that nobody can claim to own the word 'strategy' and that the term can legitimately be used in several ways. A strategy can be:

- a plan;
- a ploy;
- a pattern of behaviour;
- a position in respect to others;
- a perspective.

It is important not to see each of these Ps in isolation from each other. One of the problems of dividing ideas into frameworks like the five Ps is that they are necessarily simplified. The five Ps are not mutually exclusive, i.e. it is possible for an organization to show evidence of more than one interpretation of strategy.

Definitions

plan

A *plan* is probably the way in which most people use the word strategy. It tends to imply something that is intentionally put in train and its progress is monitored from the start to a predetermined finish. Some business strategies follow this model. 'Planners' tend to produce internal documents that detail what the company will do for a period of time in the future (say five years). It might include a schedule for new product launches, acquisitions, financing (i.e. raising money), human resource changes, etc.

ploy

A *ploy* is generally taken to mean a short-term strategy. It tends to have very limited objectives and it may be subject to change at very short notice. One of the best examples of a ploy strategy is that employed in a football match. If the opposing team has a particularly skilful player, then the team manager may use the ploy of assigning two players to mark him for the duration of the game. However, this tactic will only last for the one game – the next game will have a completely different strategy. Furthermore, the strategy will operate only as long as the dangerous player is on the pitch. If he is substituted or gets injured, the strategy will change mid-game.

Mintzberg describes a ploy as, 'a manoeuvre intended to outwit an opponent or competitor' (Mintzberg *et al.*, 1998, p.14). He points out that some companies may use ploy strategies as threats. They may threaten to, say, decrease the price of their products simply to destabilize competitors. A boss may threaten to sack an employee if a certain performance standard is not met – not because the boss intends to carry out the threat, but because he wants to effect a change in the subordinate's attitude.

A *pattern of behaviour* strategy is one in which progress is made by adopting a consistent form of behaviour. Unlike plans and ploys, patterns 'just happen' as a result of the consistent behaviour. On a simple level, small businesses like scrap dealers follow pattern strategies. They are unlikely to produce elaborate plans – they simply buy as much scrap metal as they can. If there is a batch of old scaffolding, then they buy it up without thinking about it. However, they would not buy old plastics because that would be outside their pattern of business behaviour. Eventually, following this consistent behaviour makes the scrap dealer a wealthy person – a successful strategy.

pattern of behaviour

Such patterns of behaviour are sometimes unconscious, meaning that they do not even realize that they actually following a consistent pattern. Nevertheless, if it proves successful, it is said that the consistent behaviour has *emerged* into a success. This is in direct contrast to planning behaviour.

Deliberate and emergent strategy

There is a key difference between two of Mintzberg's Ps of strategy – plan and pattern. The difference is to do with the *source* of the strategy. He drew attention to the fact that some strategies are deliberate whilst others are emergent.

Deliberate strategy (sometimes called *planned* or *prescriptive* strategy) is meant to happen. It is preconceived, premeditated and usually monitored and controlled from start to finish. It has a specific objective.

Emergent strategy has no specific objective. It does not have a preconceived route to success BUT it may be just as effective as a deliberate strategy. By following a consistent pattern of behaviour, an organization may arrive at the same position as if it had planned everything in detail. We discuss these concepts in more detail in Chapter 15.

position

perspective

A *position* strategy is appropriate when the most important thing to an organization is how it relates, or is positioned in respect to, its competitors or its markets (i.e. its customers). In other words, the organization wishes to achieve or defend a certain position. We see this a lot in sport. When a new boxing champion is crowned, his only objective is to remain the champion. He wants to retain his superior position. Accordingly, all of his efforts are invested in examining his future opponents and keeping himself in shape for the next defence of the title.

In business, companies tend to seek such things as market share, profitability, superior research, reputation, etc. It is plainly obvious that not all companies are equal when one considers such criteria. Some car manufacturers have enviable reputations for reliability and quality whilst others are not so fortunate. The competitors with a reputation to defend will use a position strategy to ensure that the reputation they enjoy is maintained and strengthened. This may even include marketing messages that point out the weaknesses in competitors' products whilst pointing out the features of their own.

Perspective strategies are about changing the culture (the beliefs and the 'feel', the way of looking at the world) of a certain group of people – usually the members of the organization itself. Some companies want to make their employees think in a certain way, believing this to be an important way of achieving success. They may, for example, try to get all employees to think and act courteously, professionally or helpfully.

Religious groups like the Church of England operate using this strategy. They have a number of core religious beliefs that they encourage all members to adopt. Then, it is argued, these beliefs will outwork themselves in actions. To be a good member of the Church of England, people must adopt the worldview of the church. The purpose of preaching, teaching, worship and other such practices is in large part concerned with further embedding Christian beliefs into the personalities of the believers. Success is achieved when all members think in the same way, i.e. they all believe in the core doctrines and work them out in their lives through good works.

The elements of strategy

Chandler's definition

Given the foregoing definitions by Mintzberg, we might think that writers in business strategy are unable to agree to a single definition of the word strategy. This is partly true, but some have tried to sum it up succinctly to make it easier for students to understand. One such definition, still widely quoted, was offered by Professor Chandler of Harvard Business School in 1962. Given that Chandler predates Mintzberg, it is not surprising that it is rather more simplistic than Mintzberg might have accepted:

Strategy is the *determination of the basic long-term goals* and objectives of an enterprise, and the *adoption of courses of action* and the *allocation of resources* necessary for carrying out these goals. (Chandler, 1962 – emphasis added)

Three components of strategy

This is a good definition because it shows the scope of what 'good' strategy is. The italics in this quote show the three important contents of strategy.

The *determination of the basic long-term goals* concerns the conceptualization of coherent and attainable strategic objectives. Without objectives, nothing else can happen. If you do not know where you want to go, how can you act in such a way as to get there?

The *adoption of courses of action* refers to the actions taken to arrive at the objectives that have been previously set. If your objective is to be in Outer Mongolia, then the actions you would take would include arranging transport. You might do this by ringing travel agents, etc.

The *allocation of resources* refers to the fact that there is likely to be a cost associated with the actions required to achieve the objectives. If the course of action is not supported with adequate levels of resource, then the objective will not be accomplished.

Hence, strategy contains three things. In order to achieve your *objective* of being in Outer Mongolia, you would take the *actions* of booking travel, taking leave from work and boarding a plane. However, the actions would not be possible if they could not be resourced. You need the *resources* of a plane with a suitably qualified pilot, an airport, money to pay for your flight and other such 'inputs.' If any one of these is missing, you will be unable to meet your objective.

Key Concepts

Resources

Resource inputs (sometimes called *factors of production*) are those essential inputs which are essential to the normal functioning of the organizational process. These are the inputs without which an organization simply could not continue to exist or meet its objectives. We can readily appreciate that human beings rely upon certain vital inputs such as air, water, nutrition, warmth, shelter, etc., but organizations have similar needs. An organization's resource inputs fall into four key categories:

1 *financial resources* – money for capital investment and working capital. Sources include shareholders, banks, bond-holders;
2 *human resources* – appropriately-skilled employees to add value in operations and to support those that add value (e.g. support employees in marketing, accounting, personnel). Sources include the

labour markets for the appropriate skill levels required by the organization;

3   *physical (tangible) resources* – land, buildings (offices, warehouses, etc.), plant, equipment, stock for production, etc. Sources include estate agents, builders, trade suppliers;

4   *intellectual (intangible) resources* – inputs that cannot be seen or felt but which are essential for continuing business success, e.g. 'know-how', legally-defensible patents and licences, brand-names, registered designs, logos, 'secret' formulations and recipes, business contact networks, databases.

Who sets objectives in an organization?

Strategic and operational objectives

The answer to this question is that it depends upon which objectives we mean. Not all objectives are the same and where they are set depends upon their scope and their level. It is here that we introduce an important distinction – that between *strategic* and *operational* objectives.

There is a clear difference between the activities at work of a managing director (the most senior person in most companies) and an office manager. The managing director will probably spend most of his or her time sitting behind a large desk, dictating letters and memos, making phone calls and, importantly, thinking. When the managing director thinks, it is usually about matters that concern the whole company – about patterns in the marketplace, the share price and its influences, the behaviour of competitors, raw material prices and the like.

The office manager is just as busy, but his or her working day is more concerned with meeting short-term deadlines and managing the people under his or her oversight. The office manager also spends some of the day thinking, but usually about issues that affect the office and its activities. Of less concern is the level of corporate taxation and of more concern is the price of the latest printer, the attitudes of the sales representatives and the deadlines they have to meet.

Both people are important in making the company successful, but they contribute in different ways. The managing director thinks and acts at the strategic level whilst the office manager is more engaged at the operational level.

The strategic level

Strategic level objectives are those taken by the most senior people in an organization. They are taken in the light of a lot of variables that can affect the organization and so the people making them must have the ability to account for a lot of factors at the same time. Hence, good strategic objective-setters will usually have strong intellectual skills and will be able to work out how external and internal influences will affect the performance of the organization. They tend to have *fairly long time horizons*, i.e. they usually try to set plans for several years into the future. Because strategic level objectives *apply to the whole organization*, they are necessarily *fairly general in nature*. They would be unlikely, for example, to detail how the objectives will affect the number of company cars the company will need or how much should be set aside for hiring new employees.

In many cases, strategic objectives will define the organization's *mission*. They are *concerned with the raison d'être* of the organization and how it will position itself in respect to its environment.

The operational level

Operational level objectives are taken by middle or lower managers in the organization. They are concerned with *shorter time periods* – usually less than one year. The purpose of operational objectives is to enable all the internal activities of the organization to act in concert towards the accomplishment of the strategic objectives. This is achieved by deconstructing the strategic objectives into their constituent parts – by asking how the strategic objectives are to be achieved. Accordingly, operational objectives are *much more detailed*. They will detail, for example, how many employees will be needed, what skills will be in particular demand and which will no longer be required, how much capital will need to be invested and on what items, and the features of proposed new products.

You may have heard terms like marketing strategy, human resource strategy and financial strategy. These are all examples of operational strategy, designed to achieve operational objectives. This is because marketing, human resources and finance are all operational functions and exist only to achieve strategic objectives.

Key Concepts

Strategic and operational objectives – a summary

Strategic level objectives	Operational level objectives
Made by senior management	Made by mid or lower level management
Longer term in timescale	Short to medium term in timescale
General in detail	Specific in detail
Concern the whole organization	Concerned with how one part of the organization will act
General – not detailed	Detailed
Set policy	Follow policy
Concerned with mission	Act in accordance with mission

Figure 1.1 Levels of decision-making in organizations.

Congruency and 'fit'

The success of strategy rests upon a very important, but rather obvious, principle. Once the strategic level objectives have been set, the operational objectives must be set in such a way so that they contribute to the achievement of the strategic objectives. In other words, the operational decisions must 'fit' the strategic objectives. This introduces the concept of *congruence*.

We can visualize the decision-making framework as a pyramid (see Figure 1.1). The top, where the strategic decisions are made, is thin whilst the bottom (operational decisions) is fatter. This representation is meant to show that strategic decisions are taken infrequently whilst operational decisions are taken often. Strategic decisions are few and far between whilst operational decisions are taken weekly, daily or even hourly. For every one strategic decision, there may be hundreds of individual operational decisions.

What matters, however, is that the levels of decision-making agree – that are congruent with each other. The only purpose of operational decisions is to facilitate the achievement of strategic objectives. Accordingly, the two levels are congruent if they purpose the same overall end.

Time and planning horizons

One of the key differences between the two levels of decision-making in organizations is the timescale with which they are concerned. Broadly speaking, the higher up an organization we look, the longer the timescale with which management is concerned. On the shop floor, operatives are typically concerned with meeting daily deadlines whilst the chief executive may be worrying about potential threats that are some years away. Meanwhile, middle managers, say those in charge of graduate recruitment or the prepa-

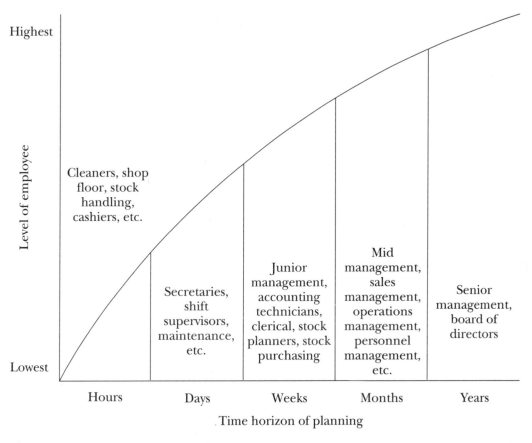

Highest

Level of employee

Cleaners, shop
floor, stock
handling,
cashiers, etc.

Secretaries,
shift
supervisors,
maintenance,
etc.

Junior
management,
accounting
technicians,
clerical, stock
planners, stock
purchasing

Mid
management,
sales
management,
operations
management,
personnel
management,
etc.

Senior
management,
board of
directors

Lowest

Hours   Days   Weeks   Months   Years

Time horizon of planning

Figure 1.2 Time horizons at levels in the organization (note that the examples on the graph
are indicative only – the actual planning timescale of each level will vary from company to
company).

ration of financial statements, will be planning a few months in advance –
possibly as far as one year ahead (see Figure 1.2).

Strategic management involves taking account of a large number of environmental variables. The longer ahead that a manager seeks to plan for,
then the more uncertainty is introduced into the analysis.

Mission and mission statements

An organization's *mission* can be described as its overarching raison d'être.
It is the objective that subsumes all others beneath it. For some organizations, the mission is very easy to articulate but for large commercial businesses it tends to be more complex.

The purposes of a mission statement

Some organizations attempt to frame their mission in a formal statement. Such a statement has a number of possible purposes. It can be used to *clearly communicate the objectives* and values of the organization to the various stakeholders' groups and it can be argued that it *assists in achieving hierarchical congruence*. It may also have an effect in *influencing the behaviour and attitudes of employees*, although this is somewhat debatable as anecdotal evidence suggests that many employees have not in fact read their organization's mission statement.

What does a mission statement contain?

The style and content of mission statements, as we might expect, varies enormously. Some are long and detailed whereas others are short and to the point. There are probably no 'rights' or 'wrongs' of how it should be presented or what it should contain – it all depends upon the organization and its culture. In practice, mission statements usually contain one or more of the following:

- some *indication of the industry* or business the organization is mainly concerned with;
- an indication of the *realistic market share* or market position the organization should aim towards;
- a brief summary of the *values and beliefs* of the organization.

Specific and *highly context-dependent objectives* are also sometimes expressed in the mission statement.

Mission statement – Nissan Motor Manufacturing (UK) Limited

In the early 1980s, the motor company Nissan made an investment of almost £1 billion in a 'greenfield' plant in Sunderland, Tyne and Wear. The building of a new installation meant that almost all employees were new to the company. There was therefore an implicit need for a clear statement of cultural norms in the business coupled with an overview of business and commercial objectives. This need was satisfied with the publication of a document called *Our Company's Philosophy*, distributed to all employees and signed by Ian Gibson CBE, Managing Director and Chief Executive, Nissan's Sunderland plants.

Nissan's *Our Company's Philosophy* reads as follows:
As a Company, we aim to build profitably the highest quality car sold in Europe. We want to achieve the maximum possible customer satisfaction and ensure the prosperity of the Company and its staff.
  To assist in this, we aim to achieve mutual trust and co-operation between all people within the Company and make NMUK a place where long-term job satisfaction can be achieved. We recognize that

people are our most valued resource and in line with this spirit believe that the following principles will be of value to all.

People
- *We will develop and expand the contributions of all staff by strongly emphasizing training and by the expansion of everyone's capabilities.*
- *We seek to delegate and involve staff in discussion and decision-making particularly in those areas in which each of us can effectively contribute so that all may participate in the efficient running of NMUK.*
- *We firmly believe in common terms and conditions of employment.*

Teamworking
- *We recognize that all staff have a valued contribution to make as individuals but in addition believe that this contribution can be most effective within a teamworking environment.*
- *Our aim is to build a Company with which people can identify and to which we all feel commitment.*

Communication
- *Within the bounds of commercial confidentiality we will encourage open channels of communication. We would like everyone to know what is happening in our company, how we are performing and what we plan.*
- *We want information and views to flow freely upward, downward and across our Company.*

Objectives
- *We will agree clear and achievable objectives and provide meaningful feedback and performance.*

Flexibility
- *We will not be restricted by the existing way of doing things. We will continuously seek improvements in all our actions.*

These are tough targets and we aim high. With hard work and good will we can get there.

(Reproduced with the permission of Nissan.)

Not all mission statements are as long and detailed as Nissan's. Others are shorter and perhaps more 'to the point'.

Mission statement – British Telecommunications plc

BT, as a very large company, expresses its objectives in a relatively brief document which is designed to communicate its objectives to its wide ranging and disparate types of employee and stakeholder. The document is divided into two parts. The first part is its Vision, and the second its Mission.

Vision
- *to become the most successful worldwide telecommunications group.*

Mission
- *to provide world class telecommunications and information products and services,*
- *to develop and exploit our networks at home and overseas, so that we can ...*
- *meet the requirements of our customers,*
- *sustain growth in the earnings of the group on behalf of our shareholders,*
- *make a fitting contribution to the community in which we conduct our business.*

(Reproduced with the permission of British Telecommunications plc.)

How do businesses set objectives?

Who 'owns' an organization?

Earlier in this chapter, we introduced the idea that strategic objectives are set by an organization's senior management, usually the board of directors. In this section, we turn to ask the question, 'Who or what influences the senior management in their objective setting?'

This question cuts to the heart of an important debate that is taking place both in universities and in business circles. We will discuss this debate at length in Chapter 14, but the issues are introduced here.

Essentially, the key question here is, 'Who owns an organization?' The presupposition is that those who own an organization will have the most leverage over the senior management when they come to set their strategic objectives. For many organizations, the answer to the question is easy, but for others it is rather more complicated.

If we were to ask who is the owner of Mr Brown's one-man-band fish-and-chip shop, then we would all agree that it is Mr Brown. If, on the other hand, we were to ask who owns the National Health Service, then we might have a much longer list of owners. Given that the majority of NHS revenue comes from the Treasury, then we might say that the taxpayers own the NHS. However, the NHS could not operate properly without its hundreds of thousands of highly-skilled employees. Other groups may also claim to be part-owners of the NHS such as the patients it treats, the companies that supply it with important equipment and medicines, the relatives of employees and patients, and many others. It is this complexity of influences that gave rise to the notion of stakeholders.

What is a stakeholder?

A stakeholder can be defined as:

any person or party that can affect or be affected by the activities and policies of an organization.

This definition draws in almost everybody that is, or may be potentially involved in the life of an organization. It consequently goes without saying that not all stakeholders are equal in their influence on an organization's objectives. In Chapter 14 we will examine this matter in more detail, but in this chapter we will confine ourselves to considering the ways in which stakeholders exert their influence on objectives.

Stakeholders and objectives

One widely-used and useful model for understanding how stakeholders exert influence on an organization's objectives was proposed by Mendelow (1991). According to this model, stakeholders can be 'ranked' depending upon two variables: the stakeholders' *interest* and *power*.

- stakeholder *power* refers to the *ability* to influence the organization;
- stakeholder *interest* refers to the *willingness* to influence the organization. In other words, interest concerns the extent to which the stakeholder cares about what the organization does.

It then follows that:

Stakeholder influence = power × interest

The actual influence that a stakeholder has will depend upon where the stakeholder is positioned with respect to ability to influence and willingness to influence. A stakeholder with both high power and high interest will be more influential than one with low power and low interest. We can map stakeholders by showing the two variables on a grid comprising two intersecting continua (see Figure 1.3).

Once constructed, we can use the map to assess two things:

1 which stakeholder is likely to exert the most influence upon the organization's objectives; and
2 the stakeholders that are most likely to be in potential conflict over strategic objectives (where two or more stakeholders are in close proximity in the high power–high interest part of the map).

The managing director and the board of directors are examples of stakeholders with both high power and high interest. This is because they not only manage the business but also depend upon it for their jobs. The bar to which employees retire after or during the day's work is an example of a stakeholder with high interest but low power (and therefore low total influence).

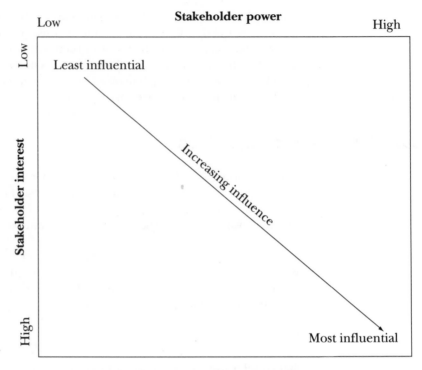

Figure 1.3 The stakeholder map (adapted from Mendelow, 1991).

What do businesses want from a strategy?

In strict terms, the most important of all objectives is to simply survive as a going concern. Other objectives depend upon the type of organization and the nature of its environment.

Economic objectives

Economic objectives are those that can be measured in financial ways. For commercial organizations, objectives will usually include measures such as *return*. Return is an accounting term to describe the proportion of either sales or investment capital that is left over as profit.

Return on sales, sometimes referred to as profit margin, is an indication of how well the company has controlled its costs; whilst *return on assets* (or *return on capital employed*) is an indication of how efficiently the company has used its investors' money. Both of these are important business objectives – to provide sufficient return to retain some profits for future investment and to provide investors with a dividend on their shareholding.

Not-for-profit organizations also have economic objectives, but they are measured in different ways. Organizations like charities, government departments and universities tend to measure economic performance by using cost–benefit or value-for-money objectives. These organizations usually rely in large part on income over which they have little control – it may, for example, be fixed by central government. The objectives set will typically involve extracting the maximum benefit in terms of outputs from the income they have. A university has a certain income which it uses as carefully as possible to ensure it can deliver its courses and research within budget.

Social objectives

We should not assume that all organizational objectives are financial in nature. Many exist, either in part or totally, to deliver social benefits. Many publicly-funded organizations such as schools, hospitals and prisons exist to deliver services to society in general. Charities and co-operatives exist primarily to provide social benefit to one or more allegedly worthwhile constituencies. For organizations of this type, economic objectives are very much secondary to their desire to deliver socially-desirable ends.

Commercial organizations are also gradually adopting social objectives in their strategic planning (see Chapter 14). Although they are usually subordinate to their economic objectives, commercial organizations may espouse social or environmental causes that they purport to believe in. They may, for example, recognize the social value of supporting local community projects or seconding (at their own expense) some of their people to serve with charities.

Growth or market share objectives

At some stages in the life of an organization, objectives concerning growth and expansion become among the most important. This is especially true of businesses who must grow and maintain market position in order to 'keep up with' or 'keep ahead of' competitors.

Size and market position offer a number of advantages and it is these that an organization seeks when growth is a key objective. Size gives an organization economy of scale advantages in both product and resource markets. It means that a larger organization attracts resource inputs at preferential unit costs compared with smaller concerns and its larger presence in its product markets increases its pricing power and its ability to subjugate competitors. We will consider this type of objective in more depth in Chapter 11.

Competitive advantage objectives

Finally, and perhaps most importantly, many strategic objectives concern the company's position in respect to its competitors. Competitive advantage objectives concern how the company's position compares with others – especially with regard to competitors. The objectives are limited to ensuring simply that 'we beat you', or 'we are better than you'. Superior performance is the only objective and if a company can achieve ascendancy over its nearest competitors, then the objective will have been accomplished.

A football team like Newcastle United operates mainly within competitive advantage objectives. Its objectives are not to be a good team as such (important though that may be), but to be a better team than its rivals. If it can win the Premiership or the FA Cup, then it matters less that they are good than that they are the best in any given season.

Summary

This chapter has discussed the meanings of the term *strategy* and introduced the concepts of deliberate and emergent strategy. It went on to explain the components of strategy (objectives, resource requirement and implementation) before discussing the levels of strategic decision-making in organizations and the important concept of hierarchical congruence. The concept of mission has been introduced and the role of stakeholders in objective-setting has been discussed. Finally, the four main 'types' of business objective have been explained.

Review and Discuss

1 What are Mintzberg's five Ps of strategy?
2 Define and distinguish between deliberate and emergent strategy.
3 What are the three components of strategy as described by Chandler?
4 Define the term 'hierarchical congruence'.
5 Why is hierarchical congruence important in successful strategy?
6 What is a mission statement?
7 In what ways might a mission statement help in achieving strategic objectives?
8 What is a stakeholder?
9 Explain how the power–interest map helps to identify the most influential stakeholders.

References and further reading

Chandler, A.D. (1962) *Strategy and Structure*. Boston, MA: MIT Press.
Mendelow, A. (1991) Proceedings of 2nd International Conference on Information Systems. Cambridge, MA.

Mintzberg, H. (1987) Five Ps for strategy. *California Management Review*, Fall. Reprinted in Mintzberg, H., Quinn, J.B. and Ghoshal, S. (1998) *The Strategy Process*, Revised European Edition. Hemel Hempstead, UK: Prentice Hall. p.13ff.

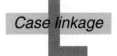

Case linkage

Three of the case studies in Part V cover the learning objectives of this chapter. You may wish to use the questions that follow.

Questions for The Gulf War (1990–91) case study.

1 Identify the key stakeholders in the case scenario.
2 In what ways did each key stakeholder contribute to the formulation of the strategic objectives?
3 Who ultimately set the strategic objectives and what were they?
4 What were the operational objectives?
5 Who was responsible for formulating the operational part of the strategy?
6 Discuss the extent to which the operational objectives were congruent with the strategic objectives.
7 Describe the resources inputs that were employed in the implementation of the strategy.
8 Which of Mintzberg's five Ps best describes the strategy followed by the allies in the Gulf War?
9 Discuss the extent to which the strategic objectives were successfully accomplished in Operation Desert Storm.

Questions for the Who Owns Newcastle United? case study.
1 Identify from the case the key stakeholders in Newcastle United plc.
2 Construct a power–interest matrix for the key stakeholders in the company.
3 Comment on the relative strengths of the most influential stakeholders.

Questions for the Cardiff Car Components case study.

1 Which of Mintzberg's five Ps best describes John Armstrong's approach to strategy?
2 Identify CCC's principal strengths.
3 Identify CCC's weaknesses.
4 Identify the opportunities open to CCC as at 1998.
5 Identify the threats that CCC might face as at 1998.

Part II

Internal analysis

Purposes of internal analysis

Internal analysis is concerned with providing management with a detailed understanding of the business, how effective its current strategies are and how effectively it has deployed its resources in support of its strategies. In recent years the importance of internal analysis has been given greater emphasis because research has suggested that it is predominantly the actions of the business itself which determine its ability to outperform its competitors. Internal analysis aims to provide the managers of a business with an understanding of its potential for competitive advantage and, equally, those areas where it must take remedial action to ensure its survival. This section of the book introduces and evaluates the main techniques employed in internally analysing the business.

Organizations may carry out an internal analysis for some or all of the following reasons:

- to identify resources, competences and core competences to be developed and exploited;
- to evaluate how effectively value adding activities are organized;
- to identify areas of weaknesses to be addressed in future strategy and its implementation;
- to evaluate the performance of products;
- to evaluate financial performance, particularly in comparison with competitors;
- to evaluate investment potential if finance is being sought from external sources;

- as a first step in assessing the suitability, feasibility and acceptability of future strategies.

What are the components of an internal analysis?

An internal analysis will cover some or all of the following aspects of the business or organization:

- resource analysis (Chapter 2);
- competence audit and analysis (Chapter 2);
- internal activities analysis by using a Porter's value chain framework (Chapter 2);
- comparative analysis (comparing performance against competitors by use of financial analysis and benchmarking) (Chapter 4);
- human resources and culture (Chapter 3);
- financial resources and financial performance (Chapter 4);
- products and their position in the market (Chapter 5).

These aspects of internal analysis are covered in Chapters 2 to 5 which form Part II of this book. A number of 'tools' and 'frameworks' will be introduced to assist the internal analysis.

Chapter 2

The business organization – competences and activities

Introduction

In Chapter 1 we encountered the concept of competitive advantage as one of the key objectives of business strategy. There has been considerable debate in the academic literature as to the causes of competitive advantage. Essentially, the debate asks the question, 'How do organizations achieve superior performance?' Two positions have emerged as the most prominent.

The *competitive positioning* school of thought, based primarily on the work of Professor Michael Porter of Harvard Business School (1980, 1985), stresses the importance of how the organization is positioned in respect to its competitive environment or industry (which we discuss in Chapter 7). The *resource* or *competence* school (Prahalad and Hamel, 1990; Heene and Sanchez, 1997) on the other hand, argues that it is the competences (abilities) of the business and the distinctive way that it organizes its activities which determines the ability to outperform competitors. As with most controversies, we suggest that both schools of thought have their merits – both are partial explanations of the source of competitive advantage.

This chapter concentrates on developing an understanding of the major factors governing the level of performance of the business, namely its resources, competences (particularly its core competences), and its 'value adding' activities.

After studying this chapter, students should be able to:

- explain the *concepts of core competences, competences, resources* and the relationships between them;
- explain the concept of the *value chain* and the value chain framework;
- explain the relationships between core competences and core activities;
- explain how the value chain framework 'works';
- explain how the configuration of value adding activities can improve business performance;
- identify the potential benefits of collaboration with suppliers, distributors and customers.

Resources, competences and core competences

Definitions

The terms *competence* and *capability*, *core competence* and *distinctive capability* are often used interchangeably in textbooks on business strategy. Although some writers (Stalk *et al.*, 1992), argue that there are significant differences between the terms *competence* and *capability* we will use the terms to mean broadly the same things based upon the following definitions.

competences

A *competence* is an attribute or collection of attributes possessed by all or most of the companies in an industry. Without such attributes a business cannot enter or survive in the industry. Competences develop from resources and embody skills, technology or 'know how'. For example, in order to operate in the pharmaceuticals industry, it is necessary to possess both the ability to manufacture medicines (by using specially-designed factory equipment) and, importantly, a detailed understanding of how medicines work on the human body. Every successful survivor in the industry possesses both of these areas of competence.

core competences

A *core competence* or *distinctive capability* is an attribute, or collection of attributes, specific to a particular organization which enables it to produce above industry average performance. It arises from the way in which the organization has employed its competences and resources *more effectively* than its competitors. The result of a distinctive capability is an output which customers value higher than that of competitors. It is based upon one or more of superior organizational knowledge, information, skills, technology, structure, relationships, networks and reputation.

resources

A *resource* is an input employed in the activities of the business. Success rests in large part upon the efficiency by which the business converts its resources into outputs. Resources fall into four broad categories – human, financial, physical (buildings, equipment, stock, etc.) and intangible ('know how', patents, legal rights, brand names, registered designs, etc.).

Competitive advantage

Competitive advantage is often seen as the overall purpose of business strategy. Some texts use the phrase *superior performance* to mean the same thing. Essentially, a business can be said to possess competitive advantage if it is able to return higher profits than its competitors. The higher profits mean that it will be able to commit more retained profit to reinvestment in its strategy, thus maintaining its lead over its competitors in an industry. When this superiority is maintained successfully over time, we refer to it as a *sustainable* competitive advantage. Competitive advantage can be lost when management fail to reinvest the superior profits in such a way that the advantage is not maintained.

How core competences 'work'

Core competences tend to be both complex and intangible so that it is necessary to explore the nature of resources and competences which underpin them before exploring the concept further (see Figure 2.1). The purpose of such analysis is to allow managers to identify which resources and competences act as the foundation of existing or potential core competences. It is extremely important to note that not all the competitors in an industry will possess core competences or distinctive capabilities (Kay, 1995). It is only those players which are producing above average performance which can be considered as possessing core competences. Those with only average or below average performance possess competences and resources (without which they could not compete in the industry at all) but not core competences (see Prahalad and Hamel, 1990; Kay, 1993; Heene and Sanchez, 1997; and Petts, 1997 for further discussion of these concepts).

Core competence (distinctive capability) = Superior employment of resources + superior development of 'general' competences

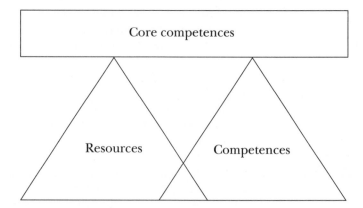

Figure 2.1 The twin sources of core competences.

We will now consider these terms in more detail.

Resource analysis

Tangible and intangible resources

Resources can be either *tangible* or *intangible.* They are the inputs which enable an organization to carry out its activities. Tangible assets include stocks, materials, machinery, buildings, human resources, finance and so on. Intangible assets include skills, knowledge, brand names and goodwill, patent rights, etc. (see Coyne, 1986; Hall, 1992). Intangible resources are often produced within the organization but tangibles are obtained from outside organizations. Such resources are obtained in resource markets in competition with businesses from within and outside the industry. Relationships with the suppliers of resources can form an important part of the organization's core competence, for example its ability to attract the most appropriately skilled human resources in the job market.

Analysing resources

When we analyse a company's resources as part of an internal analysis, several frameworks can be employed to provide a comprehensive review.

Analysis by category

Firstly, we might, for example, consider them by *category* – human, financial, production technology, information and communications technology, and materials. These resources are then evaluated quantitatively (how much or how many) and qualitatively (how effectively they are being employed). Much of this analysis is covered in Chapters 3, 4 and 5. Physical resources like buildings and machinery will typically be audited for capacity, utilization, age, condition, contribution to output and so on. Materials and stocks can be assessed on the basis of quality, reliability, availability, number of suppliers, delivery times, and unit costs. Human resources are considered in terms of numbers, education, skills, training, experience, age, motivation, wage costs and productivity in relation to the needs of the organization.

Analysis by specificity

Secondly, we can analyse resources according to their *specificity*. Resources can be specific or non-specific. For example, skilled workers tend to have specialized and industry-specific knowledge and skills. Some technology, for example computer software, is for general (non industry-specific) business use, like word-processing, database and spreadsheet software. Other computer software applications, like airline computer reservation systems, are written for highly specialized uses. Whereas non-specific resources tend to be more flexible and form the basis of competences, industry-specific resources are more likely to act as the foundations of core competences (for example the specialized knowledge of scientists in the chemical industry).

Analysis by performance

Thirdly, resources can be evaluated on the basis of how they contribute to internal and external *measures of performance*. Internal measures include their contribution to:

- business objectives and targets – financial, performance and output measures;
- historical comparisons – measures of performance over time (e.g. against previous years);
- business unit or divisional comparisons.

External measures can include:

- comparisons with competitors, particularly those who are industry leaders and those who are the closest competitors and are in its strategic grouping (see Chapter 5);
- comparisons with companies in other industries.

By employing these techniques of analysis, an organization is able to internally and externally *benchmark* its performance as a stimulus to improving performance in the future. Performance, however, is based on more than resources, and competences must be similarly analysed and evaluated.

Competences

Competences are attributes like skills, knowledge, technology and relationships that are common among the competitors in an industry. For example, all players in the pharmaceutical industry possess similar competences (basic abilities) in research and development, marketing, manufacturing and distribution. They are less tangible than resources and are consequently more difficult to evaluate. Competences are more often developed internally but may be acquired externally or by collaboration with suppliers, distributors or customers.

Competences are distinguished from core competences by the fact that they do not produce superior performance and by the fact that they are not distinctive from the competences possessed by other companies in the industry. On the other hand, competences are essential for survival in a particular line of business. Competences also have the potential to be developed into core competences.

Core competences

Distinguishing core competences from general competences

Core competences are distinguished from competences in several ways:

- they are only possessed by those companies whose performance is superior to the industry average;
- they are unique to the company;
- they are more complex;
- they are difficult to emulate (copy);
- they relate to fulfilling customer needs;
- they add greater value than 'general' competences;
- they are often based on distinctive relationships with customers, distributors and suppliers;
- they are based upon superior organizational skills and knowledge.

In the motor industry, all manufacturers have the competences and resources required to build motor vehicles, but a company like BMW has core competences in design, engine technology and marketing which act as the basis of its reputation for high quality, high performance motor cars. These core competences make it possible for BMW to charge premium prices for its products. In this way, core competences are the basis of an organization's competitive advantage.

Core competences and distinctive capabilities

Kay (1993) presents a slightly different explanation arguing that competitive advantage is based upon what he terms *distinctive capability*. Distinctive capability can develop from reputation, architecture (internal and external relationships), innovation, and strategic assets. Marks & Spencer's competitive advantage can be explained in terms of its reputation for quality, its special relationships with its suppliers and customers. Marks & Spencer has very exacting but mutually profitable relationships with the businesses who supply its products. It demands high quality at reasonable cost, and flexibility in return for large volumes of business. Its relationship with customers is based upon its reputation for good service, refunds and exchanges of goods, and high quality products. The end result is that it has a performance that is superior to most of its high street competitors.

Core competence arises from the unique and distinctive way that the organization builds, develops, integrates and deploys its resources and competences. An existing core competence can be evaluated for:

- *customer focus* – does it adequately focus on customer needs?
- *uniqueness* – can it be imitated by competitors and if so, how easily?
- *flexibility* – can it be easily adapted if market or industry conditions change?
- *contribution to value* – to what extent does it add value to the product or service?
- *sustainability* – how long can its superiority be sustained over time?

Competences, as opposed to core competences, can also be judged against these criteria in order to evaluate their potential to form the basis upon which new core competences can be built.

Core competences can never be regarded as being permanent. The pace of change of technology and society are such that core competences must be constantly adapted and new ones cultivated. A good example of the need to adapt comes from an examination of IBM. In the 1980s IBM had core competences in the design, production, marketing and sales of personal computers. The value which customers attached to these competences was lost in the late 1980s and early 1990s because competitors were able to match IBM's competences in design and production of personal computers and at a lower price. IBM had failed to adapt its core competences so that they became merely industry-wide competences. Its superiority was eroded because it failed to sustain its advantage.

Outcomes of the analyses

The aim of an analysis of resources, competences and core competences is, therefore, to:

- understand the nature and sources of particular core competences;
- identify the need for and methods of adaptation of existing core competences;

- identify the need for new core competence building;
- identify potential sources of core competence based on resources and competences;
- ensure that core competences remain focused on customer needs.

Resources, competences and core competences are obviously closely related to the ways that a business organizes and performs its value adding activities. It is therefore also necessary to analyse the way in which value adding activities are configured and co-ordinated.

Key Concepts

Competence leveraging and building
Competence leveraging
Competence leveraging refers to the ability of a business to exploit its core competences in new markets, thus meeting new customer needs. It can also refer to the ability of the business to modify and improve existing core competences.

Competence building
Competence building takes place when the business builds new core competences, based upon its resources and competences. It is often necessary to build new competences alongside existing ones when entering new markets as it is unlikely that existing competences will fully meet new customer needs.

Analysis of value adding activities

What is value adding?

Value chain analysis (Porter, 1985) seeks to provide an understanding of how much value an organization's activities add to its products and services compared with the costs of the resources used in their production. A given product can be produced by organizing activities in a number of different ways. Value chain analysis helps managers to understand how effectively and efficiently the activities of their organization are configured and co-ordinated. The acid test is how much value is added in the process of turning inputs into the outputs which are products in the form of goods and services. Value is measured in terms of the price that customers are willing to pay for the product.

Value added can be increased in two ways. It can be increased by:

1 changing customer perceptions of the product so that they are willing to pay a higher price for a product than for similar products produced by other businesses; or   *Apple*
2 reducing production costs below those of competitors.

e.g BMW

Value added

In simple terms, the value added to a good or service is the difference in the financial value of the finished product compared with the financial value of the inputs. As a sheet of metal passes through the various stages in car production, value is added so that a tonne of metal worth a few hundred pounds becomes a motor car worth several thousand pounds. The rate at which value is added is dependent upon how well the operations process is managed. If the car manufacturer suffers a cost disadvantage by, say, holding a high level of stock or working with out-of-date machinery, then the value added over the process will be lower.

There are clear linkages between value adding activities, core competences, competences and resources. Resources form the inputs to the organization's value adding activities while competences and core competences provide the skills and knowledge required to carry them out. The more that core competences can be integrated into value adding activities, the greater will be the value added.

The value adding process

Businesses can be regarded as systems which transform inputs (resources, materials, etc.) into outputs (goods and services). This is illustrated in Figure 2.2.

The activities inside the organization *add value* to the inputs. The value of the finished goods is equivalent to the price that a customer is willing to pay for the goods. The difference between the end value and the total costs is the *margin* (the quantity that accountants would refer to as the *profit margin* – before interest, taxation and extraordinary items).

The value chain

The activities of the organization can be broken down into a sequence of activities known as the *value chain* as described by Porter in 1985 (see Figure 2.3).

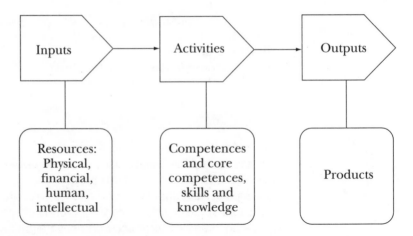

Figure 2.2 A simplified schematic of the value adding process.

The activities within the chain may be classified into *primary activities* and *support activities*. *Primary activities* are those which *directly add value* to the final product. *Support activities* do not directly add value themselves but *indirectly add value* by supporting the effective execution of primary activities. Table 2.1 describes the primary and secondary activities.

Primary activities	Inbound logistics	Receipt and storage of materials (inputs). Stock control and distribution of inputs.
	Operations	Transformation of inputs into final product.
	Outbound logistics	Storage and distribution of finished goods.
	Sales and marketing	Making the product available to the market and persuading people to buy.
	Service	Installation and after sales support.
Support activities	Procurement	Purchasing of resources.
	Technology development	Product, process and resource development.
	Infrastructure	Planning, finance, information systems, management.
	Human resource management	Recruitment, selection, training, reward and motivation.

Table 2.1 A summary of the items in the value chain.

Analysis of the value chain

An organization's value chain links into the value chains of other organizations, particularly those of suppliers and distributors. This 'chain' of value

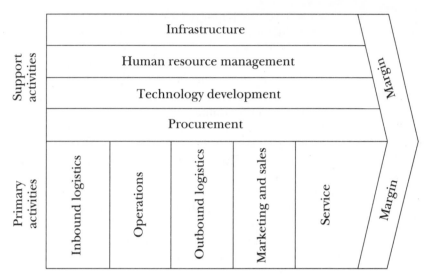

Figure 2.3 The value chain (after Porter, 1985).

chains is sometimes called the *value system* or *total supply chain*. Linkages with suppliers are known as *upstream* linkages while those with distributors and customers are *downstream* linkages.

Different types of organization will have very different value chains. For example, the value chain of Dixons, the electrical goods retailer, does not include the design and manufacture of the products it sells. Marks & Spencer's value chain does include some design but does not include manufacturing.

Similarly, not all of an organization's activities are of equal importance in adding value to its products. Those which are of greatest importance can be considered as *core activities* and are often closely associated to core competences. Thus in a fashion house like Calvin Klein, design activities are of the greatest importance in adding value and the organization's core competences are concentrated in this area.

Analysis of value adding activities helps to identify where the most value is added and where there is potential to add greater value by changing the way in which activities are configured and by improving the way in which they are co-ordinated. It is important to note that an organization's value chain is not analysed in isolation but is considered in conjunction with its external linkages to suppliers, distributors and customers.

A value chain analysis would be expected to include:

- a breakdown of all the activities of the organization;
- identification of core activities and their relationships to core competences and current organizational strategies;
- identification of the effectiveness and efficiency of the individual activities;

- examination of *linkages* between activities for additional added value;
- identification of *blockages* which reduce the organization's competitive advantage.

A useful technique in value chain analysis involves comparison with the value chains of competitors to identify the benefits and drawbacks of alternative configurations.

The aim of value chain analysis is to identify ways in which the performance of the individual activities and the linkages between them can be improved. This may involve identification of improved configurations for activities or improved co-ordination of them. It is particularly important to consider the extent to which value chain activities support the current strategy of the organization. For example, if the current strategy is based upon high quality then the activities must be configured so as to ensure high quality products. On the other hand, if the organization competes largely on the basis of price then activities must be organized so as to minimize costs.

Core activities, non-core activities and outsourcing

An increasing trend in recent years has been for organizations to concentrate on core activities associated with core competences and to outsource activities which are not regarded as core to other organizations for whom the activities are core. This is why, for example, fashion houses concentrate on design and marketing and outsource the production of their garments to businesses whose core activities are the manufacture of clothing. The combination of complementary core competences adds to the competitive advantage of all the collaborating companies. Value chain analysis should therefore also seek to identify where outsourcing might potentially add greater value than performing the activity in-house.

Summary

Internal analysis centres on the identification of the organization's potential for generating competitive advantage. This chapter has focused on the analysis of resources, competences, core competences and the value chain. Core competences and the configuration and co-ordination of value adding activities have been identified as primary sources of competitive advantage. It is important to examine the links between current strategies, core competences and core activities in the value chain as these are where the major potential for competitive advantage lies. Similarly it is important to examine other resources, competences and activities to identify the potential for building new core competences and core activities. The analysis also helps to identify opportunities for efficiency gains by re-configuring activities and by improving their integration so as to remove blockages from the system. Finally, this analysis allows a business to consider the potential of collaboration with suppliers, distributors and customers for improving performance. It is from all of this analysis that many of the elements of future strategy can be identified.

Review and Discuss

1   What are the major purposes of internal analysis?
2   Why do many writers in strategic management now consider that internal analysis is of greater importance than external analysis? Do you agree with their views?
3   Define and explain the relationships between resources, competences and core competences.
4   Explain the idea of the business as a value adding system.
5   Define and explain the relationships between primary and secondary activities.
6   What can be regarded as core activities and how do they relate to core competences?
7   What do we mean by blockages and linkages in the value chain?
8   What is the value system?
9   What do we mean by configuration and co-ordination?
10 What are the potential benefits of collaboration in the value system?

References and further reading

Coyne. K.P. (1986) Sustainable competitive advantage – what it is, what it isn't. *Business Horizons*, Jan–Feb. 54–61.

Hall, R. (1992) The strategic analysis of intangible resources. *Strategic Management Journal*, 13, 135–144.

Heene, A. and Sanchez, R. (1997) *Competence-Based Strategic Management*. London: John Wiley.

Kay, J. (1993) *Foundations of Corporate Success*. Oxford: Oxford University Press.

Kay, J. (1995) Learning to define the core business. *Financial Times*, December 1.

Petts, N. (1997) Building growth on core competences – a practical approach. *Long Range Planning*, 30 (4), August, 551–561.

Porter, M.E. (1980) *Competitive Strategy: Techniques for Analysing Industries and Competitors*. New York: Free Press.

Porter, M.E. (1985) *Competitive Advantage*. New York: Free Press.

Prahalad, C.K. and Hamel, G. (1990) The core competence of the corporation. *Harvard Business Review*.

Stalk, G., Evans, P. and Shulmann, L.E. (1992) Competing on capabilities: the new rules of corporate strategy. *Harvard Business Review*, March/April, 57–69.

Case linkage

Questions for the Kwik Save Group plc case study.

1   Identify the general competences shared by companies in the retail grocery sector.

2   Identify any distinctive capabilities (core competences) that Kwik Save may possess.

3   What are Kwik Save's core activities?

4   Why do you think Kwik Save outsources its fresh meat and greengrocery concessions?

5   Discuss the configuration of Kwik Save's value chain and its value chain linkages.

6   Identify the main threats that Kwik Save may face as a result of changes in the retail sector

Questions for the Derwent Valley Foods Ltd case study.

1   Identify the general competences shared by companies in the snack foods sector.

2   Which distinctive capabilities might DVF exploit to gain competitive advantage in its sector?

3   Which element(s) of DVF's value chain are its strongest in respect to gaining competitive advantage?

Chapter 3

Human resources and culture

Introduction

Human resources are one of the key resource inputs to any organizational process. A thorough analysis of this resource is an important part of strategic analysis and this chapter explains the human resource audit – one of the most widely used tools for this purpose.

Closely linked to the human resource is the issue of an organization's personality or culture. We define culture and then go on to explain its importance to an organization. The cultural web is discussed – a model used to explain the way that the features of culture determine the organization's paradigm. Finally, we discuss two cultural typologies.

Objectives

After studying this chapter, students should be able to:

- define and explain the importance of human resources to an organization;
- explain the purpose of a human resource audit;
- describe what a human resource gap is;
- explain what a human resource audit contains and what it can be used for;
- describe human resource benchmarking;
- explain what a critical success factor (CSF) is and how humans can be CSFs;
- define culture and explain its determinants and why it is important;
- explain the components of the cultural web and the nature of paradigms;
- describe two typologies of cultural types.

Human resources

The importance of human resources

People are an important resource to most organizations. Decisions about the future strategy of the organization are made by people and strategies are implemented by people. The success or failure of a current strategy will depend not only on decisions made in the past but also on how those decisions are being implemented now by people employed by the organization. It is therefore important to ask questions about who, how and why people are doing what they are doing and what they should do in strategic implementation. In short, human resources add value, manage the business and, conversely, can make spectacular errors that can be very costly to the organization.

An understanding of the capabilities of individuals and groups in terms of attitudes, abilities and skills, as well as an understanding of how individuals relate one to another, is an important part in the preparation and development of strategy. A key 'tool' in gaining an understanding of an organization's human resources is the human resource audit.

The human resource audit

The purpose of a human resource audit

The human resource audit is an investigation into the size, skills, structure and all other issues surrounding those currently employed by the organization. The audit reviews the ability of the human resources to implement a chosen strategy or a range of strategic options.

Most organizations employ accountants to maintain a constant review of financial resources and, each year, limited companies subject themselves (by law) to a formal external financial audit. Human resources are another resource input and are as important as, if not more important than, financial resources. An organization would be foolish to pursue a strategy without a thorough financial review, and the same is true of its people.

Once the audit has been completed, management should be able to answer the key question, 'Are the human resources in the organization capable of implementing the proposed strategy?' If any gaps are identified, then a human resource strategy may be put in place to close the gap.

Key Concepts

Human resource gaps
A 'gap' can occur in any area of human resource management. It rests upon a simple calculation:

Human resource characteristic necessary for the proposed strategy *minus* current state of the human resource characteristic *equals* the human resource gap.

Gaps can occur in particular skills. In sectors like banking, for example, skills gaps may be identified in particular computer languages. It may be that the audit reveals a deficit of 30 UNIX programmers – a negative gap. The task of the human resource department thus becomes to successfully appoint or retrain to gain the requisite number of skilled programmers.

Positive gaps may also be identified – surpluses of a particular type of employee. The human resource strategy thus becomes to put measures in place to dispose of the excess labour.

Gaps may be closed by recruitment, by retraining, by staff training and development, by redeployment, by redundancy, etc. Each of these solutions have financial and time implications.

The contents of a human resource audit

The contents of a human resource audit may vary from organization to organization depending on its size or geographic coverage. However, a typical audit checklist is as follows:

- the number of employees by a number of counting methods – the total number, by division, by location, by skill type, by grade or place in hierarchy, by age or length of service, by gender and by ethnic group;
- employee costs – usually measured by salary costs and 'add-ons' like national insurance, etc.
- the organizational structure and the position of employees within the structure;
- recruitment and selection procedures and their effectiveness;
- the quality and effectiveness of training and development programmes used;
- the level of employee motivation and morale;
- the quality of employee or industrial relations between management and employees;
- the internal and external networks that employees in the organization have developed (and their effectiveness for various purposes);

- the monitoring of the effectiveness of existing human resource policies and control procedures.

Formal and informal human resource audits

The information provided by the audit can provide management with important information about the state of the organization's human resources. In some types of organization, regular audits are essential to success. For a professional soccer club or an orchestra, the state of the human resources is completely transparent and the audit occurs continually – although it may never be formally conducted. A football team that loses every match or an orchestra that sounds terrible will have obvious human resource skill deficits. A formal audit is hardly necessary in such a circumstance.

Formal audits may be carried out by personnel specialists on a regular basis (say annually), or whenever management need the information for the purposes of a strategic analysis. Practitioners in this area make the point that the simple following of 'lists' like the one outlined above is only a starting point. As points of interest are raised, such as key skill deficiencies, then it is often a good idea to examine the reasons for the shortage as an integral part of the audit.

The outcomes of a human resource audit

The problem of measurement .

The various components of a human resource audit present differing problems of quantification. We can intuitively understand that entries like employee costs, numbers, skills shortages or surpluses can be measured in numerical terms. Industrial relations measures can usually be measured by such things as days lost through strikes, etc. Other parts of the audit present more difficulty in respect of measurement.

How, for example, might we measure staff morale or motivation? We might be able to say that staff morale is high or low, but any 'in-betweens' might be difficult to assign a value to in the same way as for, say, employee costs. The same problems arise with the levels of staff motivation and job satisfaction. It is also probably true in most organizations that large disparities exist between employees in respect to these intangibles. Some employees will be highly motivated and will enjoy good morale whilst others will not. It is for these reasons that a 'checklist' approach to human resource audit is rarely possible – it usually contains some subjective assessments of some parts of the audit.

Human resource benchmarking

The concept of benchmarking is one that we will encounter several times in this book. Essentially, benchmarking is a tool for comparing a feature of one organization with the same feature of another. It is particularly useful for comparison against the best in an industry for the feature in question. Followers of the best in the industry might then ask *why* the leader company has achieved the superior performance (see our discussion of benchmarking in finance, Chapter 4, and in operations, Chapter 12).

The feature examined in a benchmarking analysis will depend upon what the organization needs to know. If for example a company identifies a negative gap in a key skill area which it has found difficult to close (say of good quality graduates), a benchmark study will enable the company to find out about its competitors. If Company A is known to be able to attract the best graduates, then an examination of its human resource policies will enable other companies (competitors) to benchmark their own practices against it. It may be that Company A is identified as offering the best career-progression planning, the highest salaries or the best development opportunities. If this is found to be the case, then competitors will want to examine their own provision in these areas to see where they can be improved.

Lead companies may also be analysed for the ways in which they not only manage their internal human resources, but also the ways in which they interact with external sources of labour. Many high-technology companies, for example, close skills gaps by making extensive use of contract workers or consultants. The ability to attract these 'mobile' workers can be just as important as attracting permanent employees.

Identifying human resources as critical success factors

As well as using a human resource audit to identify gaps, it can also be used to establish which, if any, employees or groups of employees are critical to strategic success. These are the people that the organization's success may have been built upon in the past and it is likely that the existing structures are centred around them.

In some organizations, critical success human resources may be found on the board of directors giving strategic direction to the company as a whole. In others, they might be found in research, developing the new products upon which the future success will be built. Marketing people or operations management might also be critical in some businesses.

Key Concepts

Critical success factors
It is usually the case that there are one or more reasons why superior performers in an industry are in the positions that they are. These key reasons for success are called *critical success factors* (CSFs). Some companies have uniquely skilled employees, such as particularly important computer

programmers or research scientists. In this case, the CSF is a human resource. In other businesses, the CSF might be a unique location, a brand image, an enviable reputation, a legally-protected patent or licence, a unique production process or technology. This is not to say that other parts of the organization are unimportant, but merely that the CSF is *the* key cause of the success.

In terms of competitive strategy, the approach to a CSF is to defend it – in some cases at whatever cost it might take. This usually takes the form of 'locking it in' to ensure that the advantage is maintained or that competitors are prevented from gaining the same advantage.

Organizational culture

What is culture?

Culture is the organizational equivalent of a human's personality. One of the better definitions is that by Ralph Stacey (1996):

The culture of any group of people is that set of beliefs, customs, practices and ways of thinking that they have come to share with each other through being and working together. It is a set of assumptions people simply accept without question as they interact with each other. At the visible level the culture of a group of people takes the form of ritual behaviour, symbols, myths, stories, sounds and artefacts. (Stacey, 1996)

In simpler language, culture can be explained in terms of the 'feel' of an organization or its 'character'. Definitions can be a bit inaccessible, but the importance of an organization's culture lies in the fact that it can be 'felt' whenever it is encountered.

Organizations are as individual as people and, in many ways, there are as many cultures as there are organizations – each one is unique. This is not to say, however, that we cannot identify common features between organizational cultures.

The determinants of culture

Asking why an organization has a particular type of culture is as complicated a question as asking why a human has a particular personality. It has many possible influences, the net effect of which forge culture over a period of time. Any list would be necessarily incomplete, but following are some of the most important:

- the philosophy of the organization's founders, especially if it is relatively young;
- the nature of the activities in the business and the character of the industry it competes in;
- the nature of the interpersonal relationships and the nature of industrial or employee relationships;
- the management style adopted and the types of control mechanism, for example the extent to which management style is autocratic or democratic;
- the national or regional character of the areas in which the organization's activities are located (Schein, 1985). This in turn can affect the power distance which also influences culture;
- the structure of the organization, particularly its 'height' and 'width' (see Chapter 10);
- the dependency the organization has on technology and the type of technology employed (the growth of e-mail, for example, has had an influence on the culture of some organizations).

Key Concepts

Power distance

This is a term attributed to Hickson and Pugh (1995). They use the term to describe 'how removed subordinates feel from superiors in a social meaning of the word "distance". In a high power distance culture, inequality is accepted … in a low power distance culture, inequalities and overt status symbols are minimized and subordinates expect to be consulted and to share decisions with approachable managers.'

Why is culture important?

Culture is important because it can and does affect all aspects of an organization's activities. The metaphor of human personality may help us to understand this. Some people's personality means they are motivated, sharp, exciting to be with, etc. Others are dull, tedious, apathetic and conservative. These personality features will affect all aspects of their lives.

The same is true of an organization's 'personality'. Culture is important because of the following (not exhaustive) reasons. Culture can have an influence on:

- employee motivation;
- the attractiveness of the organization as an employer and hence the rate of staff turnover;
- employee morale and 'goodwill';
- productivity and efficiency;
- the quality of work;

- the nature of the employee and industrial relations;
- the attitude of employees in the workplace;
- innovation and creativity.

The point to make after such a list is simply that culture is *very* important. It is essential that management understand the culture of the organization both in analysing strategic position and then in the implementation of strategy.

The cultural web

One of the most commonly used ways of making sense of an organization's culture is to use the cultural web (Johnson, 1992). It is a schematic representation of the elements of an organization's culture in such a way that we can see how each element influences the paradigm (see Figure 3.1).

Paradigm
A paradigm is worldview – a way of looking at the world. It is expressed in the assumptions that people make and in their deep-rooted beliefs. The paradigm of an organization or a national culture is important because it determines how it will behave in a given circumstance. Given a certain moral dilemma or similar choice, we might expect the paradigms of an orthodox Jew and a atheist Westerner to lead them to arrive at different conclusions. The things that cause one culture to adopt one paradigm and another culture to espouse a different one are set out in the cultural web.

The main elements of the web are described below.

Stories

Stories are those narratives that people within the organization talk to each other about, what they tell new recruits and outsiders about the organization. The stories typically recount events and people from the past and present – stories of famous victories and defeats. They tend to highlight what is considered important to the members of the organization.

Routines and rituals

Routines are the procedures for doing things within the organization. They are repeated on a regular basis to the extent they are taken as 'the way things are done'. Rituals have a longer time frame and can be either formal

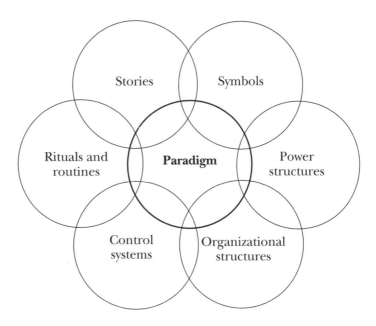

Figure 3.1 The cultural web (adapted from Johnson, 1992).

or informal. Formal routines and rituals are a part of the organization's practice, such as the 'long service award' or the company Outward Bound course that work teams might go on from time to time. Informal routines and rituals might include the way that people behave at the annual Christmas party or the extent to which colleagues do (or do not) go for a drink together after work.

Symbols

Symbolic aspects of organizational life concern those things that symbolize something to some people – a certain level of promotion, the company car they drive, the position of their office, their job title. In some companies, these symbols have no apparent importance at all. In others, they matter a great deal. The way that employees respond to these symbols can tell us a great deal about the culture.

Structure

The structure of an organization can mean more than just those formal relationships that are shown on an organization diagram. Informal structures can also exist through interpersonal relationships that transcend the formal structures. Some organizations have highly developed informal structures whilst others do not.

Control systems

The way in which activities are controlled, whether 'tight' or 'loose', is closely aligned to culture. This has a strong link to power distance and the nature of the activities that the organization is engaged in. Control systems, by definition, concern activity in which performance is gauged against a predetermined standard and the methods of both standard-setting and monitoring performance vary significantly according to culture.

Power structures

The core assumptions that contribute to the paradigm are likely to be made by the most powerful management groupings in the organization. In some companies, this power resides in the research department; in others it will be the production people or those from another department. In some organizations, there may be arguments about what is important between one or more groupings.

Each component of the cultural web exerts its own influence upon the organization's paradigm. The paradigm describes the aggregate effects of all of the cultural influences on the way the members of the organization look at the world. This can apply to regions of the world just as it applies to organizations. People indigenous to the Middle East are often thought to have a different view of the world than citizens of countries in North Western Europe. This difference is because of the influence that each component of the cultural web exerts on the national or regional paradigm.

Cultural typologies

A number of writers on organizational theory have attempted to group culture types together. The thinking behind such attempts at typology is that if organizations can describe their cultures by type, then this would help in strategic analysis. We will briefly consider two of these attempts.

Handy's culture types

Handy (1993) suggested that organizational cultures can be divided into four broad types: power cultures, role cultures, task cultures and person cultures.

Power cultures

This type of organization is dominated by either a very powerful individual or a dominant small group. It is typified by an organization that has grown as a result of entrepreneurial flair. Strategic decisions and many operational ones are made by the centre and few decisions are devolved to other managers. As the organization is dependent on the abilities and personality of the powerful individual, the ability of the organization to change in response to changes in the environment are sometimes limited by the centre.

Power cultures are common in small entrepreneurial (owner-managed) companies and in some notable larger organizations with a charismatic leader.

Role cultures

This type of culture is found in many long established organizations that have traditionally operated in stable environments. They tend to be very hierarchical and rely on established procedures, systems and precedent. They often respond slowly to change as it takes time for change to be recognized through the reporting mechanisms. Delays are also encountered in the slow, considered decision-making process.

Role cultures are common in traditional bureaucracies such as the civil service. The task of management in a role culture is to manage procedure. There is usually a high degree of decentralization and the organization is run by rules and laid-down procedures.

Task cultures

Task cultures are found in organizations engaged in activities of a non-repetitive nature, often high value one-off tasks. Activities are normally based around flexible multi-disciplinary teams containing expertise in the major disciplines required to complete the project. Teams tend to be small but flexible and find change easy to identify and adjust to. Strategic planning tends to concentrate on the task in hand.

As their name suggests, task cultures can be found in organizations that are dedicated to a particular task. Consortia that work on large civil engineering projects may demonstrate task culture as might missionary teams that work together on a medical project in the developing world.

Person cultures

Person cultures are those that exist primarily for the benefit of the members of the organization itself and, hence, they tend to be rare in commercial businesses. They can have a very different 'feel' to the other cultures as all members of the organizations work for the benefits of themselves and the other members.

They can be found in learned professional societies, in trade unions, in co-operatives, in some charities and in some religious organizations.

In reality, few organizations fit perfectly into one just classification and they may demonstrate elements of two or more. Some diversified organizations may have divisions that fall into all the categories and the cultures may change over time. Many start as power cultures and then tend towards a role culture as size increases.

Miles and Snow's culture types

Miles and Snow (1978) categorized cultures into four types, based on how they tend to react in strategic terms.

Defenders

These organizations tend to seek a competitive advantage in terms of targeting niche markets through cost reduction and specialization. They tend to operate in stable, mature markets and as the name suggests, they favour defending their current market share by service improvements or further cost savings. Defenders therefore tend to be centralized, have rigid control systems and a hierarchical management structure that does not enjoy sudden change.

Prospectors

These organizations enjoy the challenge of developing and introducing new products to the marketplace. They actively seek out new markets for their products. These favoured strategies require it to constantly monitor the environment and be willing and able to respond quickly to changes that may occur. To that end, they are decentralized and flexible.

Analyser

These organizations are 'followers' and are conservative in nature. Steady growth through market penetration is the favoured option as this can be achieved without radical changes to structure. Moves into new markets and products only occur after extensive evaluation and market research. They learn from the mistakes of others and tend to balance power between the centre and divisions with complex control systems.

Reactors

Reactors are a bit like analysers in that they tend to follow rather than innovate. They differ from analysers in that they are less conservative and sometimes behave impulsively, having failed to consider the implications of their actions fully. These organizations may lack proper control systems and typically have a weak but dominant leader.

Summary

Both human resources and organizational culture are important parts of strategic analysis. An understanding of both of these areas is a vital part of internal analysis. The state of an organization's human resources can be assessed by using a human resource audit – a tool that has its limitations, particularly in respect of measuring intangible aspects like job satisfaction, employee morale and motivation. The configuration of human resources in an organization is a major determinant of its culture. We can think of an organization's culture as its personality and we can use the cultural web to analyse it. Two ways of subdividing culture types, those by Handy and Miles and Snow, can also be useful tools in strategic analysis.

Review and Discuss

1 Why are human resources important to an organization?
2 What is the purpose of a human resource audit?
3 What is a human resource gap? Give some examples.
4 What does a human resource audit analyse?
5 What is human resource benchmarking? When might an organization use this technique?
6 What is a critical success factor?
7 What is meant by corporate culture?
8 Why is culture important to an organization?
9 What determines the culture of a business?
10 Describe the components of the cultural web.
11 What is meant by the terms power distance and paradigm?
12 Describe Handy's four culture types.
13 Describe Miles and Snow's culture types

References and further reading

Campbell, A. and Goold, M. (1987) *Strategies and Style*. London: Basil Blackwell.

Campbell, A., Goold, M. and Alexander, M. (1994) *Corporate Level Strategy*. London: Wiley.

Chandler, A (1962) *Strategy and Structure*. Cambridge, MA: MIT Press.

Goold, M. (1996) Parenting strategies for the mature business. *Long Range Planning*, June, p. 395.

Handy, C.B. (1993) *Understanding Organizations*, Fourth Edition. London: Penguin.

Hickson D.J. and Pugh D.S, (1995) *Management Worldwide*. London: Penguin.

Hofstede, G., (1980) *Culture and Organizations: Software of the Mind*. New York: McGraw-Hill.

Johnson, G. (1992) Managing strategic change: strategy, culture and action. *Long Range Planning*, 25, No. 1, 28–36.

Kay, J. (1993) *Foundations of Corporate Success*. Oxford: Oxford University Press.

Lynch, R. (1997) *Corporate Strategy*. London: Pitman.

Miles, R.E. and Snow, C.C. (1978) *Organizational Strategy, Structure and Process*. New York: McGraw-Hill.

Stacey, R. (1996) *Strategic Management and Organizational Dynamics*, Second Edition. London: Pitman.

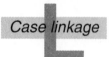

Case linkage

Questions for the Homebase case study.

1   Discuss the extent to which the human resource policies up to and during the Texas acquisition were consistent with the company's overall business strategy.

2   In what ways might Homebase have improved its knowledge of Texas, particularly in respect to its culture, before the acquisition?

3   Identify the human resource measures that Homebase took to bring the two cultures closer together and comment upon how successful you think they might have been.

Chapter 4

Financial analysis and performance indicators

Introduction

The ability to make sense of an organization's financial situation is an important part of strategic analysis. In order to carry out a financial analysis of a company's situation or of an industry, it is necessary to understand some of the fundamentals of finance and its sources. This chapter begins with a discussion of the sources of corporate finance and then goes on to discuss the costs of the various types of capital. This information helps students to make sense of a company's financial structure before the tools of conventional financial analysis are discussed. The various 'tools' for financial analysis are introduced and, finally, the concept of financial benchmarking is explained and its use in analysis is discussed.

Objectives

After studying this chapter, students should be able to:

- understand what is meant by financial analysis;
- identify the sources of funds available to companies and the relative advantages and disadvantages of each;
- assess a company's potential for further funding based on current position, future prospects and past performance;
- understand the cost and non-cost issues involved in raising and using various forms of capital;
- understand the importance of the cost of capital;
- understand the limitations of a company report and accounts as a source of data for financial analysis;
- describe the major tools that can be used to analyse a company's financial position.

An introduction to financial analysis

The importance of finance

Most university business courses have an accounting and finance content. You may consequently be familiar with some of the content of this chapter and this will be to your advantage. This chapter takes the material from the other units and develops the material into the context of strategic analysis.

Money, or the lack of it, is central to the strategic development of all organizations large or small. It is one of the key resource inputs and cannot be ignored. The most original strategies and the most complex plans for the future of a business are meaningless unless management has considered the financial position of the organization at the onset and during the period covered by the strategy. The ability of a company to finance both current and future strategies is central to any analysis of the company's position. A central theme to this chapter will be the ability of the company to finance strategies – its ability to raise the funding required for future developments.

The success or failure of the organization is judged by its ability to meet its strategic objectives. The financial information (in the form of annual corporate reports) produced by companies provides a quantifiable means of assessing success. It is important to recognize however that other quantifiable information, such as efficiency and productivity data, and non-quantifiable data such as the company's image, can also be used to make such judgements. In this chapter we will examine the value of information extracted from corporate reports as a source from which judgements can be made.

Corporate reports are, however, just one source of information about a company's financial state. Managers have a number of ways of gathering information about their own and competitors' finances and we will discuss these later in the chapter.

Sources of corporate funding

Financial resources, as we have already learned, are an essential input to strategic development. Capital for development can be raised from several sources and these are summarized here.

Key Concepts

Capital
Accountants use the term capital to describe one particular type of 'money'. It is usually contrasted with revenue. *Revenue* is money that is earned through normal business transactions – through sales, rents or

whatever the company 'does' through its normal activities. *Capital* is money that is used to invest in the business – to buy new equipment, new capacity, extra factory space, etc. The investment of capital enables the business to expand and, through that expansion, to increase its revenue and profits in future years. Capital can be raised from shareholders, through retained profits, through rights issues, through loan capital or through the disposal of assets.

Share capital

For limited companies, a sizeable proportion of capital is raised from shareholders (the financial owners of the company) in the form of share capital.

Historically, share capital has comprised the majority of capital for a limited company's start up and subsequent development. In return for their investment, shareholders receive a return in accordance with the company's performance in a given year in the form of a dividend. The dividend per share is taken as an important measure, by shareholders, of the company's success in its chosen strategy. Shares also confer on their holders a right to vote on company resolutions at annual or extraordinary company meetings *pro rata* with the size of their holding. It follows of course that a shareholding in excess of 50 per cent confers total control over a company's strategy.

Under normal circumstances, share capital is considered to be permanent – it is not paid back by the company. It is thus unlike other forms of capital (e.g. loan capital). The shareholders' only 'payback' is in the form of dividends and through capital growth – an increase in the value of the shares. Shareholders who wish to divest their stock in a company must usually sell it via a stock exchange (in the case of shares in a public limited company) or through a private sale (in the case of a private company). In exceptional circumstances, some companies offer a 'buyback' of their own shares. In recent years, Barclays plc and BP have offered this facility. Between February 1996 and February 1997 Barclays plc bought back some 104 million shares from its shareholders in order to increase its control over its own strategy.

Shareholders can be individuals or 'institutional shareholders'. Some individuals hold their personal share portfolio but the vast majority of shares are held by institutional shareholders such as pension funds, life assurance companies and investment trusts. The Annual Report & Accounts of Vickers plc is not untypical when in 1995 it stated that 94 per cent of its ordinary share capital, in terms of volume, were held by institutional shareholders with Schroder Investment Management Ltd being the largest with 14.2 per cent. The profile of shareholders varies from company to company and from country to country.

Key Concepts

Share value and share volume

Share value is the price of a given company's shares at a given point in time. Like any other commodity, its value is determined by the forces of supply and demand. Given that in normal circumstances the supply is fixed over the short to medium term, its price is determined by how many people want to buy it. If the market has confidence in a company's prospects, its price will rise. If a company's prospects are considered poor, fewer people will want to buy its shares and the price will fall.

Share volume is the number of shares held by a shareholder. The larger the volume, the more influential the shareholder will be in the company's affairs.

Total share volume is the total number of shares that a company has issued for sale to the stockmarket or to employees of the organization. Broadly speaking, larger companies have greater share volumes than smaller concerns

Rights issue capital

From time to time, a company may seek to increase its capital for expansion by means of a *rights issue*. This is when a company issues new shares to the stockmarket, normally giving its own shareholders the first refusal *pro rata* with their current proportion of the company's share volume.

The decision to go for a rights issue may well be a strategic decision for management because it can impact on the ownership of the company. If existing shareholders do not exercise their right to buy, then it is likely that ownership will be diluted – i.e. shareholders will find that they own a lower percentage of share volume than they used to.

Those shares not taken up by shareholders, who may be unable or unwilling to buy them, are normally covered by *underwriters* (institutional investors) at a price agreed, in advance. Underwriting is an important 'technical' feature of new share issues and as such is a major cost in the process. A rights issue is sometimes seen as a reward to loyal shareholders.

A variation on a rights issue is *placing*. A placing involves the selling of shares direct to a small number of investors, usually large financial institutions. This may be marginally cheaper than a rights issue, but its major advantage is its flexibility in enabling new shareholders to have significant, possibly strategic, holdings.

Retained profit as a source of capital

Shareholders provide other funds for development by agreeing not to receive all the company's profits in a given year. *Retained profit,* that element of operating profit not paid to shareholders in the form of dividend, is arguably the most common method of funding strategic developments, particularly if the company is quite old in terms of years. By using this form of funding, organizations save on the costs involved in using alternatives – such as fees to merchant banks, lawyers and accountants. It also means management do not have to reveal nor justify their strategies to others and risk their plans becoming known to competitors.

It should be recognized that retained profits do not constitute a loss to shareholders as such, because the value of the organization and consequently the share price is normally increased when these funds are used for reinvestment. It is however important that companies recognize the need to balance the proportion of profits distributed and retained in order to satisfy those shareholders who need regular funds flow themselves (such as insurance and pension companies).

Loan capital

An important consideration in the use of retained profits to fund corporate development is clearly the ability of the company to actually make a profit that can be, at least in part, distributed to shareholders as dividends. Whilst a company may make a profit from its normal activities after taxation, some profits may be required to meet the cost of other forms of *debt finance* or loans.

Debt finance is shown in the balance sheet under two headings, *Creditors: amounts following within one year* and *Creditors: amounts falling due after more than one year*. The form of borrowing with most impact on strategic development is that falling due after more than one year – long-term debt. This form of borrowing can take a number of forms. In addition to the use of long-term bank loans, a company can use debentures, convertible loan stock or corporate bonds.

Debt finance is normally for a set period of time and at a fixed rate of interest. The interest must be paid every year, regardless of the level of profit (referred to as *servicing* the debt). The interest rate for this source is normally less than the cost of share capital (when the dividend payable on the shares is taken into account).

Comparing share capital and loan capital

Each of the types of capital described above has its pros and cons. Share capital has the advantage that the amount paid on the capital is dependent upon company results. A company can decide not to pay a dividend if profits are poor in any given year. Loan capital, by contrast, must be serviced regardless of results in much the same way that a mortgage on a house must be repaid regardless of other commitments.

Offsetting this advantage is the fact that share capital is permanent. As long as the company exists, it has an obligation to repay a dividend to its shareholders. Loan capital has the advantage to the company that it is time limited. Servicing the capital is restricted to the term of the loan (like a mortgage on a house) and when it is finally repaid in full, the business has no further obligation to the lender.

The fact that the repayment of debt finance takes precedence over dividends on shares means that shareholders bear an increased risk. If the company performs badly, their return on investment will be small or non-existent in a given year. Against this possibility, they usually expect to receive higher returns compared with providers of loan capital in the years when profits are good.

Key Concepts

Loan capital – a summary
Interest on debt capital must be paid regardless of the level of profit. Interest on debt capital takes priority over dividends to shareholders.

In practice, business profits can vary significantly over time. In some years, it is preferable to use loan capital, especially when interest rates are low and profits are high. In other years, when profits are lower and interest rates are higher, share capital works out cheaper. The fact that the benefits are so finely divided means that most companies opt to use an element of both. The relationship of debt capital to shareholder capital is referred to as the company's *gearing ratio.*

Gearing is an indication of how the company has arranged its capital structure. It can be expressed as either:

$$\frac{\text{borrowed capital (i.e. debt)}}{\text{total capital employed (i.e. borrowings plus shareholders' capital)}}$$

or, as:

$$\frac{\text{borrowed capital (i.e. debt)}}{\text{shareholders' capital (i.e. equity)}}$$

Both are usually expressed as percentages by simply multiplying the quotient by 100. It is not important which one is used unless we are comparing the gearing of two or more companies.

Other sources of capital

Whilst the foregoing are the most common mechanisms of raising capital for development, others are available under some circumstances.

One such method is to dispose of existing fixed assets. This can range from selling of a factory to selling a subsidiary to a third party. Assets sales can offer the benefits of reducing liabilities (if the facility is loss-making) or of selling off non-core activities.

The realizable price for the asset will depend on the timing of its sale. In the summer of 1998, overcapacity in the microchip industry meant that two factories in the North East of England (Siemens and Fujitsu) were unsaleable as 'going concerns'.

Finally, marginal improvements in a company's capital situation can be achieved by improving the management of working capital. Over the course of a financial year, small savings can accumulate to significant proportions, increasing both profitability and capital for reinvestment. This can be achieved by:

- extending the time taken to pay creditors;
- getting debtors to pay sooner; or
- more efficiently controlling stocks

Working capital
Working capital is the amount of money that a company has tied up in the normal operation of its business. Working capital comprises money tied up in:

- stocks;
- debtors (money owed to the business);
- creditors (money the company owes);
- cash or current bank deposits.

A company's objective is usually to minimize this figure.

Cost of capital

Availability of capital (where to get it from) is one issue when examining a company's capital funding, but another equally important consideration is its cost. We learned above that providers of loans or share capital (equity) both require a return on their investments. Management therefore need to know what return (profit) they need to make in order to meet the minimum requirements of capital providers. Failure to achieve this minimum will make the raising of future funds all the more difficult. The cost of capital can be seen as the minimum return required on the company's assets, which in turn may influence the objectives of the company.

cost of capital

At its simplest, the *cost of capital* can be viewed as the annual amount payable (as a percentage) against the principal amount of money. Most of us will be aware that the return payable on such things as loans varies between lenders and over time as interest rates rise or fall. The cost of loans on a credit card is, for example, much higher than a mortgage loan (where the security against the loan is mainly responsible for the difference). Some fortunate people are able to borrow money interest-free (zero cost of capital).

cost of debt capital

The *cost of debt capital* is relatively easy to calculate as it tends to correspond closely to the prevailing rate of interest. If the loan is to be repaid at a fixed rate, the calculation is even more straightforward. Loans up to a certain amount are granted tax exemption by HM Inland Revenue and this may be deducted from the interest rate before arriving at the final annual cost of loan capital.

cost of share capital

Calculating the *cost of share capital* is slightly more complex as it contains more variables. Accounting academics spend a great deal of time discussing what should and should not be included in this calculation and how each component should be weighted. Reasons for this complexity include the indefinite nature of the funding, the opportunity cost of undistributed profits and shareholders' expectations. These mean that some models try to include components for inflation, industry averages and attitudes towards risk.

At its simplest, the cost of share capital can be calculated as follows:

$$\text{Cost of share capital (equity) as a percentage} = \frac{\text{Current net dividend per share}}{\text{Current market price of share}} \times 100 + \text{Average percentage annual growth rate}$$

Example

The market price for shares was 400p per share and the annual dividend was 20p. If growth in profits averages 10% per annum, this gives:

Cost of share capital = (20/400) × 100 + 10%
= 15%

Models of capital costing

The CAPM model

The *Capital Asset Pricing Model* (CAPM) is a more complex but widely-used model for calculating the cost of share capital.

Cost of share capital = Ri +β (Rm – Ri)

The model takes into account the competitor financial products available to potential investors. These range from the percentage return on virtually risk free government bonds (Ri) to a component covering the average interest for the share (equity) markets overall (Rm). The final elements of the model represents the company itself, or more correctly its position relative to the market overall. The β coefficient is a measure of the volatility of the company's financial returns.

The CAPM model does have a number of drawbacks which need to be recognized. Firstly, the shares of the company need to be traded on a stockmarket. This means that the cost of equity in private companies cannot be calculated using this model. Secondly the volatility of share prices in recent years causes problems in arriving at a date for 'acceptable' returns. The dynamic and complex nature of many industries and markets also suggest that historical data has limited value.

CAPM model
Assume that risk-free government bonds were trading at 4% and the average return on the market was 10%. Also assume that the volatility of the company had been calculated at 1.1 (meaning the shares fluctuated slightly more than the market average).

Cost of share capital (equity) = 4%+1.1(10% – 4%) = 10.6%

The WACC model

Whereas the CAPM model is used to calculate the cost of share capital, the *Weighted Average Cost of Capital* (WACC) can be used to determine the overall cost of funding to a company. The calculation of this information is relatively simple:

WACC = (Proportion of loan finance × cost of loan finance) + (proportion of shareholders' funds × cost of shareholders' funds)

WACC model
Assume that a company had £30 million of loan capital and £70 million equity funding. The cost of each type had been calculated as 5% and 15% respectively, the calculation would be as follows

Type of capital	Proportion	Cost (after tax)	Weighted cost
Loan Finance	0.3	5%	1.5%
Shareholders' Funds	0.7	15%	10.5%
Total	1.0		12.0%

Why calculate the cost of capital?

The cost of capital is usually an important figure to calculate because if it works out to be too high, the development that it is intended to fund may not be viable. Given that both debt and share capital attract servicing costs, the profit returns must exceed these servicing costs to the extent that the proposal is economically attractive.

If the projected returns on a strategic development (such as a new factory facility) are not much more than the projected servicing costs, then management will have to make a judgement as to whether the investment is actually 'worth the risk'.

The whole situation is rendered more complex if debt capital is obtained at a variable rate of interest. Interest rates can vary substantially throughout an economic cycle and depend upon such things as government inflation targets, the currency exchange value and the national rate of capital deposition.

There are no guidelines as to the ideal capital structure – the balance between debt and equity finance. The optimal structure will vary from company to company, from industry to industry and from year to year. Some companies will calculate their WACC and include factors which are difficult to quantify, such as the degree of risk faced by the industry, trends in interest rates and even the cost and availability of funds to competitors.

Financial analysis

The basics

We would usually employ an analysis of a company's financial situation as part of an internal strategic analysis. We may wish to understand a company's finances in order to make an assessment of its 'health' or its readiness to undertake a phase of strategic development.

There are three areas of financial analysis:

● longitudinal analysis (sometimes called trend analysis);
● cross-sectional analysis (or comparison analysis);
● ratio analysis.

A comprehensive analysis of a company's financial situation would normally involve an element of all three of these analyses. The one thing to bear in mind when looking at accounting statements is that they contain numbers in isolation. An accounting number on its own is just that – a number. In order to make any sense of it, we must compare it with other accounting numbers.

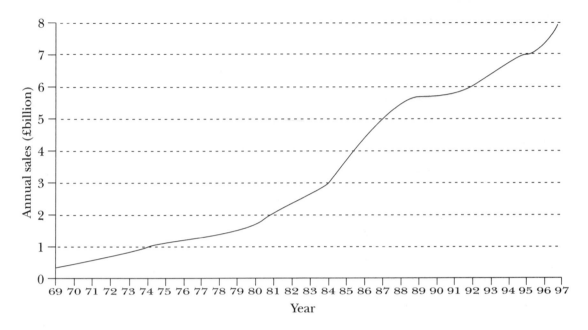

Figure 4.1 A simple longitudinal analysis: annual sales for Marks & Spencer plc (1969–97).

Longitudinal analysis

The simplest means of assessing any aspect of a company's finances is to compare the data for two or more years and see what has increased and what has decreased over that time period, and by how much. It goes without saying that the longer back in time we look, then the better idea we will get as to its current position in its historical context (see for example Figure 4.1). Many company corporate reports provide a five or ten year record and this can help us in constructing a longitudinal analysis.

The easiest way to perform this form of analysis is to conduct an initial scan of the figures to identify any major changes between the years. This involves simply looking along each line in turn, and highlighting any larger than normal increases or decreases, for example a scan along five years of stock figures from the balance sheet below clearly indicates that something happened in year 4. Not only did the figure more than double, it reverted to the 'normal' trend the following year.

Year	1	2	3	4	5
Stock	300	330	370	800	450

Anomalies like these may need further investigation. Questions need to be asked – or rather answers found – to explain the reasons for such an increase. The impact of the 'blip' on the year's performance must be assessed, as must its impact on current performance. Further investigation of the balance sheet or profit and loss account, together with any notes to the accounts, may provide some clues. It may be important to discover how such an increase was financed, why there was a need to carry such high levels of stock and the impact of such levels on suppliers and customers.

The initial scan may need to be followed by a more detailed analysis which calculates the year-on-year increase/decrease in percentage terms. It is sometimes helpful to plot trends on a graph against time (such as in Figure 4.1). This can help to highlight changes at particular points in time.

The identification of trends, in terms of say turnover, costs or of some items of a balance sheet (such as stocks) can therefore be valuable in our financial analysis. Such trends should, however, be seen in their context. An organization operating in a static or slow growth market may judge a 1 per cent year-on-year increase in turnover as a great success, whereas a company in a buoyant market would judge a 1 per cent increase as a failure.

Cross-sectional analysis

Whilst longitudinal analysis helps us to assess performance against a historical trend, it tells us nothing of the company's performance against that of competitors or of companies in other industries. If we were, for example, to identify strong sales growth of 10 per cent a year in a longitudinal analysis of Company A's financial statements we might be tempted to think that the company was performing well. If we were then to compare this company with its competitors only to find that the industry average rate of growth was 15 per cent, then we would wish to modify our initial assessment of Company A's performance.

Key Concepts

Financial statements

One of the conditions placed upon limited companies is the requirement to file an audited annual report and accounts. There are five compulsory components to this document as set out in the UK in the Companies Act (1985 as amended): chairman's statement, auditor's report, profit and loss statement, balance sheet and cash-flow statement. The accounting rules by which they are to be constructed are prescribed in financial reporting standards (FRSs) to ensure that all companies mean the same thing when they make an entry in one of the statements. When they are completed (following the company's financial year end), they become publicly available. Each shareholder receives a copy, and a copy is lodged at UK Companies House in Cardiff or London.

It is for the purposes of comparisons of this nature that cross-sectional analyses are important. As well as comparing accounting numbers like turnover, it is often helpful to compare two or more companies' ratios (see next section) such as return on sales or one of the working capital ratios.

Ratio analysis

The third important tool in the analysis of company performance is *ratio analysis*. A ratio is a comparison (by quotient) of two items from the same set of accounts. Given that there are a lot of numbers in a set of accounts, it will not come as a surprise to learn that a large number of ratios can be drawn – some of which are more useful than others.

Ratio analysis is an area of some academic debate and, accordingly, the way in which ratios are expressed may vary between accounting and strategy textbooks. What is important therefore is to employ a consistent approach to ratio analysis, especially in longitudinal and cross-sectional analyses.

For most purposes, we can divide ratios into five broad categories:

1 performance ratios;
2 efficiency ratios;
3 liquidity ratios;
4 investors' ratios;
5 financial structure ratios.

Performance ratios

As their name suggests, performance ratios test to see how well a company has turned its inputs into profits. This usually involves comparing *return* (PBIT or profit before interest and tax) either against turnover or against its capital. This is because the rates of tax and interest payable vary. Using profit after interest and tax would distort the performance figure.

Return on capital employed (ROCE) is perhaps the most important and widely used measure of performance. It indicates the return being made compared with the funds invested. At its simplest, it is this figure that tests the gains of investing in a business as opposed to simply placing capital on return in a bank

Where an organization can break down its figures by divisions or subsidiaries, individual performance can be measured and decisions relating to continued ownership made.

Return on equity or *return on ordinary shareholders' funds* gives an indication of how effectively the share capital has been turned into profit (i.e. it does not take account of loan capital). This ratio should be used carefully as the capital structure of the company can affect the ratio.

Return on sales, or *profit margin*, either net or gross, is a popular guide to the profitability of a company. This ratio assesses the profit made per £ sold. Return on sales tends to vary from industry to industry and between companies within an industry. Food retailers typically make between 5 and 12 per cent whilst companies in the pharmaceuticals sector rarely make less than 20 per cent. Figure 4.2 shows an analysis of Marks & Spencer's return on sales.

Performance ratios
Each can be expressed as a percentage by multiplying the ratio by 100:

Return on capital employed = Profit before interest and tax (PBIT – from P&L account)/total capital employed (i.e. one side of the balance sheet)

Return on shareholders' funds = PBIT/shareholders' funds (from balance sheet

Net return on sales = PBIT/total sales (also called turnover or revenue)

Gross return on sales = Gross profit/total sales

Note: Gross profit is the profit after direct costs (i.e. conversion costs) have been deducted from sales, but before indirect (i.e. administrative) costs. Gross margin is an indication of how effectively a company has managed its wages, energy and stocks.

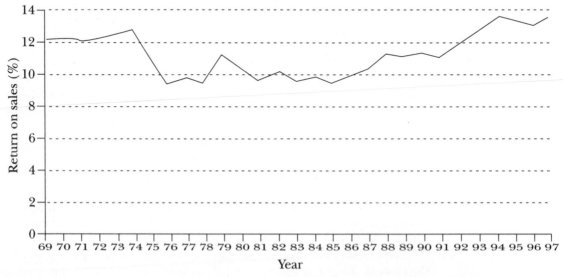

Figure 4.2 A longitudinal analysis of Marks & Spencer plc return on sales, 1969–97.

Efficiency ratios

These ratios show how efficiently a company has used its assets to generate sales. We can use any one of a number of a company's inputs to test against sales or profits. Common efficiency ratios include *sales per employee* and *profit per employee*, both of which test the efficiency with which a company uses its labour inputs.

Efficiency

The term efficiency is used in many ways – not just in accounting. We may speak of an efficient engine or the efficiency of a heating system in a house. At its simplest, efficiency is a comparison of a system's output to its inputs with a view to testing how well the input has been turned into output. It follows that a more efficient system will produce more output for a given input than a less efficient one.

It can be expressed mathematically as a quotient:

Efficiency = (Work output/work input) × 100 (to arrive at a percentage)

Other commonly used efficiency ratios are *asset turnover* and a variant of this, *fixed asset turnover*. A high level of asset turnover indicates that the company is using its assets efficiently and, conversely, a low level may indicate that the company is suffering from overcapacity. Stock turnover gives an indication of how well the company controls its stocks. A company that keeps stock moving will generally have a higher stock turnover than one that has piles of unsaleable or obsolete materials.

Efficiency ratios
Sales per employee (£) = Total sales (from P&L)/number of employees (usually found in the notes to the accounts)

Profit per employee (£) = PBIT/number of employees

Stock turnover = Cost of sales (from P&L)/value of stock (from balance sheet)

Stock turnover is measured in times – i.e. the number of times the total stock is turned over in a given year.

Liquidity ratios

These ratios test the company's ability to meet its short-term debts – an important thing to establish if we have reason to believe the company is in trouble. Essentially, they ask the question, 'Has the company enough funds to meet what it owes?'

The *current ratio* is the best known liquidity ratio. It is a measure of a company's total liabilities in comparison to its total assets and is thus calculated entirely from balance sheet figures. It is used to assess the company's ability to meet its liabilities by the use of its assets such as stock, debtors (receivables) and cash.

The *acid test ratio* is a variant of the current ratio and tests the company's ability to meet its short-term liabilities using its cash or 'near cash' assets. Many textbooks suggest a ratio of 2:1 should be a target for this ratio and a target of 1:1 should be sought for the acid test ratio. These are simple guides and should not be taken as the norm for all industries. For example, many companies in the retail industry have few debtors and have high stock turnover but still have creditors – as a result their current ratio is below 2:1.

Investors' ratios

This family of ratios test for things that are important to a company's investors – usually its shareholders or potential shareholders. There are three that are widely used.

Earnings per share (EPS) is calculated by dividing profit after interest and tax (called earnings) by the number of shares. It shows how much profit is attributable to each share. The *price earnings ratio* (P/E) gives an indication of the stock market's confidence in a company's shares. It is the current market price of the company's ordinary shares divided by its EPS at the last year end and it follows therefore that the P/E varies with the share price. Broadly speaking it is a way of showing how highly investors value the earnings a company produces. A high P/E ratio (where the price is high compared with the last declared EPS) usually indicates growth potential whilst a low P/E suggests static profits. The P/E ratio for quoted companies is regularly published in the financial press.

Dividend yield is the third widely used investors' ratio. Potential shareholders often want to know what the most recent return on the share was in terms of percentage. Dividend yield is calculated by dividing the dividend per share at the last year end by the current price (and then multiplying by 100 to arrive at a percentage).

Example

Investors' ratios
EPS = Profit after interest and tax/share volume

P/E = Price of share (as of 'today')/EPS at most recent year end

Dividend yield = (Gross dividend per share/current price of share) × 100

Financial structure ratios

We encountered financial structure above when we discussed the relative merits of loan and share capital. The way in which a company 'mixes' these forms of capital is referred to as its financial (or capital) structure.

The *gearing ratio* looks at the relationship between all the borrowings of the company (including short-term borrowings), and all the capital employed by the company. This provides a view of the extent to which borrowing forms part of the total capital base of the company and hence the risk associated with rising interest rates.

The *debt/equity ratio*, a variation on the gearing ratio, uses the shareholders' funds in the calculation rather than the total capital employed. This ratio provides a more direct comparison between the funds attributed to shareholders and liability of the company to loan providers.

Example

> **Financial structure ratios**
> **Gearing = Debt capital (typically borrowings due after one year)/debt capital plus shareholders' funds**
>
> **Debt/equity ratio = Debt capital (borrowings due after one year)/shareholders' funds**

Using ratios in financial analysis

Compared with simply looking at accounting numbers, ratios provide a way of making some sense of published accounts. However, if we place a ratio within its longitudinal or cross-sectional context, its usefulness is maximized.

If we take return on sales as an example, we would usually want to know how Company A's figure this year compares not only with last year's (i.e. is it more or less), but also with Company A's competitors. This enables us to assess how Company A is performing over time and to make a judgement on its competitive position in its industry. This is because profitability is an important indicator of competitive success.

Limitations of financial information

For most purposes in strategic analysis, we can accept the proposition that the data we collect from a company's annual accounts is accurate and provides a truthful statement on its financial position. From time to time, however, we may need to qualify our analysis for one or more reasons.

Firstly, whilst the financial statements are audited for accuracy, other parts of the annual report are not. If our financial analysis consists of an examination of the entire document and not just the accounting sections, then we would need to be aware of this. Additional disclosures made in corporate reports may serve a number of purposes. Some commentators have suggested that such disclosures may be something of a public relations and marketing exercise.

Secondly, we should remember that the financial information in a corporate report is historical, often published up to three months after the period it represents. Whilst this historical information can be used to judge past performance, it may have limited use in predicting future performance. The balance sheet shows the financial position at 'a moment in time' (at the year end). It does not (unlike the P&L) summarize a full year's trading and things can sometimes change quickly after the year end.

In an attempt to avoid this potential problem, Stock Exchange quoted companies are required to produce *interim reports*, normally half yearly and unaudited, which show their profit and turnover for that period. Quoted companies are also required to provide the Stock Exchange with information that may have a significant impact on its prospects such as changes on the board or anything that gives rise to a 'profits warning'.

Thirdly, those who prepare a company's financial statements (the financial accountants) sometimes have cause to 'hide' bad news so as to avoid alarming the company's investors. It is possible to employ legal financial restructuring so as to make some figures appear better than perhaps they are. A year-on-year increase in the value of fixed assets, for example, may appear at first glance to be healthy, but it may be that the company has accumulated a high amount of debt to finance it. It is for this reason that we sometimes need to examine all parts of a company's financial statements to spot any countervailing bad news that has been obscured by the company in its reporting.

Other analysis tools

Whilst the majority of situations can be made sense of using the above 'tools', two others that are sometimes useful are discussed here.

Financial benchmarking

Inter-company comparison or *benchmarking* is a variation on cross-sectional analysis. It usually involves an analysis of 'like' companies, usually in the same industry though it can occasionally be an inter-industry analysis.

In order to make the benchmarking analysis meaningful, the company selection should usually be guided by similarity by:

- company size (i.e. they should be comparable in terms of turnover, market value or similar);
- industry (in that the companies produce similar products); and
- market (i.e. the companies share a similar customer base).

In practice, sample selection for benchmarking study always involves some compromise because no two companies are in all respects directly comparable. Many companies, for example, operate in more than one industry and this may render problematic any comparisons with another company that operates in only one industry.

The practice of inter-company (cross-sectional) analysis using financial data has been undertaken by accountants for many years. Benchmarking, however, can be used to compare financial and, importantly, non-financial information between two or more companies.

Benchmarking is now used to compare the effectiveness of various processes, products and procedures against others. The objective is to identify where superior performance is found in whatever variable that is being used for comparison. Once the company with the highest performance is identified, the exercise becomes to explore the reasons behind the superior performance.

The benchmarking process therefore involves decisions on:

- what are we going to benchmark? (financial or non-financial data)
- who are we going to benchmark against? (sample selection)
- how will we get the information?
- how will we analyse the information?
- how will we use the information?

The value of benchmarking is in identifying not only which company has the superior performance in a sector but also *why* this is the case. If, for example, our analysis throws up the fact that Company X enjoys a return on sales significantly higher than the other companies in the sector, then Company X occupies the profitability benchmark in that sector. The other companies may then wish to examine the practices within Company X that give rise to this level of performance.

For non-financial indicators, our analysis may highlight the fact that Company Y is able to attract the best-qualified people within a key category of personnel, for example the best scientists or computer programmers. In this case, Company Y demonstrates the benchmark in successful recruitment. Other companies who are unable to attract the best personnel would usually wish to examine Company Y to see why it is so successful in this regard.

Common-sizing accounts

Commonly sized accounts are particularly useful in cross-sectional analyses but can also be used to analyse the same company's accounts from year to year. If we were, for example, to examine the P&L or balance sheets of two companies in the same industry, we may at first be unable to make sense of differences between the two. The two separate accounts can be analysed by making the totals of both equal 100 and then dividing each entry by the resultant quotient accordingly. A simplified example of commonly sized accounts is shown in Table 4.1.

	Company A £M	Common size	Company B £M	Common size
Sales	113.4	100	224.6	100
Cost of sales	65	57.31922	112	49.86643
Gross profit	48.4	42.68078	112.6	50.13357
Administrative costs	33.7	29.71781	67	29.83081
Operating profit	14.7	12.96296	45.6	20.30276

Table 4.1 Simplified P&L accounts for two hypothetical companies.

From Table 4.1, we can make comparisons between the cost structures of the two companies despite the fact that Company B has approximately twice the turnover of Company A. We can tell, for example, that overall, Company B is better at controlling costs than Company A – as evidenced by the fact that its operating profit is 20.3% compared with Company A's figure of 12.9%. We could draw comparable conclusions from other commonly sized components of the accounts.

Summary

An analysis of a company's financial position is an indispensable part of any strategic review. Decision-makers need to know whether or not the company has the level of funding required to finance their strategies and, if not, financial resource will have to be raised.

It is usually important to know where a company has obtained its capital and the cost of this capital. Both share capital and loan capital have their advantages and disadvantages for use in strategic development. It is important to note whether or not current levels of profitability are sufficient to service the costs of capital.

There are a number of tools which we can use to make sense of a company's financial statements. Longitudinal analysis examines trends over time while cross-sectional analysis compares a company's finances against its competitors'. Ratio analysis enables us to make sense of accounts by dividing one accounting number by another. Benchmarking enables us to compare one company's performance on a number of fronts with similar companies.

Review and Discuss

1 Why is money important to a business?
2 Define and distinguish between revenue and capital.
3 Define and distinguish between share capital and loan capital.
4 What are the advantages of employing share capital for development?
5 What are the advantages of employing loan capital for development?
6 What is a rights issue?
7 What is meant by the cost of capital?
8 Define and distinguish between longitudinal and cross-sectional analyses.
9 What are the main categories of accounting ratios?
10 Explain what is meant by benchmarking.

References and further reading

Allen, D. (1997) *An Introduction to Strategic Financial Management*. London: CIMA/Kogan Page.

Department of Trade & Industry (1992). *Best Practice Benchmarking*. London: DTI.

Camp, R.C. (1994). *Business Process Benchmarking*. ASQC Quality Press.

Ellis, J. and Williams, D. (1993) *Corporate Strategy & Financial Analysis*. London: Pitman Publishing.

Franks, J.R. and Broyles, J.E. (1979). *Modern Managerial Finance*. London: John Wiley.

Higson, C. (1995) *Business Finance*. Oxford: Butterworth-Heinemann.

Mott, G. (1991). *Management Accounting for Decision Makers*. London: Pitman Publishing.

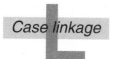

Case linkage

Questions for the Kwik Save Group plc case study.

1 Chart and comment upon the longitudinal trends from the Kwik Save accounts in:
 a) turnover;
 b) profit before interest and tax;
 c) shareholders' funds.
2 Comment upon the performance of the group over time for return on sales and return on net assets.
3 Identify any 'points of interest' in the Kwik Save accounts that might be of concern to investors and/or creditors.

Chapter 5

Products and markets

Introduction

The way in which an organization relates to its markets is one of the most important aspects of competitive strategy. The idea of a market as a place where buyers and sellers come together can apply to both inputs and outputs. Product markets are those in which an organization competes for sales whilst resource markets are those in which an organization competes for its resource inputs.

In this chapter, we discuss the key elements of this system – the nature of markets and the nature and importance of products. The way in which an organization configures itself in respect to these elements is crucial to the success of business strategy.

Objectives

After studying this chapter, students should be able to:

- explain the term *market* and describe three ways by which markets can be defined;
- describe market segmentation and explain the ways that markets can be segmented;
- describe three ways of approaching market segmentation;
- explain the term product and describe Kotler's five levels of product benefit;
- describe and criticize Copeland's product typology;
- understand the stages in and uses of the product life cycle;
- explain the concept of portfolio;
- describe the composition and limitations of the Boston matrix.

Ways of defining and understanding markets

Defining markets and market share

Economists refer to a market as a system comprising two 'sides'. The demand side comprises buyers or consumers of a product or resource whilst the supply side produces or manufactures the same.

In strategy, we often use the term slightly differently. By market, we usually mean a group of actual or potential customers with similar needs or wants (the demand side). We usually refer to the supply side as an industry.

The definition and boundaries of an organization's markets represent a key starting point for the formulation of strategy, and provide a basis for measuring competitive performance. The analysis and definition of markets will provide key information concerning threats and opportunities.

Market share is a measure of an organization's performance with regard to its ability to win and retain customers. It can be measured either by volume or by value. Volume measures concern the organization's share of units sold to the market (e.g. number of barrels of oil sold by an oil company in proportion to the total number of barrels sold). Value measures concern the sales turnover of one company in proportion to the total value of the market.

We can also define the boundaries of markets in different ways. If different companies define a market in different ways, it is not surprising that the sum of their claimed market share may add to more or less than one hundred per cent. The grocery market, for example, may mean different things to different companies. One might include just the English market for groceries whilst another might measure it for the whole of the UK. It is clearly important, therefore, that market share measures are stated explicitly with the market boundaries clearly defined.

There are three ways in which markets are commonly defined:

- definition based on product;
- definition based on need satisfaction or function performed;
- definition based on customer identity.

We will briefly examine each of these in turn.

Definition based on product

If someone working for an organization is asked what market they are in, a common reply will be to describe the products that are produced and/or sold. Thus, we would have examples like 'consumer detergents' or 'industrial machinery'. If the product definition is wide, this type of definition is close to describing an industry. Since government economic statistics are often produced on this basis, markets defined in this way often have the advantage of ease of measurement.

A drawback of this approach is that it sometimes fails to take into account that a product may provide a range of different benefits, and the same need might be met by different products, often derived from completely different technology. This can lead to a failure to recognize threats that may come from a different industry altogether. Cinema and computer games appear to be entirely different products with different markets, but they both may compete for customers' discretionary income and time if they are considered as part of the 'leisure' market.

An advantage of a product-based definition of markets can be that economies of scale of production may be gained by the sharing of a particular production process. Taken to extreme, this can lead to a view of a market as the market for the products that a company happens to make, even where they have little in common apart from a production process. An example of this would be a company using a plastic moulding machine. If the company were to utilize the machine seven days a week, twenty-four hours a day, it would be efficient in production terms. However, if the range of products included golf tees, toys and components for the motor industry the different end customers would make it very difficult to sell the products economically. It would have sacrificed marketing synergy for production efficiency, and to analyse its customer base it would have to recognize that it operated in several markets.

Definition based on need satisfaction or function performed

The reason why consumers purchase a good or service is to gain *utility*. The concept of utility infers that whenever a consumer makes a purchase, they make a cost–benefit calculation wherein they make the judgement that the benefit they will get from the product is worth more than the price paid. This understanding enables the organization to understand its markets according to customers' perceptions.

Whilst need satisfaction definition can lead to a more open-minded approach to the formulation of strategy, its weakness can be that very broad definitions can lead to a view of markets that do not allow a practical approach to decision-making. A cinema chain, for example, might define itself as being in the 'leisure' market, but it is probably wise for cinema companies to also consider threats and opportunities that might arise from television, bars, computer games, holidays, etc. Opportunities only arise from leisure activities that the company's competences would allow it to enter (see Chapter 2), and threats would come from activities that would be likely to substitute customers' business.

Key Concepts

Needs and wants

Whenever a customer makes a purchase decision, he or she expects to gain a benefit from the product purchased. This benefit satisfaction is usually expressed as a *need* or a *want*. The difference between the two is in the perception of the consumer – one customer's want is another's need. The practical use of the distinction is in the price responsiveness of the product. Generally speaking, customers who need – or who believe they need – a product will be less price sensitive than those who merely want it. Hence, the greater the felt need, the more price inelastic the demand.

Definition based on customer identity

Groups of customers have requirements in common, and differ from other groups of customers. In this way, the *identity* of customers can be used to define markets. We could, for example, consider the 'office consumables market' a quite distinct market. The market might be for products as diverse as pencils, pens, envelopes, computer disks, etc. but the market could clearly be seen as for things that offices in organizations need to buy on a regular basis.

In terms of strategy formulation, the advantage of this approach is that it allows accurate targeting of the customer, so that efficient use can be made of advertising, mail shots, personal selling, etc. Its main disadvantage is that whilst marketing economies may be made, there is a risk that a number of different technologies need to be employed, so that it would be uneconomic to produce all the items required, and some or all of the products sold would have to be bought in. We can contrast this with the product definition approach in that with this some marketing may have to be subcontracted, whereas with the customer identity approach some manufacturing is likely to be outsourced.

Combined definition

In practice, most businesses serve several markets with a range of products. They will define their markets with a combination of the ways listed here, and to the extent that one or another approach is uppermost, the advantages and disadvantages that we have already encountered will apply. A key task for management at strategic level is to produce combinations that gain synergistic benefits and that enable opportunities to be best chosen and exploited. In cases where change in aspects of the technology of supply, or the characteristics of markets take place so that synergies previously achievable are no longer there, a case exists for restructuring an organization to divest itself of some activities and/or to acquire new ones.

In terms of working out competitive success in markets, a key concept is that of the *served market* – that part of a market that the company is in. It is on that basis that the measure of market share is most meaningful.

Market segmentation

Target marketing and market segmentation

Markets are rarely completely homogeneous. Within markets there are groups of customers with requirements that are similar, and it is this similarity of needs and wants that distinguishes one market segment from another. These 'submarkets' are known as *market segments*. By considering the extent to which the segments should be treated differently from others, and which ones will be chosen to serve, organizations can develop target markets and gain a focus for their commercial activity.

This process of segmentation represents a powerful competitive tool. It is true to say that a business will prosper by giving the customer what the customer wants. Since not all customers are likely to want the same thing, then identifying subgroups and attending to their requirements more exactly is a way of gaining competitive advantage. We might say that it is better to be hated by half of potential customers and loved by the other half than to be quite liked by them all. The latter is a recipe for being everyone's second choice, and underlines the dangers of placing too much reliance on averages in market research.

By identifying a specific market segment and concentrating marketing efforts at the segment, many organizations can build a mini-monopoly in the segment. Many organizations that have each identified a highly specific segment can each succeed and gain reasonable profits by configuring their internal activities precisely to meet the needs and wants of the customer group.

For the most part, we can assume that segments exist naturally in most markets, and it is up to organizations as to how to exploit the differences that exist in the submarkets. We do, however, have to recognize that activities of companies can also shape the segments to some extent. We could expect, for example, that men and women may buy differently. If, in those markets, suppliers offer and promote different products to men and women, then this tendency will be reinforced.

Three approaches to segment marketing

Three broad approaches are recognized in respect to the ways that an organization can approach marketing to market segments (or submarkets).

Undifferentiated marketing

The first approach in relating to segmentation is called *undifferentiated* marketing. This means that the organization denies that its total markets are segmented at all and relates to the market assuming that demand is homogeneous in nature. The economies of a standardized approach to marketing outweighs any advantages of segmenting the market.

Undifferentiated marketing is appropriate when the market the organization serves is genuinely homogeneous in nature. In Chapter 13 we will encounter this concept in the context of internationalization and globalization. Companies like Coca-Cola, Levi jeans and McDonald's employ this strategy successfully because demand for their products does not vary from country to country. Organizations that adopt this approach have standard products, standard packaging and advertising that is very similar in a number of countries.

Differentiated marketing

Companies that adopt *differentiated* marketing recognize separate segments of the total market and treat each segment separately. Different segments need not always be different in every respect – it could be that some standard products can be promoted differently to different segments because of certain similarities or common characteristics. In other cases the product will be substantially or completely different and marketing to each segment will necessitate a distinctive approach to each one.

Concentrated marketing

An extreme form of differentiated marketing is *concentrated* marketing, where an organization's effort is focused on a single market segment. In return for giving up substantial parts of the market, an effort is made to specialize in just one niche, and so we may see this referred to as 'niche marketing'. This approach offers the advantage that the organization can gain a detailed and in-depth knowledge of its segment which, in turn, can enable an ever-improving match between the product and the customer requirement. The disadvantage relates to the extent to which the company may become dependent upon the one segment it serves. Any negative change in the demand pattern of the segment will leave the supplier vulnerable because of the narrowness of its market portfolio (see later in this chapter).

A company operating with a large product range in many markets will typically use a multifocus strategy – a combination of the above.

Product positioning

Product positioning is the way in which a product or a brand is perceived in relation to preferences of segments of the market, and in relation to competitive products. Thus, in a particular alcoholic drinks market, attributes thought to be important by customers might be alcoholic strength (weak

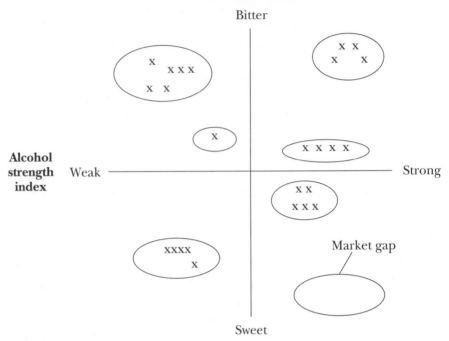

Figure 5.1 The product positioning framework.

versus strong) and taste (bitter versus sweet). There may be groups of customers with preferences for any combinations of these attributes, and a range of competing products that by means of the products themselves and their advertising and promotion are seen to occupy a particular position. This can often be represented by a product positioning diagram, as shown in Figure 5.1. The oval shapes on the chart represent the preferences of a group of customers and the customer perceptions of existing products are marked by an 'x'.

If an organization finds a group of customers with a particular requirement for a combination not currently offered, it will literally have discovered a 'gap' in the market (see the 'gap' on the bottom right of the chart). More likely, it will have to make the best of subtle differences in position, since all major combinations may be filled.

Bases for segmentation

What is a segmentation base?

A segmentation base is a way of distinguishing one customer type from another. There are potentially limitless ways that markets can be divided into segments, and the ultimate segment would be one customer. In practice, a number of criteria typically have to be met before a base for dividing a market can be considered to be commercially viable. The major criteria for establishing market segments are:

- market size;
- identifiability of the segment;
- measurability of the segment;
- accessibility to the segment;
- buying behavioural characteristics of the segment.

We will briefly examine these criteria in turn.

Market size

Smaller segments may allow more and more exact matching of customer requirements, but this comes at a cost as economies of scale of marketing and manufacturing are lost. If an advertisement is produced, there will be fixed costs of production and design, whether it is run once or several times. In production, separate tooling might be required to produce different versions of a product. Companies can reduce the cost by producing different versions of a product with a large number of common components.

In the twenty-first century, some of the assumptions we have long held that limit the smallest segments that can be economically reached are likely to change. Flexible manufacturing technology is reducing the minimum production runs that are economic for a separate product. In advertising, we are used to the concept of broadcasting. In the future we shall have to become used to the concept of 'narrowcasting', as a revolution in media takes place. At present, if a company advertises on television, and its product is only of interest to city dwellers, it is also paying to reach all the rural viewers. Cable technology allows organizations to direct adverts much more accurately at prospective customers. The same process is taking place in mail shots where most mail shots can now be very accurately aimed, and the Internet allows people to select what they want to see. The result of this process will be that very great rewards will be available to organizations that can come up with sophisticated segmentation strategies, as opposed to straightforward old-style mass marketing.

Identifiability of the segment

Ultimately, whatever base is being used for segmentation, we should still be able to answer the question as to *who* is in the segment, even if this is a bit indistinct. Otherwise the organization will not be able to reach the segment effectively.

Measurability of the segment

If we cannot measure the size of the segment that using a particular base would create, then we would not be in a position to judge its potential. Any organization that adopts a marketing strategy without an accurate knowledge of the size of the market segment cannot be sure that it has the optimal level of information upon which to make important investment decisions.

Accessibility to the segment

Any market segment identified must obviously be reachable in an organization's marketing communications. However, in order for marketing communications to be cost-effective, they must be aimed at the target segment and not at others. This latter issue requires a careful examination of media and how effectively each of the media reaches the target segment within cost constraints.

Buying behavioural characteristics of the segment

Even if all the other criteria can be met, it is pointless to divide a market up in a way that does not represent real or potential differences in buying behaviour. The whole point of market segmentation is to identify subgroups of a market that share commonalities such that their buying behaviour will be similar. If this is not the case for some reason, the exercise is useless.

Typical bases for segmentation of markets

In consumer markets (as distinct from industrial markets) we use the ways in which people naturally differ to divide markets up. The most commonly used 'people dividers' are:

1 demographic variables such as difference by age, stage of family life cycle, gender, income, occupation, education, race, religion;
2 geographic variables such as difference by country, region, type of housing/neighbourhood (geodemographic), etc.;
3 psychographic variables which exploit the lifestyle, personality or intelligence differences between people;
4 behavioural variables such as attitudes to brand loyalty, frequency of use (heavy or light usage), consumption occasion, etc.

Key Concepts

Demographic variables
In consumer markets, market segments are most commonly defined by using demographic variables. It is self-evident that people can be divided from each other in many ways and the more variables that are applied to a total market, the smaller and more homogeneous the segment becomes.

The most commonly used demographic variables are those that are readily identifiable. Differences such as sex, age, occupation, type of residence and stage of family life cycle are all easy to identify. Less easy – and therefore less usable – are differences such as religious affiliation, sexual orientation, political persuasion and musical preferences. The paradox is that some of this latter category of variables are very powerful in respect of their ability to predict patterns of demand.

Products

Product definition

We can define a product as anything that is offered for sale, so that the product might be a physical good, or could be a service. A good is tangible and is something that can be owned. A service is something that is done on the buyer's behalf and is intangible in nature. Some products contain both a good and a service element such as when we might commission a plasterer to repair a wall in a house (the good being the bag of plaster and the service being the application by the tradesman).

Of value in product strategy is a consideration of how value might be added to the product from the point of view of the customer. To do this, it can be helpful to consider the product's features and benefits in a number of levels. Different approaches can give different numbers of levels. We shall consider here a five-level model (Kotler, 1997).

Kotler's five 'levels' of product benefit

Core and basic benefits

Kotler proposes at the most fundamental level the 'core benefit' provided by the product. In a car, for example, this would be the ability to transport. Since all the products on the market will provide this benefit, this will rarely be the level on which companies compete. Added to the core benefit is the *basic product* which would include everything that would be required to make the product practical in use. For the car, this might include the seats, appropriate controls, and legal safety equipment.

Expected, augmented and potential benefits

The next level is the expected product. Here we have all that the customer has come to expect in a product. In our example of a car, this might include a radio, comprehensive guarantee, and certain levels of performance. The *augmented product* goes beyond the customer's expectations to provide something extra and desirable, for example air conditioning and an on-board satellite navigation system in a car. At the final level is the *potential product* – the product level that encompasses all that the product might ultimately become, but currently does not incorporate. An (albeit unlikely) example would be a car company considering a driverless car. There are already driverless trains, and arguably the technology exists to make it possible to produce a driverless car, even if the technical and commercial risks might make a prudent organization leave its development of such a vehicle to the future.

Competition of augmented benefits

In mature markets, competition is normally at the augmented product level, and the basic product is taken for granted. What is in the expected product in one market may be in the augmented product in another. Air conditioning might be a bonus in a temperate climate, but a necessity in a tropical one. Thus, a car company that had gained a competitive advantage by superior reliability would lose that advantage once all cars had become reliable. It then has to be able to offer something else or face a lack of competitiveness. Over time, the augmented product becomes the expected product, so there has to be a continuous search for something extra to offer.

Augmentation adds to costs, and the company has to consider whether the customer will be willing to pay for the extra costs in the final price. Sometimes, after a period of rivalry where competitors try to compete by adding more and more features and cost, a market segment emerges for a basic stripped down low-cost version that just supplies the expected benefits.

Copeland's product typology and strategy

There is a commonly held view that different types of products need to be managed and brought to market in different ways. *Services*, for example, cannot be stored, must be consumed at the point of production, are intangible, and it is difficult to judge quality in advance. As a result of these factors, we might anticipate off-peak pricing offers, the need for supplier credibility, and difficulties in advertising not experienced by physical products. *Industrial products* are less likely to be sold direct to the end user than consumer products, with advertising being relatively more important for consumer products and high quality personal contact being relatively more important for industrial products (hence the use of sales representatives to speak directly to industrial buyers).

There have been a number of attempts to build on product characteristics to produce classification systems for products that will serve as a comprehensive guide. A system based on dividing consumer products into *convenience, shopping, and speciality goods* (Copeland, 1923) has endured and is one of the most popular product classification systems used at the present time.

Convenience goods

Convenience goods are products where purchase is relatively frequent, at low prices, and the customer sees little interest or risk in the purchase. Examples would include low price confectionery, batteries, carbonated drinks. As a consequence, the customer will typically buy the product available in the most convenient outlet, and the supplier will have to make the product available in as many outlets as possible. Point of sale display and simple reminder advertising with little information content are likely to be important.

Shopping goods

In contrast, shopping goods are those that are typically more expensive, of more interest to the purchaser, and some risk is seen in the purchase. Examples would include cars, personal computers and cameras. The customer will typically 'shop around' to make comparisons and gather information. These goods do not, therefore, have to be available in all possible outlets, and promotional material will usually have a high information content. In some categories of shopping goods such as personal computers, customers can demonstrate a very high level of technical knowledge that assists them in their purchase and producers must usually satisfy customers on a technical level before a sale is made.

Speciality goods

Speciality goods are seen as products that are so differentiated from others, often carrying considerable prestige, that customers may insist on only one brand. High prices, high levels of service, and restricted distribution would be appropriate. An example would be that of Hasselblad cameras, which dominate certain parts of the professional photography market. There is no need or benefit for the products to be available in every camera shop, but they would tend to appear in shops where customers would expect a high level of service and expertise.

Limitations of Copeland's framework

The use of such classification systems is widely accepted by both managers and academic researchers. It is easy to show how they work in practice, and a multitude of examples can be produced to show how appropriate they are. A strong argument against their slavish adoption is that they can exhibit circular logic. In other words, we examine how a product is marketed, and on this basis assign it to a particular classification. We then use that to say how it *should* be marketed. This is a recipe for staying with the status quo, and companies adopting this practice, even if implicitly, will never lead with new product strategies. Over time, many products will gradually change from shopping goods to convenience goods. Thus, some watches will be speciality goods, some will be shopping goods, and now the lowest priced watches on the market are convenience goods.

Changes in technology and customer taste or fashion may also create opportunities for things to be done differently, and there may always be part of a market that will respond to an approach that is different from the

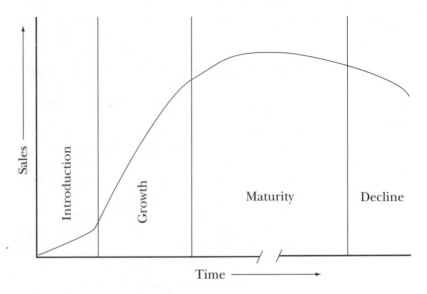

Figure 5.2 The product life cycle.

norm. Some organizations recognized that technology in reducing transaction cost could make telephone banking viable. Avon cosmetics was built on the basis that some customers would be prepared to buy cosmetics from people selling it on their doorsteps as opposed to buying in conventional retail outlets.

Product type may be a useful starting point to guide management thinking, but it is not a substitute for creativity and analysis.

The product life cycle

Uses of the product life cycle

The product life cycle concept is based on the analogy with living things, in that they all have a finite life. All products would be expected to have a finite life, whether it be long or short. The life cycle can operate at an individual product level, or a product type, or at a product class level, where arguably 'market life cycle' would be a more appropriate term. At individual product level, the product life cycle is a useful tool in product planning, so that a balance of products is kept in various stages of the life cycle (see Figure 5.2).

At the product class level, we can use the product life cycle concept to analyse and predict competitive conditions and identify key issues for management. It is conventionally broken into a number of stages as shown in the diagram. We shall explore the key issues posed by the different stages.

The introduction stage

The introduction stage follows the product's development. It is consequently new to the market and will be bought by 'innovators', a term used to describe a small proportion of the eventual market. The innovators may not be easy to identify in advance and there are likely to be high launch and marketing costs. Because production volumes are likely to be low (because it is still at a 'pilot' stage), the production cost per unit will be high.

The price elasticity of demand will strongly influence whether the product is introduced at a high 'skimming' price, or a low 'penetration' price. Price skimming is appropriate when the product is known to have a price inelastic demand such as with new pharmaceuticals or defence equipment. Penetration is appropriate for products with price elastic demand and when gaining market share is more important than making a fast recovery of development costs.

'Pioneer' companies (those who are first to the market with a particular product) are usually forced to sell the product idea in addition to an existing brand, and the early promotion may help competitors who enter the market later with 'me too' versions of the product idea.

Entering the market at an early stage is usually risky. Not only will the company be incurring a negative cash flow for a period, but many products fail at this stage. Against this risk is the prospect of increasing market share in the new product area faster than the 'me toos' such that the first product may become the industry standard in future years.

The growth stage

During the growth stage, sales for the market as a whole increase and new competitors typically enter to challenge the pioneer for some of the market share. The competitors may develop new market segments in an attempt to avoid direct competition with the established pioneering market leader.

The market becomes profitable and funds can be used to offset the development and launch costs. This is an important time to win market share, since it is easier to win a disproportionate share of new customers than later on to get customers to switch brands. As new market segments emerge, key decisions will need to be made as to whether to follow them or stay with the original. It has been shown (Brown, 1991) that the calculator market, for example, was based originally on scientists and engineers, then business use, then university students and finally the biggest part of the market was to schoolchildren. A pioneer wishing to stay in all these markets would have to make the brave decision to move out of organization-to-organization business into a mass consumer market.

The maturity stage

Maturity is reached when a high proportion of people who will eventually purchase a product have already purchased it once. It is likely to be the longest stage, but depending on the market, this could range from days or weeks to many decades or even centuries. It is important at this stage either to have achieved a high market share, or to dominate a special niche in the market. It can be expensive and risky to achieve large market share changes at this time, so that some companies prefer to concentrate their competitive efforts on retaining existing customers, and competing very hard for the small number of new customers appearing.

It has been pointed out that market shares amongst leading competitors are often very stable over extremely long periods of time (Mercer, 1993), and this may be used as a criticism of the product life cycle concept. However, over the time of maturity in the market, companies have to be vigilant in detecting change in the market, and be ready to modify or improve products and to undertake product repositioning.

The decline stage

It is part of product life cycle theory that all markets will eventually decline, and therefore companies have to be ready to move to new markets where decline is felt to be inevitable, or to be ready with strategies to extend the life cycle if this is felt to be feasible. Appropriate extension strategies could include developing new uses for the product, finding new users, and repositioning the product to gain a presence in the parts of the market that will remain after the rest of the market has gone. Even where markets have reached an advanced stage of decline, there may remain particular segments that can be profitable for organizations able to anticipate their existence and dominate them.

Companies that succeed in declining markets usually adopt a 'milking' strategy wherein investment is kept to a minimum and take up any market share that may be left by competitors that have left the market because of the decline. There is a certain recognition that death will come eventually and thus any revenues that can be made in the interim are something of a bonus.

Remember

The human life cycle metaphor
The concept of life cycle does not just apply to products, it also applies to humans. Human beings undergo a life cycle that has a huge bearing, not just on our biological changes but also on behaviour.
We undergo *introduction* when we are conceived and grow inside our mothers. After birth, we begin to grow – a process that continues until,

after puberty, we reach our full height and weight. Our *maturity* phase is the longest. For most people, it will last from our mid-teens until the time when our faculties begin to fail us – perhaps in our sixties or seventies. When we reach old age, we begin to *decline*. Our eyesight may begin to deteriorate, we slow down and we may lose some of our intellectual sharpness. Finally, when decline has run its course, life is no longer viable, and we *die*.

Criticisms of the product life cycle

The product life cycle appears to be both widely understood and used (Greenley and Bayus, 1993). Despite this, some important criticisms have been made. Whilst it is easy to go back into history and demonstrate all the features of the concept, it is hard to forecast the future, and in particular hard to forecast turning points. Not to try to do so at all, however, would seem to avoid confronting hard strategic issues.

Another criticism is that life cycles may sometimes not be inevitable as dictated by the market, but created by the ineptitude of management. If management assume that decline will come, they will take the decision to reduce investment and advertising in anticipation of the decline. Not surprisingly, decline does come, but sooner than it otherwise would have done had the investment not been withdrawn.

New product development

The importance of new products

Change in society, markets, economies and society has led to a shortening of life cycles, and this has intensified the need for most organizations to innovate in terms of the products that they offer. New products can provide the mechanism whereby further growth can take place. Increasing competition, often itself coming from new or modified products, means that innovation is frequently not an option, but a necessity.

'Newness' can vary from restyling, or minor modification, to producing products that are 'new to the world' that lead to new markets. The higher the degree of newness, the more likely it is that major gains in sales and profits may be made, but at the same time the risks of incurring high costs and market failure are also increased. A single new product failure, if big enough, could bankrupt an organization. It is generally accepted that a very large proportion of new products fail, although precise quantification is impossible as many new products may be kept on the market despite not meeting their original objectives.

Organizations are faced with a dilemma in the management of new product development: new product development is essential, but is also fraught with risks. The successful management of the dilemma is often to produce a large number of new product ideas, most of which will never reach the market because they have been weeded out by an appropriate screening process.

New product idea generation

Ideas for new products can come from many sources. The greater the range of sources used, the more likely it is that a wide range and large number of new ideas will be produced (Sowrey 1990).

Ideas from customers

For most organizations, the most important source of new ideas will be the customers. Obtaining ideas from customers is a good way of ensuring that ideas are produced that will produce products as a result of 'market pull'. This means that there will be a market for the products that result because they are specifically requested by the customers. Surveys and focus groups can help to produce ideas. The more straightforward approaches may give ideas for improvements, but more subtle approaches may reveal new needs.

Eric von Hippel (von Hippel, 1978) showed that a very successful approach for new ideas in industrial markets was to work with lead customers (respected, technically advanced buyers) to overcome their particular problems, and then to use the resulting new products to sell to other customers. Sometimes the products may require modification for the other customers at some cost, but the products then have unique value for these customers and price inelasticity of demand (Coates and Robinson, 1995).

Ideas from research and development

R&D departments are useful at idea generation when a market opportunity has been identified but a solution has not yet been found. In this respect, R&D can lead to competitive advantage as developments in the pharmaceuticals industry have proven on several occasions (e.g. the introduction of the anti-impotence drug Viagra by Pfizer Pharmaceuticals).

In some organizations, ideas emerge from R&D without a trigger from marketing intelligence. This is called 'technological push' and can sometimes lead to overspecified and high cost products. At other times, technological push can result in a genuine breakthrough that marketing people can then 'run with'.

Other sources of ideas

It is impossible to construct a comprehensive list of sources of new products but the following have proven themselves to be useful in the past:

- advertising agencies (who sometimes have their 'finger on the pulse' of market requirements);
- consultants (who may carry out market research on a company's behalf);
- universities and other academic institutions;
- competitors (where an organization copies a competitive product);
- suppliers (who may have devised a way to use a component or material);
- employees, sometimes through 'employee idea' schemes;
- distributors and agents.

Screening

Once ideas for a new product have been generated, a company must then sift through them to develop only those with genuine potential – a process known as *screening*. As far as possible, the screening process has to attempt to avoid two potential types of errors – GO errors, where products are developed that ultimately fail, or do not meet objectives, and DROP errors, where ideas are abandoned that would ultimately have succeeded. GO errors are recognizable, at least by the organization that makes them, but most DROP errors are unrecognized because the project has not gone ahead (unless of course a competitor makes a success of an idea that has been abandoned).

In practice, the screening process is normally multi-stage, with at least some kind of review at several points in the process. Since risks may be high, and organizational politics may play a part, it is usually recommended that in at least one of the stages, a formal process is undergone where the idea is evaluated against predetermined objective criteria.

Development

The stages in development will vary according to the nature of the product and the work required to develop a new version, but it is important to include stages of the screening process before activities that involve the commitment of large amounts of finance, and it would not make sense to spend large amounts in developing a new product without producing evidence that there would be some demand for it. Stages in the process are typically as follows:

1 initial appraisal;
2 detailed business analysis and investment appraisal;
3 technical development;
4 market testing;
5 launch.

A traditional view of the development process is that one stage should precede another. With increasing competition, reducing time to market has become very important in many industries. To reduce the time to market, some of the activities may go on at the same time, sometimes known as *parallel processing*. This puts a premium on good communications in the company between functions such as technical R&D and marketing. To avoid the delays and complications that might be involved in handing a project from one function in the organization to another, multi-disciplinary teams known as *venture teams* may be created, and in some circumstances the team may be given the new product to manage when it is on the market. If such a team is created, it is likely that higher management will make the GO or DROP decisions to avoid the risk of the bias of an enthusiastic but optimistic team taking over.

Product portfolio theory

What is a portfolio?

The notion of portfolio exists in many areas of life, not just for products. Underpinning the concept is the need for a business to spread its opportunity and risk. A broad portfolio signifies that a business has a presence in a wide range of product and market sectors. Conversely, a narrow portfolio implies that the organization only operates in few or even one product or market sector.

A broad portfolio offers the advantage of robustness in that a downturn in one market will not threaten the whole company. Against this advantage is the problem of managing business interests that may be very different in nature – the company may be said to lack strategic focus. An organization operating with a very narrow portfolio (i.e. just one sector) can often concentrate wholeheartedly upon its sector but it can become vulnerable if there is a downturn of demand in the one sector it serves.

The BCG matrix

The Boston Consulting Group matrix offers a way of examining and making sense of a company's portfolio of product and market interests. It is a way of viewing the entire product range to see a company's products as a collection of items in the way that a holder of shares in several companies might consider the decisions on what to do with the shares.

One way of looking at the products in a portfolio would be to consider each product in its position in the product life cycle and aim to have a balance of products in each stage. A more sophisticated approach is based on the idea that market share in mature markets is highly correlated with profitability, and that it is relatively less expensive and less risky to attempt to win share in the growth stage of the market, when there will be many new cus-

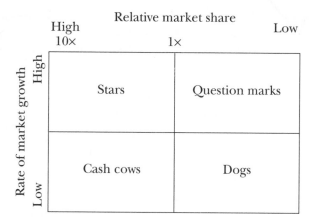

Figure 5.3 The Boston Consulting Group matrix.

tomers making a first purchase. This is the approach taken by the BCG matrix. It is used to analyse the product range with a view to aiding decisions on how the products should be treated in an internal strategic analysis. Figure 5.3 shows the essential features of the Boston matrix.

The market share measure

The horizontal axis is based on a very particular measure of market share. That measure is share relative to the largest competitor. A product with a share of 20 per cent of the market, where the next biggest competitor had a share of 10 per cent, would have a relative share of 2, whereas a product with a market share of 20 per cent and the biggest competitor also had 20 per cent would have a relative share of 1. The cut-off point between high and low share is 1, so high market share products in this analysis are market leaders. This arrangement of scale is sometimes described as being *logarithmic* in nature.

The market growth measure

The vertical axis is the rate of market growth, with the most relevant definition of the market being served. A popular point used to divide high and low growth in the market is 10 per cent year-on-year growth, but the authors have found it useful in practical situations to use growth that is faster than the rate of growth in the economy as a whole, which, after inflation is usually between 1 per cent and 2.5 per cent a year.

Using the BCG matrix

Cash cows

A product with a high market share in a low growth market is normally both profitable and a generator of cash. Profits from this product can be used to support other products that are in their development phase. Standard strategy would be to manage conservatively, but to defend strongly against competitors. Such a product is called a *cash cow* because profits from the product can be 'milked' on an ongoing basis. This should not be used as a justification for neglect.

Dogs

A product that has a low market share in a low growth market is termed a *dog* in that it is typically not very profitable. To cultivate the product to increase its market share would incur cost and risk, not least because the market it is in has a low rate of growth. Accordingly, once a dog has been identified as part of a portfolio, it is often discontinued or disposed of.

More creatively, opportunities might be found to differentiate the dog and obtain a strong position for it in a niche market. A small share product can be used to price aggressively against a very large competitor as it is expensive for the large competitor to follow suit.

The matrix does not have an intermediate market share category, but there are large numbers of products that have large market share but are not market leaders. They may be the biggest profit earners for the companies that own them. They usually compete against the market leader at a disadvantage that is slight, but real. Management need to make very efficient use of marketing expenditure for such products and to try to differentiate from the leader. They should not normally compete head on, especially on price, but attempt to make gains if the market changes in a way that the leader is slow to exploit.

Stars

Stars have a high share of a rapidly growing market, and therefore rapidly growing sales. They may be the sales manager's dream, but they could be the accountant's nightmare, since they are likely to absorb large amounts of cash, even if they are highly profitable. It is often necessary to spend heavily on advertising and product improvements, so that when the market slows, these products become cash cows. If market share is lost, the product will eventually become a dog when the market stops growing.

Question marks

Question marks are aptly named as they create a dilemma. They already have a foothold in a growing market, but if market share cannot be improved they will become dogs. Resources need to be devoted to winning market share, which requires bravery for a product that may not yet have large sales, or the product may be sold to an organization in a better position to exploit the market.

Limitations of the BCG matrix

Accurate measurement and careful definition of the market are essential to avoid mis-diagnosis when using the matrix. Critics, perhaps unfairly, point out that there are many relevant aspects relating to products that are not taken into account, but it was never claimed by the Boston Consulting Group that the process was a panacea, and covered all aspects of strategy. Above all, the matrix helps to identify *which* products to push or drop, and *when*. It helps in the recognition of windows of opportunity, and is strong evidence against simple rules of thumb for allocating resources to products.

Composite portfolio models

The limitations of the BCG matrix have given rise to a number of other models that are beyond the scope of this text. A leading example is the General Electric matrix. Whilst the Boston matrix is intended for products, but may be used for strategic business units that are fairly homogeneous, the General Electric matrix is mainly applied to strategic business units such as the subsidiaries of a holding company. The model rates *market attractiveness* as high, medium or low; and *competitive position* as strong, medium or weak. Strategic business units are placed in the appropriate category, and although there is no automatic strategic prescription, the position is used to help devise an appropriate strategy.

Summary

Splitting markets up into segments can be used as a competitive tool, and there are many different ways in which market segments might be chosen. The concept of the augmented product is a tool to examine how features and benefits might be produced to provide a competitive edge. The product life cycle shows how a number of strategic issues might be anticipated at different stages, and the management of the product portfolio must deal with the management of a whole product range. Aspects of product innovation may be viewed by examining the processes of new idea generation and new product screening.

Review and Discuss

1 Define the term *market*.
2 What is the difference between a market and an industry?
3 What is a market segment?
4 Explain the variables that can be applied to segment markets.
5 Explain why Coca-Cola and a supplier of a regional food (like black pudding) adopt a different approach to market segmentation.
6 Explain Kotler's five levels of product benefit.
7 What is meant by core benefit?
8 Explain Copeland's product typology.
9 What are the stages of the product life cycle?
10 Define and distinguish between skimming and penetration strategies.

11 What is a portfolio?
12 Explain the pros and cons of having a broad product and market portfolio.
13 What are the benefits of using the BCG matrix to analyse a company's product and market portfolio?

References and further reading

Aaker, D.A. (1995) *Strategic Market Management*, Fourth Edition. New York: John Wiley.

Brown, R. (1991) The S-curves of innovation. *Journal of Marketing Management,* 7, No. 2, 189–202.

Coates, N. and Robinson, H. (1995) Making industrial new product development market led. *Marketing Intelligence and Planning,* 13, No. 6, 12–15.

Copeland, M.T. (1923) Relation of consumers' buying habits to marketing methods. *Harvard Business Review,* 1 (April), 282–289.

Doyle, P. (1994) *Marketing Management and Strategy.* Englewood Cliffs: Prentice Hall.

Greenley, G.E. and Bayus, B.L. (1993) Marketing planning decision making in UK and US companies: an empirical comparative study. *Journal of Marketing Management,* No. 9, 155–172.

Jobber, D. (1995) *Principles and Practice of Marketing.* New York: McGraw-Hill.

Kotler, P. (1997), *Marketing Management Analysis, Planning, Implementation, and Control,* Ninth Edition. Englewood Cliffs: Prentice Hall.

Lancaster, G, and Massingham, L. (1993) *Marketing Management.* London: McGraw-Hill.

Mercer, D. (1993) Death of the Product Life Cycle. *Admap,* September, 15–19.

Sowrey, T. (1990) Idea generation: identifying the most useful techniques. *European Journal of Marketing,* 42, No. 5, 20–29.

von Hippel, E. (1978) Successful industrial products from customer ideas. *Journal of Marketing,* 42, No. 1, January, 39–49.

Case linkage   Questions for the Ben & Jerry's case study.

1 What are the core benefits of ice cream as a general product category?
2 What are the expected benefits of ice cream?
3 Describe the augmented features of Ben & Jerry's products.
4 Comment on the robustness of Ben & Jerry's product and market portfolio.

5 Where do you think that super-premium ice cream is on the product life cycle? Give reasons for your answer

Questions for the Dansk Tyggegummi Fabrik A/S case study.

1 Which demographic variables did DTF use in segmenting its markets?
2 Identify the core and premium benefits of Dirol.
3 Comment upon the extent to which DTF has related to the specific preferences of its various international markets.
4 Compare the positions on the product life cycle of Wrigley's traditional brands of chewing gum and Dandy's dentally active products. Comparing this with their respective market shares, which company would represent a better investment?

Part III
External analysis

Introduction

The external environment is a bit like an onion. It comprises concentric strata of influences that can affect an organization. We considered the internal environment in Part II of the book. In this section, we look at the external environment.

The micro or 'near' environment is the sphere in which the organization interacts often – usually on a day-to-day basis. Any changes in the microenvironment can affect an organization very quickly and, sometimes, very dramatically.

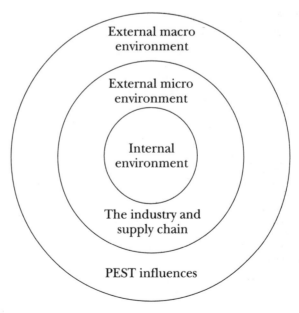

A schematic of the external environment

In the case of most organizations, the microenvironment comprises influences from the competitive environment – its industry and markets. In Chapter 7, we discuss two models for making sense of this important stratum of influence – Porter's five forces model and the resource or core competence based model.

The macroenvironment contains a number of influences that affect not only an organization itself, but also the rest of the players in the industry. Most textbooks, and this one is no exception, employ the STEP model to make sense of this stratum of environmental influence (sometimes expressed as PEST analysis).

Socio-demographic, technological, economic and political influences are usually beyond an organization's ability to influence. Strategy usually therefore rests upon an organization's ability to cope with any changes in the macroenvironment. A key skill in strategic management is that of predicting changes in any of the STEP influences and of accounting for potential changes in strategic formulation. We consider the macroenvironment in Chapter 6.

In Chapter 8, we introduce the strategic postures that organizations might adopt as a result of their external analyses. In this respect, Chapters 7 and 8 are naturally linked – Chapter 8 explains the implications of an organization's position in its microenvironment upon its competitive strategy.

Chapter 6

Analysis of the macroenvironment

Introduction

The most widely used technique for analysing the macroenvironment is known as STEP analysis. STEP analysis divides the influences in the macroenvironment into four categories:

- *social influences* – social, cultural and demographic forces;
- *technological influences* – products, processes, IT, communications and transport;
- *economic influences* – fiscal and monetary policy, incomes, living standards, exchange rates, etc.;
- *political influences* – governmental, legal and regulatory influences.

It is this framework which is explained and explored in this chapter.

Objectives

After studying this chapter, students should be able to:

- explain what is meant by the macroenvironment;
- explain Ginter and Duncan's mechanisms of carrying out macroenvironmental analysis;
- describe the components of each of the four STEP influences;
- describe how the STEP factors are interlinked and interrelated.

The macroenvironment

What is the macroenvironment?

We refer to the macroenvironment as the broad environment outside of an organization's industry and markets. It is generally beyond the influence of the individual business but can have significant impact on the microenvironment (industry and market) in which the business operates. The macroenvironment is sometimes referred to as the *far* or *remote* environment because it tends to exert forces from outside the organization's sphere of influence and the forces are usually beyond control.

Changes in the macroenvironment can be of immense importance to an organization. They can bring about the birth or death of an entire industry, they can make markets expand or contract, they can determine the level of competitiveness within an industry and many other things. It is therefore essential that managers are alert to actual and potential changes in the macroenvironment and that they anticipate the potential impacts on their industry and markets.

Conducting macroenvironmental analysis

Ginter and Duncan (1990) state that:

macroenvironmental analysis involves:

- *scanning* macroenvironments for warning signs and possible environmental changes that will affect the business;
- *monitoring* environments for specific trends and patterns;
- *forecasting* future directions of environmental changes;
- *assessing* current and future trends in terms of the effects such changes would have on the organization.

In their paper, Ginter and Duncan give the example of the sportswear manufacturers Adidas and Converse, whose failure adequately to analyse the macroenvironment caused them to miss the opportunity of catering for the premium (upper priced) segment of the running shoe market. Nike, on the other hand, more accurately predicted the strength of demand in the segment and exploited the market opportunities much more successfully.

The same authors go on to identify the potential benefits of macroenvironmental analysis as:

- increasing managerial awareness of environmental changes;
- increasing understanding of the context in which industries and markets function;
- increasing understanding of multinational settings;
- improving resource allocation decisions;
- facilitating risk management;
- focusing attention on the primary influences on strategic change;
- acting as an early warning system, providing time to anticipate opportunities and threats and devise appropriate responses.

Limitations of macroenvironmental analysis

We should be careful to note that macroenvironmental analysis has its limitations and pitfalls. At its root, the macroenvironment can be extremely complex and at any one time there may be conflicting and contradictory changes taking place. The pace of change in many macroenvironment situations is increasing and becoming more turbulent and unpredictable. This degree of uncertainty has, to some extent, cast some doubt over the value of carrying out a macroenvironmental analysis at all. By the time that an organization has come to terms with one major change in the macroenvironment, another change often occurs that requires even more attention and action.

Accordingly, those managers that are concerned with strategic analysis must:

- be aware of the limitations and inaccuracies of macroenvironmental analysis;
- carry out the analysis continuously (because it changes so frequently);
- constantly seek to improve sources of information and techniques for its analysis;
- use the information as one source of organizational learning (alongside other information-gathering activities – see Chapters 7 and 15);
- use the information to inform future strategy.

With these points in mind, macroenvironmental analysis is a valuable mechanism for increasing strategic awareness of managers.

STEP analysis

Overview of the STEP influences

The complexity of the macroenvironment makes it necessary to divide the forces at work into the four broad categories we have already encountered (see Figure 6.1). It is important to remember that the four categories are interrelated and constantly interact with each other. In the process of STEP analysis (sometimes called PEST analysis) it is therefore important to explore and understand the relationships between the forces at work. It is equally important to identify the relative importance of the influences at work for the business, its industry and its markets. Finally, because of the uncertainty of the effects of macroenvironmental change on the microenvironment (see Chapter 7), it is essential that a range of possible outcomes of the changes are identified and considered. Techniques for such analysis are considered in a later section of this chapter.

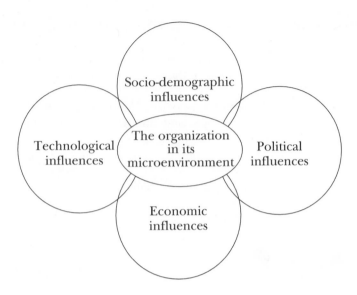

Figure 6.1 The STEP environment.

Socio-demographic influences

Analysis of the social environment is concerned with understanding the potential impacts of society and social changes on a business, its industry and markets.

For most analyses, analysis of the social environment will require consideration of:

- *social culture* (values, attitudes and beliefs) – its impact on demand for products and services, attitudes to work, savings and investment, ecology, ethics, etc.;
- *demography* – the impact of the size and structure of the population on the workforce and patterns of demand;
- *social structure* – its impact on attitudes to work and products and services.

Social culture

The cultures of countries in which a business operates can be of particular importance. The culture of a country consists of the values, attitudes and beliefs of its people which will affect the way that they act and behave (or, put simply, its 'personality'). There are important cultural differences between all countries. Culture can affect consumer tastes and preferences, attitudes to work, attitudes to education and training, attitudes to corruption and ethics, attitudes to credit, attitudes to the social role of a business in society and many other things.

Demography

Demographic trends are similarly important. Demography is the social science concerned with the charting of the size and structure of a population of people. The size of the population will obviously be a determinant of the size of the workforce and the potential size of markets. Just as important will be the structure of the population. The age structure will determine the size of particular segments and also the size of the working population. The size and structure of the population will constantly be changing and these changes will have impact on industries and markets.

Social structure

Social structure is strongly linked to demography and refers to the ways in which the social groups in a population are organized. There are a number of ways of defining social structure such as by sociodemographic groupings, by age, sex, location, population density in different areas, etc. The social structure will affect people's lifestyles and expectations and so will strongly influence their attitudes to work and their demand for particular products and services.

Among the most important general changes in recent years in the social environment have been in people's attitudes to the natural environment (see Chapter 14). Increasing awareness of the problems caused by pollution and the exhaustion of non-renewable resources have caused businesses in many industries to rethink the way that they produce their products and the composition of the products themselves. Similarly, changes in social structure (upward mobility), lifestyle (increased leisure) and demography (ageing populations in developed countries) have significantly altered many market and industry structures.

Technological influences

Analysis of the technological environment involves developing an understanding of the effects of changes in technology on all areas of a business and its activities, including:

- products and services;
- production processes;
- information and communications;
- transport and distribution;
- society, politics and economics.

Changes in technology affect the products available to consumers and businesses, the quality of the products and their functionality. For example, the development of the microprocessor has made possible the development of many new products including the personal computer, automatic washing machines and programmable video recorders. Production processes in many industries have been transformed and automated by Computer Aided Design (CAD) and Computer Aided Manufacturing (CAM). This has speeded design processes, transformed working practices and increased the efficiency of production.

Developments in information and communications technology (ICT), like the development of personal computers (PCs), networks, satellite, cable and digital communications, and the Internet together with rapid advances in software, have all contributed to revolutionizing the way that business is conducted in many industries. Activities are now better co-ordinated, research and development is speeded up, thus making businesses more flexible and responsive.

Similarly, changes in transport technology have revolutionized business and have changed societies and cultures. It is possible to transport materials, components and products with far greater speed and at much lower cost as a result of developments in road, rail, sea and air transport. These improvements in transport have also increased the amount of personal and business travel that people undertake. Increasing personal travel has had significant influence on the patterns of consumption in many countries. For example, in the UK patterns of food and alcohol consumption have altered dramatically. In the markets for alcoholic drinks, lager consumption has increased, partly as a result of the increased mobility that modern transport systems have brought about.

Interestingly, it is in the technological environment that it is sometimes possible for large organizations actually to exert influence rather than be the recipients of it. IBM's role in the development of the PC, Philips' development of the compact disc, Microsoft's developments in operating systems and software are all examples of the impact of individual (albeit large) businesses on general levels of technology.

As a consequence it is important that organizations monitor changes in the technologies that can affect their operations or their markets. In most industries, organizations must be flexible and be ready to innovate and to adopt new technologies as they come along. The way in which (and the extent to which) organizations do or do not employ the latest technology can be an important determinant of its competitive advantage.

Economic influences

Analysis of the economic environment will centre on changes in the macro-economy and their effects on business and consumers. It is important to remember that, because governments intervene (to varying extents) in the operation of all countries' economies, many factors classed as political in this chapter will have important economic implications.

Broadly speaking, the regulation of a national economy is brought about by two key policy instruments – fiscal policy and monetary policy. These policy instruments, alongside influences from international markets, determine the economic climate in the country in which a business competes. From these, a number of other, vital economic indicators 'flow' and it is these that organizations experience – either for good or ill.

Key Concepts

Fiscal and monetary policy

Fiscal policy is the regulation of the national economy through the management of government revenues and expenditures. Each fiscal year, a government raises so much in revenues (such as through taxation) and it spends another amount through its various departments (such as on health, education, defence, etc.). The government is able to influence the economic climate in a country by varying either or both of these sides of the fiscal equation.

Monetary policy is the regulation of the national economy by varying the supply and price of money. Money supply concerns the volume of money (in its various forms) in the economy and the 'price' of money is the base rate which determines the interest rate that banks and other lenders charge for borrowings.

In the UK, the Chancellor of the Exchequer is in charge of fiscal policy whilst monetary policy is overseen by the Monetary Policy Committee of the Bank of England.

When the effects of fiscal and monetary pressure work themselves out in the economy, they can affect any or all of the following economic factors:

● economic growth rates (the year-to-year growth in the total size of a national economy, usually measured by gross domestic product);
● levels of income in the economy;
● levels of productivity (i.e. output per worker in the economy);
● wage levels and the rate of increase in wages;
● levels of inflation (i.e. the year-to-year rise in prices);
● levels of unemployment;
● balance of payments (a measure of the international competitiveness of one country's economy against its international competitor countries);
● exchange rates (the exchange value of one currency against another).

Economic growth, exchange rates, levels of income, inflation and unemployment will all affect people's ability to pay for products and services and hence affect levels and patterns of demand. Similarly, levels of productivity, wage levels, levels of inflation and exchange rates will affect costs of production and competitiveness. All of these indicators must be monitored in comparison to those faced by competitors abroad to provide indications of changes in international competitiveness.

Political, governmental, legal and regulatory influences

The political environment is defined as that part of the macroenvironment which is under either the direct control or influence of the government. Governments have direct control or influence over:

- *legislation and regulation* – this covers laws that influence employment, consumer protection, health and safety at work, contract and trading, trade unions, monopolies and mergers, tax, etc.;
- *economic policy* – particularly over fiscal policy. Governments usually set policy over the levels of taxation and expenditure in the country;
- *government-owned businesses* – nationalized industries. Some governments retain control over key strategic industries and the way in which these are controlled can have 'knock-on' effects to other parts of the country;
- *government international policy* – government intervention to influence exchange rates, international trade, etc.

The objectives that a government may have towards the regulation of business will depend in large part upon the political leaning of the governing party. Most governments have, however, sought to construct policy over a number of key areas of business activity:

- control of inflation (such as to improve international competitiveness);
- promotion of economic growth and investment;
- control of unemployment;
- stabilization of exchange rates;
- control of balance of payments;
- control of monopoly power, both by businesses and trade unions;
- provision of public and merit goods like health, education, defence, etc.;
- control of pollution and environmental protection;
- redistribution of incomes (to varying degrees);
- consumer protection;
- regulation of working conditions;
- regulation of trade.

To varying degrees, all businesses will be affected by political influences. Accordingly, it is important for managers to monitor government policy to detect changes early so as to respond effectively.

Another important aspect of the political environment is *political risk* and its potential effects on business. Political risk is particularly important in international business. Whilst Europe and North America are comparatively politically stable, other parts of the world like Eastern Europe, South America and parts of the Middle East have undergone periods of instability.

It is therefore necessary to monitor closely the political situation in these areas when trading with them as the political risks are large. Even in more stable areas, political uncertainty can be higher at, for example, election times or when other political crises arise.

The relationships between the STEP influences

The example of ecological concern

A temptation when carrying out a STEP analysis is to think of each influence as separate when in fact they are often interlinked. Increasing concerns about ecology and 'green issues' provide a good example of this. In recent years there has been an important social trend which has changed people's attitudes towards the effects of products and production processes on the environment. Whereas twenty years ago most consumers showed little concern for the long-term effects of products and processes on the natural environment, today people are increasingly aware of the need to protect it. This has led to pressure on governments to introduce legislation and other measures to control pollution. The combined desire of consumer for products which are themselves environmentally friendly and which have been produced by 'green' methods has resulted in the realization by business that there are profits to be made by being environmentally friendly. This, in turn, has led to research and development aimed at designing products and processes which are less damaging to the environment. Among the numerous examples are aerosols which do not use CFCs, catalytic converters for automobile engines, unleaded fuel, reduced use of fuels which produce gases which damage the ozone layer and so on.

In this example, the effects of ecological issues on business, social factors (increased awareness) have impacted on political factors (legislation) and the two forces together have produced technological change (products and processes which are less damaging to the environment). Accordingly, a macroenvironmental analysis should recognize the ways in which the four STEP factors might be linked to each other.

Using the STEP analysis

How to carry out a STEP analysis

Now that we know what the STEP influences are and how they are interrelated, we turn to actually using the framework in strategic analysis. We generally think of the analysis as falling into four stages:

1 scanning and monitoring the macroenvironment for actual or potential changes in social, technological, economic and political factors;

2 assessing the relevance and importance of the changes for the market, industry and business;

3 analysing each of the relevant changes in detail and the potential relationships between them;

4 assessing the potential impact of the changes on the market, industry and business.

What to analyse

When managers carry out a STEP analysis as part of a strategic analysis (and the same is true of students examining a case study), they would normally examine how each factor might impact upon:

- *the internal parts of an organization* – the effects of STEP factors on the organization's core competences, strategies, resources, and value system;
- *an organization's markets* – the effects of STEP factors on product markets (market size, structure, segments, customer wants, etc.) and resource markets;
- *the industry in which the organization competes* – the effects of STEP factors on the five competitive forces (buyer power, supplier power, threat of entry, threat of substitutes, competitive rivalry – see Chapter 7).

Summary

Analysis of the macroenvironment is primarily concerned with providing insight into the future facing a business organization. The complexity and turbulence of the environment make prediction of the future problematic. Analysis, however, informs managers in their strategic decision-making. The complexity of the environment is simplified by breaking it down into the smaller social, technological, economic and political environments. These environments can then be analysed for their potential effects on the business and its microenvironment. The process of macroenvironmental analysis must be continuous to cope with the pace of change.

Review and Discuss

1 What does the term 'macroenvironment' mean?
2 Explain how the business, microenvironment and macroenvironment relate to each other.
3 Describe the components of each of the STEP factors.
4 Define and distinguish between fiscal and monetary policy.
5 What is demography and why is it important in macroenvironmental analysis?
6 Discuss the argument that suggests that turbulence and uncertainty render analysis of the macroenvironment less useful.
7 Explain the stages in a macroenvironmental analysis.

References and further reading

Chakravarthy, B. (1997) A new strategy framework for coping with turbulence. *Sloan Management Review*, Winter, 69–82.

Elenkov, D.E. (1997) Strategic uncertainty and environmental scanning: the case for institutional influences on scanning behaviour. *Strategic Management Journal*, 18, No. 4, 287–302.

Fahey, L. and Narayanan, V.K. (1986) *Macroenvironmental Analysis for Strategic Management*, West Publishing.

Ginter, P. and Duncan, J. (1990) Macroenvironmental analysis. *Long Range Planning*, December.

Helms, M.M. and Wright, P. (1992) External considerations: their influence on future strategic planning. *Management Decision*, 30, No. 8, 4–11.

Levitt, T. (1983) The globalization of markets. *Harvard Business Review*, May/June.

Makridakis, S. (1990) *Forecasting, Planning, and Strategy for the 21st Century*. New York: Free Press.

Mintzberg, H. (1991) *The Strategy Process – Concepts, Contexts, Cases*. Englewood Cliffs: Prentice Hall.

Sanchez, R. (1995) Strategic flexibility, firm organization, and managerial work in dynamic markets: a strategic options perspective. *Advances in Strategic Management*, 9, 251–291.

Sanchez, R. (1995) Strategic flexibility in product competition. *Strategic Management Journal*, 16 (Summer), 135–159.

Strebel, P. (1992) *Breakpoints*. Cambridge, MA: Harvard Business School Press.

Turner, I. (1996) Working with chaos. *Financial Times*, October 4.

Chapter 7

Analysis of the competitive environment

Introduction

In the introduction to Part III, we encountered the idea that an organization's external environment comprises two strata – the macroenvironment and the microenvironment. We considered the macroenvironment in Chapter 6 (using the STEP framework). In this chapter, we turn to an analysis of the microenvironment.

The microenvironment comprises those influences that the organization experiences frequently. For most businesses, it concerns the industries in which they operate. Within this arena, businesses may compete with each other or, in some circumstances, collaboration may be more appropriate. We discuss two models for industry analysis in this chapter. Then we discuss the scope of collaborative behaviour, before considering the way in which competitors in an industry fall into strategic groups.

Objectives

After studying this chapter, students should be able to:

- explain the importance of industry and market analysis;
- describe the construction and application of Porter's five forces framework;
- explain the limitations of Porter's five forces framework;
- define and distinguish between competitive and collaborative behaviour in industries;
- describe and explain the limitations of the resource-based model of industry analysis;
- define strategic groups and describe their usefulness in industry analysis.

Industries and markets

The importance of industry and market identification

Some strategic management texts wrongly use the terms *industry* and *market* interchangeably. Kay (1995) points out that to confuse the two concepts can result in a flawed analysis of the competitive environment and, hence, in flawed strategy. Modern businesses (especially larger companies) may operate in more than one industry and in more than one market. Each industry and market will have its own distinctive structure and characteristics which will have particular implications for the formulation of business strategy. Kay (1993) also points out that a distinctive capability, or core competence, 'becomes a competitive advantage only when it is applied in a market or markets.' Industries are centred on the supply of a product while markets are concerned with demand. It is important, therefore, to understand and analyse both industries and markets to assist in the process of strategy selection.

Key Concepts

Industry and market
Industries *produce* goods and services – the supply side of the economic system.
   Markets *consume* goods and services that have been produced by industries – the demand side of the economic system.

The industry

It is sometimes difficult to define a particular industry precisely. Porter (1980) defines an industry as a group of businesses whose products are close substitutes, but this definition can be inadequate because some organizations and industries produce a range of products for different markets. Alternatively, organizations can be grouped according to the similarity of their production processes. Two major official classifications of industries, employing this means of grouping, are the *Standard Industrial Classification* (SIC) of economic activity in the UK and the *Nomenclature Générale des Activités Economiques dans les Communautés Européennes* (NACE) of the European Union. These classifications, mainly used by investors and stockmarkets, can be extended to define an industry as a group of businesses which share similar products, processes, technologies, competences, suppliers and distribution channels. Analysis of these features of an industry will inform the process of strategy formulation.

The competitors in a given industry may produce products for more than one market. For example, businesses in the 'white goods' industry produce both washing machines and refrigerators. The materials, technology, skills and processes employed in the manufacture of both products are very similar. The materials used are obtained from similar suppliers and the products are sold to consumers through the same distributors (e.g. the main electrical retail multiples). There is clearly, therefore, an identifiable 'white goods' industry. Yet both these products (washing machines and refrigerators) satisfy very different customer needs, are used for entirely different purposes and are therefore sold in separate markets. One make of washing machine competes with another, while one make of refrigerator competes with another.

The market

While an industry is centred upon producers of a product or service, a market is centred on customers and their requirements (needs and wants). A particular market consists of a group of customers with a specific set of requirements which may be satisfied by one or more products. Analysis of a market will therefore involve gaining understanding of customers, their requirements, the products which satisfy those requirements, the organizations producing the products and the means by which customers obtain those products (distribution channels).

As well as selling their products in markets, businesses also obtain their resources (labour, materials, machinery, etc.) in markets – referred to as resource markets. Additionally, most businesses are interested in markets for substitute products and they will also be keen to investigate new markets for their products.

The relationship between a business, its industry and markets

Analysis of its industry and markets allows a business to:

- identify other industries where it may be able to deploy its core competences;
- understand the nature of its customers and their needs;
- identify new markets where its core competences may be exploited (see Chapter 2 for a discussion of core competences);
- identify threats from existing and potential competitors in its own and other industries;
- understand markets from which it obtains its resources.

Analysis of the competitive environment (industry and market) is equally as important to the development of an organization's future strategy as is internal analysis (which was the subject of Part II of this book). The industry and market context will play an important role in shaping an organization's competences and core competences. The core competences of a business must continually be reviewed in relation to changing customer needs, competitors' competences and other market opportunities.

Industry analysis

What is industry analysis?

Industry analysis aims to establish the nature of the competition in the industry and the competitive position of the business. Industry dynamics, in turn, are affected by changes in the macroenvironment (see Chapter 6). For example, ageing populations in many developed countries have significantly affected the need to develop drugs suitable for treating the ailments of older people. There is a danger that industry analysis can be seen as a 'one-off' activity but, like all components of the strategic process, it should be undertaken on an ongoing basis. The industry analysis framework developed by Porter (1980) is the most widely used and is explained in this section.

Microenvironment and macroenvironment

The most commonly used frameworks for analysing the external business environment distinguish between two levels or strata of environmental influence:

- The *micro (or near) environment* is that which immediately surrounds a business, the parts of which the business interacts with frequently and over which it may have some influence. For most purposes, we can identify competitors, suppliers and customers as comprising the main constituents of this stratum of the environment.
- The *macro (or far) environment* comprises those influences that can affect the whole industry in which a business operates. The macroenvironment comprises influence arising from political, economic, socio-demographic and technological factors. The nature of these factors normally means that individual businesses are unable to influence them – strategies must usually be formulated to cope with changes in the macroenvironment.

Porter's five forces model of industry analysis

Porter (1980) developed a framework for analysing the nature and extent of competition within an industry. He argued that there are five competitive forces which determine the degree of competition within an industry (see Figure 7.1). Understanding the nature and strength of each of the five forces within an industry assists managers in developing the competitive strategy of their organization. The five forces are:

- the threat of new entrants to the industry;
- the threat of substitute products;
- the power of buyers or customers;
- the power of suppliers (to businesses in the industry);
- rivalry among businesses in the industry.

By determining the relative 'power' of each of these forces, an organization can identify how to position itself to take advantage of opportunities and overcome or circumvent threats. The strategy of an organization may then be designed to exploit the competitive forces at work within an industry.

When using Porter's framework it is important to identify which of the five forces are the key forces at work in an industry. In many cases, it transpires that one or more of the five forces prove to be 'key forces' and the strategic analysis must focus on these if it is to use the framework fruitfully. The dynamic nature of the competitive environment (meaning that it is constantly changing) means that the relative strength of the forces in a par-

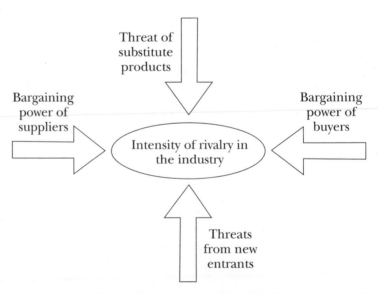

Figure 7.1 Porter's five forces framework (adapted from Porter, 1980).

ticular industry will change over time. It is therefore important that the five forces analysis is repeated on a regular basis so as to detect such changes before competitors and allow an early adjustment of strategy. Before any conclusions can be drawn about the nature of competition within an industry each of the five forces must be analysed in detail.

We will now discuss each of the five forces in turn.

Force 1: The threat of new entrants to the industry

The threat of entry to an industry by new competitors depends upon the 'height' of a number of entry barriers. Barriers to entry can take a number of forms.

The capital costs of entry

The size of the investment required by a business wishing to enter the industry will be an important determinant of the extent of the threat of new entrants. The higher the investment required, the less the threat from new entrants. The lower the required investment, the greater the threat.

Brand loyalty and customer switching costs

If the players in an industry produce differentiated products and customers are brand loyal, then potential new entrants will encounter resistance in trying to enter the industry. Brand loyalty will also be an important factor in increasing the costs for customers of switching to the products of new competitors.

Economies of scale available to existing competitors

If existing competitors are already obtaining substantial economies of scale it will give them an advantage over new competitors who will not be able to match their lower unit costs of production.

Access to input and distribution channels

New competitors may find it difficult to gain access to channels of distribution which will make it difficult to provide their products to customers or obtain the inputs required

The resistance offered by existing businesses

If existing competitors choose to resist strongly it will make it difficult for new organizations to enter the industry. For example, if existing businesses are obtaining economies of scale it will be possible for them to undercut the prices of new entrants because of their cost advantage. In some cases, existing competitors may make price cuts or increase marketing expenditure in order to deter new entrants.

If barriers to entry make it difficult for new competitors to enter the industry then this will limit the amount of competition within it. As a result, competitors within the industry will attempt to seek to strengthen the barriers to entry by cultivating brand loyalty, increasing the costs of entry and 'tying up' input and distribution channels as far as is possible.

Force 2: The threat of substitute products

A substitute can be regarded as something which meets the same needs as the product of the industry. For example, an individual wishing to cross the English Channel can choose to travel by ferry, by hovercraft or by the train service through the channel tunnel. These products all provide the benefit to the customer of crossing to France, despite the fact that ferry and rail services are provided by different industries. The extent of the threat from a particular substitute will depend upon two factors.

The extent to which the price and performance of the substitute can match the industry's product

Close substitutes whose performance is comparable to the industry's product and whose price is similar will be a serious threat to an industry. The more indirect the substitute, the less likely the price and performance will be comparable.

The willingness of buyers to switch to the substitute

Buyers will be more willing to change suppliers if switching costs are low or if competitor products offer lower price or improved performance. This is also closely tied in with the extent to which customers are brand loyal. The more loyal customers are to one supplier's products (for whatever reason) then the threat from substitutes will be accordingly reduced.

Key Concepts

Switching costs

One of the key strategic manoeuvres in maintaining customer loyalty is to increase the cost – to the customer – of changing to a new supplier. If switching costs are high, then customers will have an economic disincentive to switch and hence will tend to stay with the existing supplier. For direct substitutes, switching costs are usually very low. It costs nothing, for example, to switch brands of coffee or washing powder.

For indirect substitutes, there are likely to be higher actual or perceived switching costs. If buyers have had to make an investment in order to accommodate one supplier's product, then switching may involve extra investment which would act as a disincentive to switch. Switching costs may be financial, but may also be expressed in terms of lower quality, reduced confidence in the competitor's product or poorer product performance.

Competitors in an industry will attempt to reduce the threat from substitute products by improving the performance of their products, by reducing costs and prices, and by differentiation.

Key Concepts

Direct and indirect substitutes

There are very few products for which there is no substitute. A substitute can be defined as a product that offers substantially equivalent benefits to another. This criterion – that of receiving equivalent benefits – can be met in two ways: directly and indirectly.

Direct substitutes are those that are the same in substance. In the consumer goods sectors, direct substitutes are simply competitive brands. Nescafé and Maxwell House are direct competitors in the instant coffee market and Crown and Dulux white emulsions are direct competitors in the retail decorative paint sector.

Indirect substitutes are those that are different in substance but which can, in certain circumstances, provide the same benefit. For bridge construction, the same structural benefits can be provided by steel, wood or concrete. Hence, in the construction market, these three are indirect substitutes – but only in this market. In the automotive industry, concrete is not an indirect substitute for steel.

Force 3: The bargaining power of buyers

The extent to which the buyers of a product exert power over a supplying organization depends upon a number of factors. Broadly speaking, the more power that buyers exert, the lower will be the transaction price. This has obvious implications for the profitability of the supplier.

The number of customers and the volume of their purchases

The fewer the buyers and the greater the volume of their purchases the greater will be their bargaining power. A large number of buyers each acting largely independently of each other and buying only small quantities of a product will be comparatively weak.

The number of businesses supplying the product and their size

If the suppliers of a product are large in comparison to the buyers, then buying power will tend to be reduced. The number of suppliers also has an effect – fewer suppliers will tend to reduce the bargaining power of buyers as choice and the ability to 'shop around' is reduced.

Switching costs and the availability of substitutes

If the costs of switching to substitute products are low (because the substitutes are close in terms of functionality and price), then customers will be accordingly more powerful.

We should bear in mind that buyers are not necessarily those at the end of the supply chain. At each stage of a supply chain, the bargaining power of buyers will have a strong influence upon the prices charged and the industry structure.

In the supply chain for beer, for example, the buyers include consumers, wholesalers, supermarket chains, public houses and restaurants. The amount of power which each buyer exerts can differ substantially. Supermarket chains can exert far greater pressure on brewers than can individual consumers.

Force 4: The bargaining power of suppliers

Businesses must obtain the resources that they need to carry out their activities from resource suppliers. These resources fall into the four categories we have previously encountered: human, financial, physical and intellectual (see the Key Concept on page 9).

Resources are obtained in resource markets where prices are determined by the interaction between the businesses supplying a resource (suppliers) and the organizations from each of the industries using the particular resource in question. It is important to note that many resources are used by more than one industry. As a result, the bargaining power of suppliers will not be determined solely by their relationship with one industry but by their relationships with all of the industries that they serve.

The major factors determining the strength of suppliers are discussed below.

The uniqueness and scarcity of the resource that suppliers provide

If the resources provided to the industry are essential to it and have no close substitutes then suppliers are likely to command significant power over the industry. If the resource can easily be substituted by other resources then its suppliers will have little power. It is for this reason, for example, that people with rare or exceptional skills can command higher salaries than lesser-skilled people.

The cost of switching to another resource

If the resource can easily be substituted then switching costs will be low. If there is high labour turnover or low penalty clauses in debt rescheduling, then the power over suppliers of these resources will be increased.

How many other industries have a requirement for the resource

If suppliers provide a particular resource to several industries then they are less likely to be dependent upon one single industry. Thus, the more industries to which they supply a resource, the greater will be their bargaining power.

The number and size of the resource suppliers

If the number of organizations supplying a resource is small and the buyers are large, then the greater will be their power over the organizations in any industry. If the suppliers are small and there are a large number of them, they will be comparatively weak, particularly if they are small in comparison to the organizations buying the resource from them. For example, most of Marks & Spencer's suppliers are weak because they are small in comparison to the retailer. Marks & Spencer has a number of suppliers and is able to switch suppliers if necessary to gain lower input costs or higher quality.

In short, suppliers to an industry will be most powerful when:

- the resource that they supply is scarce;
- there are few substitutes for it;
- switching costs are high;
- they supply the resource to several industries;
- the suppliers themselves are large;
- the organizations in the industry buying the resource are small.

When the opposite conditions apply then suppliers will be weak.

Force 5: The intensity of rivalry among competitors in the industry

Businesses within an industry will compete with each other in a number of ways. Broadly speaking, competition can take place on either a price or a non-price basis.

Price competition involves businesses trying to undercut each other's prices which will, in turn, be dependent upon their ability to reduce costs of production. Non-price competition will take the form of branding, advertising, promotion, additional services to customers and product innovation. In some industries competitive rivalry is fierce, while in others it is less intense or even genteel.

In Figure 7.1, we see that the other four forces point in towards this fifth force. This representation is intentionally to remind us that the strength of this force is largely dependent upon the contributions of the other four that 'feed' it. In particular, however, the intensity of competition in an industry will depend upon the following factors.

The height of entry barriers and the number and size of the competitors in the industry

If there are few, large competitors in the industry, then it is likely that this is due to high entry barriers. Conversely, an industry of many, smaller competitors is likely to be the result of lower entry barriers. Competitive rivalry on both a price and non-price basis will be higher in the industry comprising the more and smaller competitors.

The maturity of the industry

If the product is mature and the industry is subject to 'shakeout' then competition will be more intense (see our discussion of this in Chapter 5).

The degree of brand loyalty of customers

If customers are loyal to brands then there is likely to be less competition and what competition there is will be non-price. If there is little brand loyalty then competition will be more intense.

The power of buyers and availability of substitutes

If buyers are strong and there are close substitutes available for the product then the degree of competitive rivalry will be greater.

A high degree of rivalry will usually compromise the potential profitability of an industry and will typically result in innovation which stimulates consumer demand for the products of the industry. In recent years, many industries have become more competitive.

The five forces framework and profitability – a summary

As has been discussed, a relationship can be established between a company's position in respect to the five forces and its potential profitability. Table 7.1 shows a summary of how the five forces can help to determine company and industry profitability.

Force	Profitability will be higher if there is/are	Profitability will be lower if there is/are
Bargaining power of suppliers	weak suppliers	strong suppliers
Bargaining power of buyers	weak buyers	strong buyers
Threat of new entrants	high entry barriers	low entry barriers
Threats from substitute products	few possible substitutes	many possible substitutes
Competitive rivalry	little rivalry	intense rivalry

Table 7.1 Porter's five forces and profitability – a summary (after Campbell, 1997).

Limitations of the five forces framework

Despite its obvious value as a tool for managers seeking to understand the competitive environment better, Porter's framework is subject to several important limitations. These are considered and then some suggestions are made for modifications to improve the value of the framework as an analytical tool. The major limitations of the framework are as follows.

It claims to assess industry profitability

Porter (1980) argues that the framework makes it possible to assess the potential profitability of a particular industry. While there is some evidence to support this claim, there is also strong evidence to suggest that company-specific factors are more important to the profitability of individual businesses than industry factors (Rumelt, 1991).

It implies that the five forces apply equally to all competitors in an industry

In reality, the strength of the forces may differ from business to business. The framework implies that if, for example, supplier power is strong then this will apply to all the businesses in the industry. In fact, supplier power may differ from business to business in the industry. Larger businesses will face less of a threat from suppliers than will smaller ones. Similarly, businesses with strong brand names will be less susceptible to buyer power and substitutes than those with weaker brands.

It does not adequately cover product and resource markets

The concepts of buyer power and supplier power relate to the markets in which a business sells its products and obtains its resources. The conditions in both sets of markets are, however, somewhat more complex than Porter's framework implies (see Chapter 5).

An alternative approach to competitive and collaborative analysis

Competitive and collaborative arenas

It is not always the case that businesses in an industry compete with each other – they might, from time to time, have reasons to collaborate with each other. Accordingly, in some 'arenas' businesses compete whilst in others they may work together.

At the root of this understanding is the fact that organizations and industries are *open systems* – they interact with many environments. The 'arenas' in which the organization operates are:

- *the industry* – the industry within which the organization currently deploys its resources and competences in producing products;
- *resource markets* – the markets from which the organization, its competitors and other industries obtain their resources;
- *product markets* – markets where the organization sells its products. These can be subdivided into markets for the organization's products, markets

for substitute products, and new markets to which the organization may be considering entry;

● *other industries* – where businesses possess similar competences to those of the organization. Such industries are important for two reasons. The first is that the business may be considering entry to them. The second is that the organizations in these industries are potential competitors who may enter the business's industry and markets.

Each of these arenas must be analysed as they directly affect an organization's competitive positioning and hence its chances of outperforming competitors.

The competitive and collaborative arena framework builds upon Porter's five forces framework but explicitly recognizes that the competitive environment is divided into the four separate but interrelated arenas above.

A resource-based approach to environmental analysis

Limitations of existing frameworks of analysis

This chapter has so far concentrated on explaining the traditional strategic management frameworks employed in the analysis of the competitive environment. The resource-based approach to strategic management, which emphasizes the importance of core competence in achieving competitive advantage, employs a different approach to analysis of the competitive environment. There are several limitations to existing (traditional) frameworks:

● they do not sufficiently integrate external and internal analysis (Sanchez and Heene, 1997);
● they presuppose that businesses are naturally competitive and not collaborative in their behaviour;
● they tend to emphasize product and service markets rather than those where organizations obtain their resources;
● they do not adequately recognize the fact that organizations themselves may alter their own competitive environments by their competence leveraging and building activities (see the Key Concept on page 32);
● they do not adequately recognize the fact that organizations currently outside a company's industry and market may pose a significant competitive threat if they possess similar core competences and distinctive capabilities;
● similarly they do not recognize that the leveraging of existing competences and the building of new ones may enable businesses to compete outside their current competitive arenas.

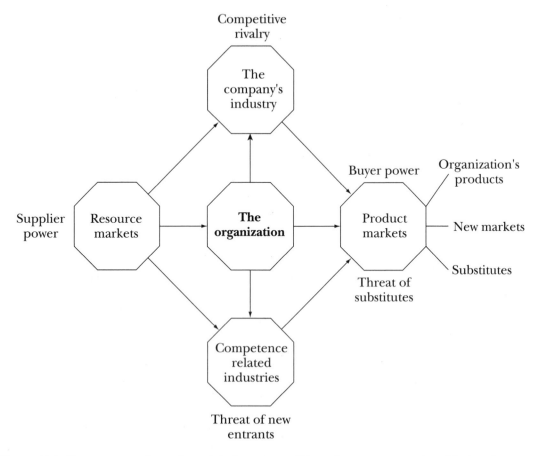

Figure 7.2 The resource-based model of strategy. (*Note* Competence-related industries are those where businesses possess similar competences to those of competitors.)

The resource-based framework

A resource- based framework for analysis of the business and its competitive environment is shown in Figure 7.2. Analysis is divided into five interrelated areas:

1 the organization;
2 its industry;
3 product markets (existing markets, markets for substitutes, potential new markets);
4 resource markets;
5 other industries.

The significance of each area is considered below.

The organization

The 'organization' concerns the configuration of the internal value chain, its competences, resources and core competences and is discussed in Part II of this book (particularly in Chapter 2).

The organization's industry

The organization's industry consists of the business and a group of companies producing similar products, employing similar capabilities and technology.

Analysis of the industry therefore examines over time (for each player in the industry):

- the skills and competences of the competitors;
- the configuration of value adding activities;
- the technologies employed;
- the number and relative size of competitors in the industry;
- the performance of competitors (particularly in financial terms);
- ease of entry to and exit from the industry;
- strategic groupings (see later in the chapter for a discussion of this concept).

This analysis will assist the organization in gaining greater understanding of its core competences, its major competitors and their core competences, and competitive and collaborative opportunities and threats.

Product markets

Product markets are those where businesses deploy their competences and sell their products and services. A business may operate in one or more product markets. In addition, a business will be interested in understanding markets to which it is considering entry on the basis of its core competences and also markets for substitute products. Each of these markets will have its own characteristics and each market can be analysed in terms of:

- customer needs and motivations;
- unmet customer needs;
- market segments and their profitability;
- the number of competitors to the market and their relative market shares;
- the number of customers and their relative purchasing power;
- access to distribution channels;
- potential for collaboration with customers;
- ease of entry;
- potential for competence leveraging;
- need for new competence building.

Unless an organization's products and services are sold at a profit the business will ultimately fail. Market-driven businesses, which set out to meet existing customer needs, anticipate their currently unmet needs and actually seek to shape the needs of their customers, are likely to be the most successful. For example, the Dutch electronics company Philips created a new customer need when it developed and launched the CD format for music and computer software.

Market subgroups

An important part of understanding the market is identifying subgroups within the market that share common needs. Such shared characteristics will cause specific customer groups to have different needs and to act and behave differently from other customer groups (or *segments*). Fundamentally, segmentation means subdividing the total market into customer subgroupings, each with their own distinctive attributes and needs. Customer groups are commonly segmented according to demographic variables (or 'people dividers') like age, sex, occupation, socio-economic grouping, race, lifestyle, buying habits, geography (i.e. where they live). When customers are other businesses, they can be grouped by the nature of the business, organization type and by their size. Each segment is then analysed for its size and potential profitability, for customer needs and for potential demand, based on ability and willingness to buy. Segmentation analysis assists in the formulation of strategy by identifying particular segments and consumer characteristics which can be targeted. Computer games, for example, are largely targeted upon young males between the ages of 11 and 25, whilst Findus Lean Cuisine frozen recipe dishes are reputedly targeted at women aged between 25 and 45 in socio-economic groups ABC1. This is not to say that other groups and individuals do not play computer games or consume Lean Cuisine, but that the segment identified is the largest and most profitable for the products in question. We discuss the concept of market segmentation in more depth in Chapter 5.

Customer motivations

Once market segments have been identified, they must be analysed to reveal the factors which influence customers to buy or not buy products. It is particularly important to understand factors affecting customer motivations like:

- sensitivity to price;
- sensitivity to quality;
- the extent of brand loyalty.

Differences in customer motivations between market segments can be illustrated by reference to the market for air travel. The market can be segmented into business and leisure travel. Customers in each group have very different characteristics and needs. Business travellers are not particularly price-sensitive but are sensitive to standards of service, to scheduling, and to availability of connections. Leisure travellers are generally much more price rather than service conscious and are less sensitive to scheduling and connections. Market research has an important role to play in building understanding of customer needs so that they can be targeted by appropriate product or service features.

Potential new markets are those where the product or service bought by customers is based upon similar competences to those of the organization or where customer needs are similar to those of customers in the business's market. If conditions are favourable the organization may consider using its current competences to enter new markets. Of course it may also have to build new competences in order to be able to meet new customer needs.

Resource markets

Resource markets are those where organizations obtain finance, human resources, materials, equipment, services, etc. It is evident that businesses will normally operate in several such markets, each with its own characteristics, depending upon the company-specific resources that are required. Resource markets can be analysed in terms of:

- resource requirements;
- number of actual and potential resource suppliers;
- size of suppliers;
- supplier capabilities and competences;
- potential for collaboration with resource suppliers;
- access by competitors to suppliers;
- the nature of the resource and the availability of substitutes.

By analysing each of its resource markets, the managers of a business can identify the extent of competition that they face from suppliers of resources, the competition that they face from other competitors using the same resources, and the potential for collaboration with suppliers (if appropriate).

Competence-related industries

Other industries comprising businesses possessing similar competences and which often produce products or services which are substitutes for those of the business in question must also be analysed. This analysis is necessary for three reasons. Firstly, the organization may face a threat from other competitors possessing similar competences which may seek to enter its industry and markets. Secondly, the organization may be able to enter industries where competences are similar to those which it already possesses. Thirdly, the organization may be able to enter the markets currently served by competitors in the competence-related industry. Competence-related industries can be analysed for:

- key competences of the businesses in the industry;

- the number and size of the businesses in the industry;
- the threat from competitors in such industries who may leverage their competences to enter the markets of the business;
- opportunities for the business to leverage its existing competences and build new ones in order to enter competence-related industries and their markets;
- substitutability of the products of the industry for those of the business – how close the substitute product is to satisfying the same consumer demands as the business's product or service.

A summary of the resource-based model

The competence/resource-based model is more complex that the five forces framework but offers a more comprehensive analytical framework. It enables an organization to establish the extent of competition within its own industry and market. It also enables the organization to assess the threat of competition from competitors in industries where similar competences to their own are employed. Equally, based on this model, the organization is able to identify other markets which it may be able to enter by leveraging its existing competences and by adding new ones.

Once adapted the framework enables managers to:

- understand the nature of competition within the industry and markets (both product and resource) in which they operate;
- understand the threat from competitors in other industries;
- understand potential opportunities in new industries and markets

Strategic group and competitor analysis
What are strategic groups?

A business can rarely confine its analysis to the level of the industry and markets in which it operates. It must also pay particular attention to its closest competitors, known as its strategic group (Porter, 1980). Strategic groups cannot be precisely defined but they consist of organizations possessing similar competences, serving customer needs in the same market segment and producing products or services of similar quality. Such analysis allows the managers of a business to compare its performance with that of its closest competitors in terms of profitability, market share, products, brands, customer loyalty, prices and so on. In this way managers are able to benchmark the performance of their organization against their closest rivals.

In the automotive industry, for example, we can observe a number of important strategic groupings. Although Lada and BMW are both motor manufacturers – and hence are technically competitors – they operate in quite different strategic groups. They are unlikely to appeal to the same customers and their products, dealership networks, brand identities and prices are quite different. BMW's strategic group (that grouping of producers in the automotive industry that compete with each other directly) includes Lexus, Mercedes Benz, Jaguar and Audi.

Industry and market critical success factors

In any industry and its associated markets, there will be certain factors which are of fundamental importance to the success of the businesses operating within that competitive environment. These are known as critical success factors (CSFs – see the Key Concept on page 43).

CSFs differ between individual industries and markets. In the pharmaceutical industry CSFs will be in the areas of research and development and production. CSFs will differ between the markets for drugs available over the counter and those available only on prescription. CSFs for the over-the-counter market will centre on advertising and linkages to retail pharmacy groups while those for the prescription market are likely to focus on clinical trials and linkages to governments and doctors. In this way pharmaceutical companies must develop competences which concentrate on the industry and market CSFs.

Summary

Competitive analysis is intended to increase managers' understanding of the industry and markets in which their business operates. The process begins with a clear identification of those industries and markets and their key characteristics. The process then allows managers to develop a detailed picture of the industry in which they operate, the markets for their products, the markets where they obtain their resources, their strategic grouping, markets that they may wish to enter in the future, and industries with related competences. This analysis will enable managers to identify: critical success factors in their industry and markets; needs and opportunities for competence building and leveraging; and the potential for collaboration with suppliers, distributors, customers and competitors.

Review and Discuss

1 Define and distinguish between an industry and a market.
2 What is the purpose of industry analysis?
3 Explain how Porter's five forces framework works as a tool of industry analysis.
4 What are the limitations of the five forces framework?

5 Explain what entry barriers are and the link between their 'height' and the profitability of an industry.
6 Define and distinguish between competition and collaboration.
7 What is a resource market?
8 Explain how the resource-based model aids the understanding of industry analysis.
9 What is a strategic group?

References and further reading

Aaker, D.A. (1992) *Strategic Market Management.* New York: John Wiley.

Abell, D.F.(1980) *Defining the Business: The Starting Point of Strategic Planning.* Englewood Cliffs: Prentice Hall.

Arthur, W.B. (1996) Increasing returns and the new world of business. *Harvard Business Review*, 74, July–August.

Baden-Fuller, C. and Stopford, J. (1992) *Rejuvenating the Mature Business.* Oxford: Routledge.

Campbell, D. J. (1997) *Organizations and the Business Environment.* Oxford: Butterworth-Heinemann (see especially Chapter 20).

Chakravarthy, B. (1997) A new strategy framework for coping with turbulence. *Sloan Management Review*, Winter, 69–82.

D'Aveni, R.A. (1994) *Hypercompetition: Managing the Dynamics of Strategic Manoeuvring.* New York: Free Press.

Ginter, P. and Duncan, J.(1990) Macroenvironmental analysis. *Long Range Planning*, December.

Hamel, G. and Prahalad, C.K. (1989) Strategic intent. *Harvard Business Review*, 67, No. 3.

Hamel, G. and Prahalad, C.K. (1994) *Competing for the Future.* Cambridge, MA: Harvard Business School Press.

Heene, A. and Sanchez, R. (1997) *Competence-Based Strategic Management.* New York: John Wiley.

Helms, M.M. and Wright, P. (1992) External considerations: their influence on future strategic planning. *Management Decision*, 30, No. 8.

Kay, J. (1993) *Foundations of Corporate Success.* Oxford: Oxford University Press.

Kay, J. (1995) Learning to define the core business. *Financial Times*, December 1.

Lindsay, W. K. and Rue, L. W. (1980) Impact of organization environment on the long range planning process. *Academy of Management Journal*, 23.

McGahan, A.M. and Porter, M.E. (1997) How much does industry matter, really? *Strategic Management Journal*, 18 (Summer special issue), 15–30.

McGahan, A.M. and Porter, M.E. (1997) The persistence of profitability: comparing the market-structure and Chicago views. Manuscript, Harvard Business School.

Porter, M.E. (1979) How competitive forces shape strategy. *Harvard Business Review*, March/April.

Porter, M.E. (1980) *Competitive Strategy: Techniques for Analysing Industries and Competitors*. New York: Free Press.

Porter, M.E. (1985) *Competitive Advantage*. New York: Free Press.

Prahalad, C.K. and Hamel, G. (1990) The core competence of the corporation. *Harvard Business Review*.

Rumelt, R.P. (1991) How much does industry matter? *Strategic Management Journal*, 12, No. 3.

Simonian, H. (1996) Star parts for bit players. *Financial Times*, October 28.

Strebel, P. (1992) *Breakpoints*. Cambridge, MA: Harvard Business School Press.

Turner, I. (1996) Working with chaos. *Financial Times*, October 4.

Case linkage

Questions for the UK paint industry case study.

1 Using your general knowledge, generate a list of the indirect substitutes for decorative paint.
2 From the information given in the case, construct a five-forces analysis for a typical company in the decorative paint industry.
3 From your five-forces analysis, predict, in general terms, the average level of return on sales for a competitor in the decorative paint industry (i.e. high, medium, low). Give reasons for your prediction.
4 Identify and describe the bases on which paint companies might fall into strategic groups.

Questions for the Ben & Jerry's case study.

1 Discuss the extent to which a company with a market share of 70 per cent would have bargaining power over its buyers (or distributors).
2 Explain why Pillsbury was unable to exert its natural bargaining power over its buyers.
3 What does the case tell us about the limitations of the five forces framework?

Chapter 8

Strategies – core competence, generic and hybrid strategies

Introduction

The study of strategic management offers several explanations of how competitive advantage can be achieved and sustained. This chapter focuses on two of the major explanations of competitive advantage: competitive positioning and core competence.

The *competitive positioning* approach is based largely upon Porter's generic strategy framework (Porter, 1980, 1985). The *core competence* or *resource-based* approach explains competitive advantage in terms of the development and exploitation of an organization's core competences (see Chapter 2). These two approaches can be seen as complementary and mutually enriching rather than mutually exclusive. The two frameworks are first explored separately and then the linkages between them are developed.

The chapter ends with a discussion of the general mechanisms that organizations employ to grow and develop in order to sustain and develop their competitive advantage. We use the Ansoff matrix as a starting point for this discussion.

After studying this chapter, students should be able to:

- explain the concept of competitive advantage;
- describe and evaluate Porter's generic strategy framework;
- explain the concept of hybrid strategy;
- explain the role of core competences and distinctive capabilities in building competitive advantage;
- explain the role of the value chain in linking core competences and generic strategies;
- identify the strategic growth options available to the business;
- identify where core competences and strategies can be exploited.

Michael Porter's generic strategies

Introduction

Perhaps the oldest and best known explanation of competitive advantage is given by Porter in his *generic strategy* framework. Although this framework has been increasingly called into question in recent years, it still provides useful insight into competitive behaviour. The framework and its limitations are considered in this section.

According to Porter (1985), competitive advantage arises from selection of the generic strategy which best fits the organization's competitive environment and then organizing value adding activities to support the chosen strategy. There are three main alternatives:

- *differentiation* – creating a customer perception that a product is superior to that of competitors' products so that a premium price can be charged;
- *cost leadership* – being the lowest cost producer of a product so that above-average profits are earned even though the price charged is not above average;
- *focus* – utilizing either a differentiation or cost leadership strategy in a narrow profile of market segments (possibly just one segment).

Porter's generic strategy framework

Porter argues that an organization must make two key decisions on its strategy (see Figure 8.1):

- Should the strategy be one of differentiation or cost leadership?
- Should the scope of the strategy be broad or narrow?

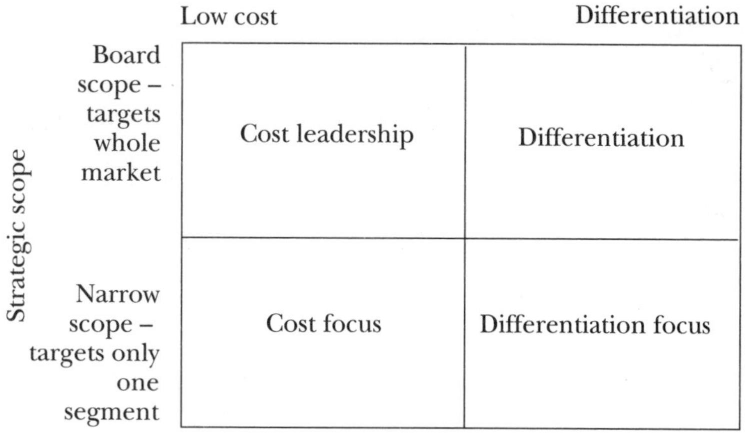

Low cost   Differentiation

Board
scope –
targets
whole   Cost leadership   Differentiation
market

Narrow
scope –   Cost focus   Differentiation focus
targets only
one
segment

Figure 8.1 The generic strategy framework (adapted from Porter, 1985).

In other words, the organization must decide whether to try to differentiate its products and sell them at a premium price or whether to gain competitive advantage by producing at a lower cost than its competitors. Higher profits can be made by adopting either approach. Secondly, it must decide whether to target the whole market with its chosen strategy or whether to target a specific segment or niche of the market (see Figure 8.2).

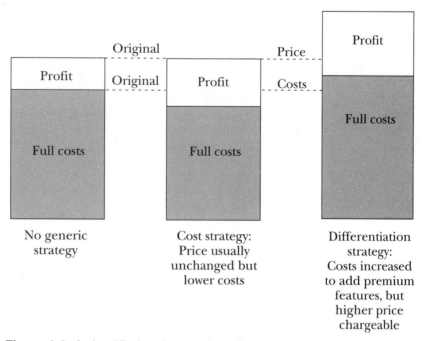

Figure 8.2 A simplified understanding of cost and differentiation strategies (note that price = full costs plus profits).

Cost leadership strategy

A cost leadership strategy is based upon a business organizing and managing its value adding activities so as to be the lowest cost producer of a product (a good or service) within an industry. There are several potential benefits of a cost leadership strategy:

- the business can earn higher profits by charging a price equal to, or even below, that of competitors because its costs are lower;
- it allows the business the possibility to increase both sales and market share by reducing price below that charged by competitors (assuming that the product's demand is price elastic in nature);
- it allows the business the possibility to enter a new market by charging a lower price than competitors;
- it can be particularly valuable in a market where consumers are price sensitive (see Figure 8.3);
- it creates an additional barrier to entry for organizations wishing to enter the industry.

Value chain analysis is central to identifying where cost savings can be made at various stages in the value chain and its internal and external linkages (see Chapter 2).

A successful cost leadership strategy is likely to rest upon a number of organizational features. Attainment of a position of cost leadership depends upon the arrangement of value chain activities so as to:

- reduce costs by copying rather than originating designs, using cheaper materials and other cheaper resources, producing products with 'no frills', reducing labour costs and increasing labour productivity;
- achieving economies of scale by high volume sales, perhaps based on advertising and promotion, allowing high fixed costs of investment in modern technology to be spread over a high volume of output;
- using high volume purchasing to obtain discounts for bulk buying of materials;
- locating activities in areas where costs are low or government help (e.g. grant support) is available;
- obtaining 'learning curve' economies (see the Key Concept on page 233).

A cost leadership strategy, coupled to low price, is best employed in a market or segment where demand is price elastic. Under such circumstances sales and market share are likely to increase significantly thus increasing economies of scale, reducing unit costs further, so generating above-average profits.

Price elasticity of demand

Economists use the term *price elasticity* to describe the extent to which the volume of demand for a product is dependent upon its price. The coefficient of elasticity is expressed in a simple equation:

Ep = percentage change in quantity/percentage change in price

The value of Ep (price elasticity) tells us the price responsiveness of the product's demand. If, for any given price change, Ep is more than −1, it means that the change in price has brought about a higher proportionate change in volume sold. This relationship between price change and quantity is referred to as price elastic demand.

Demand is said to be price inelastic if the quantity change is proportionately smaller than the change in price (resulting in an Ep of less than −1). The larger the value of Ep, the more price elastic the demand and, conversely, the nearer Ep is to 0, the more price inelastic the demand.

The price elasticity of demand (the value of Ep) is dependent upon the nature of the market's perception of a product. Products tend to be price elastic if the market sees a product as unnecessary but desirable. Products will have price inelastic demand if the customer perceives a need for a product rather than a want (such as the demand for most medicines, tobacco, etc.)

Alternatively, if a price similar to that of competitors is charged accompanied by advertising to boost sales, similar results will be obtained.

Discount retailers like Comet and Argos can be regarded as basing their strategies mainly on cost leadership. Both offer a 'no frills' service and discount prices, relying on low costs, high volume sales and economies of scale to earn their profits. On a global basis, Toys 'R' Us offer warehouse style shopping, relying on low costs and high volume to earn above-average profits.

Differentiation strategy

A differentiation strategy is based upon persuading customers that a product is superior to that offered by competitors. Differentiation can be based on premium product features or simply upon creating consumer perceptions that a product is superior. The major benefits to a business of a successful differentiation strategy are:

- its products will command a premium price;
- demand for its product will be less price elastic than that for competitors' products;
- above-average profits can be earned;
- it creates an additional barrier to entry to new businesses wishing to enter the industry.

A business seeking to differentiate itself will organize its value chain activities to help create differentiated products and to create a perception among customers that these offerings are worth a higher price.

Differentiation can be achieved in several ways:

- by creating products which are superior to competitors' by virtue of design, technology, performance, etc.;
- by offering superior after-sales service;
- by superior distribution channels, perhaps in prime locations (especially important in the retail sector);
- by creating a strong brand name through design, innovation, advertising, and so on;
- by distinctive or superior product packaging.

A differentiation strategy is likely to necessitate emphasis on innovation, design, research and development, awareness of particular customer needs and marketing. To say that differentiation is in the eyes of the customer is no exaggeration. It could be argued that it is often brand name or logo which distinguishes a product rather than real product superiority. For example, men's shirts bearing the logo of Ralph Lauren, Calvin Klein or Yves St Laurent command a price well above that of very similar shirts which bear no logo. There is little empirical evidence of objectively better design or of better quality materials. Differentiation appears merely to be based on the fact that the designer's name is fashionable and that its products bear the logo.

A strategy like this is employed in order to reduce price elasticity of demand for the product so that its price can be raised above that of competitors without reducing sales volume, so generating above-average profits.

Focus strategy

A focus strategy is aimed at a segment of the market for a product rather than at the whole market. A particular group of customers is identified on the basis of age, income, lifestyle, sex, geography, or some other distinguishing demographic characteristic. Within the segment a business employs either a cost leadership or a differentiation strategy.

The major benefits of a focus strategy are:

- it requires a lower investment in resources compared with a strategy aimed at an entire market;
- it allows specialization and greater knowledge of the segment being served;
- it makes entry to a new market less costly and more simple.

A focus strategy will require:

- identifying a suitable target customer group which forms a distinct market segment;
- identifying the specific needs of that group;
- establishing that the segment is sufficiently large to sustain the business;
- establishing the extent of competition within the segment;
- producing products to meet the specific needs of that group;
- deciding whether to operate a differentiation or cost leadership strategy within the market segment.

An example of a business which pursues a focus strategy is Ferrari which targets the market for high performance sports cars (a relatively small number of customers in relation to the total market for cars). Ferrari, unlike Toyota or Fiat, does not produce family saloons, minis, 'off-road' vehicles or 'people carriers'. It produces only high performance cars. Its strategy is clearly one of differentiation based on design, superior performance and its Grand Prix record which allows it to charge a price well above that of its competitors.

Many businesses use a focus strategy to enter a market before broadening their activities into other related segments.

Criticisms of Porter's generic strategy framework

A critical evaluation of the framework

In recent years Porter's generic strategy framework has been the target of increasing criticism (see for example Johnson and Scholes, 1993, 1997 (especially the *strategy clock* model); Cronshaw *et al.*, 1990; Miller, 1992; Mintzberg, 1991). At least six objections to Porter's model have been advanced.

A business can apparently employ a successful hybrid strategy without being 'stuck in the middle'

Porter argued that a business must choose between a differentiation and a cost leadership strategy. To be 'stuck in the middle' between the two, he argued, will result in sub-optimal performance. There is plenty of evidence to suggest, however, that some companies with lower than industry-average costs can nevertheless sell their products on the basis of differentiation. A good example of this is Nissan, the Japanese motor manufacturer, whose unit costs are among the lowest in the industry but whose prices are comparable to or above the average. It is able to charge a premium price because customers perceive its products to be extremely reliable and as having a high level of specification as standard. A business like Nissan can thus be regarded as having a *hybrid strategy* which combines elements of differentiation with price and cost competitiveness. A successful hybrid strategy will be based upon a conscious decision by senior managers to combine differentiation with price and cost control. Under such circumstances a business can be successful. When a business slips into the situation unconsciously it can still be regarded as being 'stuck in the middle' but is less likely to be successful.

Cost leadership does not, in and of itself, sell products

Buying decisions are made upon the basis of desirable product features or upon the price, not on the basis of the unit cost itself. This criticism is less valid if a company competes in an industry on the basis of price.

Differentiation strategies can be used to increase sales volumes rather than to charge a premium price

Porter's work does not consider the possibility that a business employing a differentiation strategy might choose not to charge a premium price, but rather to increase sales and market share by forgoing the premium price for an introductory period. This criticism, however, does not fundamentally undermine Porter's thinking.

Price can sometimes be used to differentiate

Porter does not consider the possibility that price may be used to differentiate a product. Mintzberg (1991) argues that price, along with image, support, quality and design, can be used as the basis of differentiation.

A 'generic' strategy cannot give competitive advantage

It is evident that in order to outperform competitors a business must do things better than and differently from them. The word 'generic' could be construed to imply that Porter is arguing that there are general recipes by which competitive advantage can be achieved. This, however, is not the case. Porter's framework is merely a framework by which competitive strategies can be grouped to assist in understanding and analysis.

The resource/competence-based strategy has arguably superseded the generic strategy framework

The resource-based approach argues that it is the core competences of the individual business which give it competitive advantage and not generic strategies. In fact the two approaches do not preclude each other. The relationships between the two approaches are discussed in a later section of this chapter.

Despite these criticisms, Porter's work can, in modified form, constitute the basis of a useful framework for categorizing and understanding sources of competitive advantage. The idea of a hybrid strategy is discussed below.

Hybrid strategies

There is a significant body of evidence that suggests that successful strategy can be based upon a hybrid (a mixture) of differentiation, price and cost control (see Figure 8.3). The hybrid strategy framework developed here is based upon the following assumptions:

1 the strategy can employ a combination of differentiation, price and cost control;
2 differentiation can be used as the basis for charging a premium price or in order to increase sales and/or market share;
3 there are clear linkages between core competences, strategy and value adding activities;
4 the framework is not intended as a recipe for competitive advantage but rather as a way of grouping different strategies.

The extent of differentiation, price and cost control will depend upon the nature of the market in which the business is operating. In markets where consumers show a preference for quality then the emphasis will be less on price and costs whilst in markets where demand is price sensitive the emphasis will be on keeping both price and costs as low as possible. Of course, organizations may also seek to shape customer attitudes by advertising and promotion so as to modify market conditions.

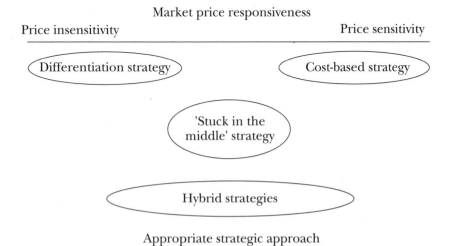

Figure 8.3 Hybrid strategy.

Competence-based competitive advantage

The generic strategy model is not the only one which seeks to provide an explanation of the sources of competitive advantage. The *competence* or *resource-based model* emphasizes that competitive edge stems from attributes of an organization known as *competences* or *capabilities*, which distinguish it from its competitors allowing it to outperform them (see Chapter 2).

Core competence and distinctive capabilities

Chapter 2 explained the ways in which internal analysis makes it possible to better understand core competences by a process of deconstructing them into the component resources and competences which act as their foundation. This chapter builds upon this analysis to explore the ways in which existing competences can be extended and new ones cultivated. It goes on to examine how and where these core competences can be exploited so as to acquire and prolong competitive advantage. Much of the recent attention to the concept of core competence is based upon the work of Prahalad and Hamel (1989, 1990), Stalk, Evans and Shulmann (1992), who advocate the idea of competing on the basis of capabilities, and Kay (1993) who advances the idea that competitive advantage is based upon distinctive capability.

Core competences

Perhaps the best known explanation of core competence is that provided by Prahalad and Hamel (1990):

Core competences are the collective learning of the organization, especially how to co-ordinate diverse production skills and integrate multiple streams of technologies. (Prahalad and Hamel, 1990)

Prahalad and Hamel specify three tests to be applied in the identification and development of core competence. A core competence should:

- equip a business with the ability to enter and successfully compete in several markets;
- add greater perceived customer value to the business's products and services than that perceived in competitors' products;
- be difficult for competitors to imitate.

According to Prahalad and Hamel, there are many examples of core competence resulting in competitive advantage. Philips' development of optical media, including the laser disc, has led to a whole range of new hi-fi and information technology products. Honda's engine technology has led to advantage in car, motor-cycle, lawn-mower and generator businesses. Canon's expertise in optics, imaging and microprocessor controls has given access to diverse markets including those for copiers, laser printers, cameras and image scanners.

Prahalad and Hamel argue that competitive advantage is likely in practice to be based upon no more than five or six competences. These competences will allow management to produce new and unanticipated products, and to be responsive to changing opportunities, because of production skills and the harnessing of technology. Given the turbulent business environment in many industries, such adaptability is essential if competitive advantage is to be built and sustained.

Distinctive capabilities

Kay (1993) has taken the concept of capability, initially identified by Stalk, Evans and Shulmann (1992), to develop a framework which explains competitive advantage in terms of what he defines as *distinctive capability* (see also Chapter 2). This idea of distinctive capability has much in common with that of core competence in that it views competitive advantage as being dependent upon unique attributes of a particular business and its products.

According to Kay (1993), distinctive capability results from one or more of the following sources:

- *architecture* – the unique network of internal and external relationships of a business which produces superior performance. These can be unique relationships with suppliers, distributors or customers which competitors do not possess. Equally, the unique relationships may be internal to the business and based upon the way that it organizes its activities in the value chain;
- *reputation* – this stems from several sources including superior product quality, characteristics, design, service and so on;
- *innovation* – the ability of the business to get ahead and stay ahead of competitors depends upon its success in researching, designing, developing and marketing new products. Equally it depends upon the ability of the business to improve the design and organization of its value adding activities;
- *strategic assets* – businesses can also obtain competitive advantage from assets like natural monopoly, patents and copyrights which restrict competition.

Core competence, distinctive capability and competitive advantage

So what do the concepts of core competence and distinctive capability add to our understanding of competitive advantage? Firstly, they provide us with insight into how a business can build attributes which can deliver superior performance. Secondly, they inform the process of determining where such competence and capabilities can be exploited.

The process of building new core competences or extending existing ones must take into account the following considerations.

Customer perceptions

Competences, capabilities and products must be perceived by customers as being better value for money that those of competitors. The business's reputation can be particularly important in this regard.

Uniqueness

Core competences must be unique to the business and must be difficult for competitors to emulate. Similarly there must be no close substitutes for these competences.

Continuous improvement

Core competences, products and services must be continuously upgraded to stay ahead of competitors. Product and process innovation are particularly important.

Collaboration

Competitive advantage can result from the business's unique network of relationships with suppliers, distributors, customers and even competitors. There is the potential for 'multiplier effects' resulting from separate businesses' complementary core competences being combined.

Organizational knowledge

Competences must be based upon organizational knowledge and learning. Managers must improve the processes by which the organization learns, builds and manages its knowledge. Knowledge is, today, potentially the greatest source of added value (see for example Hall, 1992).

Core competence, generic strategy and the value chain – a synthesis

How the different approaches 'agree'

It has been argued (see for example Heene and Sanchez, 1997) that the resource or competence-based approach is largely incompatible with the competitive positioning or generic strategy approach advocated by Porter (1980, 1985). Mintzberg *et al.* (1995), however, make the case that the two approaches are in many respects complementary rather than mutually contradictory. Perhaps the best way of illustrating the linkages between the approaches is through the value chain of the organization.

As competitive advantage is based upon the unique approach of the individual business to its environment, it is not possible to identify a one-for-all prescription which will guarantee superior performance in all situations. Both the competitive positioning and the resource-based approach, however, provide frameworks which allow broad sources of competitive advantage to be categorized for the purposes of analysis and development of future strategy. A differentiation strategy, for example, will be likely to be dependent upon core competences in areas of the value chain like design, marketing and service. Similarly a cost or price-based strategy may well require core competences in value chain activities like operations (production), procurement and perhaps in marketing. It is much less likely that a cost leader will have core competences based on design and service. Possible relationships between core competences, generic strategies and the value chain are shown in Table 8.1.

Value chain activity	Areas of competence associated with differentiation strategies	Areas of competence associated with cost/price based strategies
Primary activities		
Inbound logistics	Control of quality of materials	Strict control of the cost of materials. Tendency to buy larger volumes of standard inputs.
Operations	Control of quality of output, raising standards	Lowering production costs and achieving high volume production
Marketing and sales	Sales (and customer relations) on the basis of quality technology, performance, reputation, outlets, etc.	Achieving high volume sales through advertising and promotion
Outbound logistics	Ensuring efficient distribution	Maintaining low distribution costs
Service	Adding to product value by high quality and differentiated service	Minimal service to keep costs low
Support activities		
The business's infrastructure	Emphasis on quality	Emphasis on efficiency and cost reduction
Human resource development	Training to create a culture, skills which emphasize quality, customer service, product development	Training to reduce costs
Technology development	Developing new products, improving product quality, improving product performance, improving customer service	Reducing production costs and increasing efficiency
Procurement	Obtaining high quality resources and materials	Obtaining low cost resources and materials.

Table 8.1 Core competences, generic strategies and the value chain.

Where to exploit core competences and strategies

As core competences and business strategies are developed, it is necessary to decide where they can be exploited. Core competences and strategies can be targeted on existing customers in existing markets or it may be possible to target new customers in existing markets. Alternatively it may be possible to target new customers in new markets. These markets may be related to markets currently served by the organization or they may be unrelated markets. The organization may also consider employing its competences in a new industry. These decisions, on where to deploy core competences, are concerned with determining the *strategic direction* of the business. Once this decision has been made then decisions must be made on the *methods* to be employed in following the chosen strategic direction.

The process of exploiting existing core competences in new markets is known as competence leveraging. In order to enter new markets it is often necessary for the organization to build new core competences, alongside the existing core competences which are being leveraged, so as to satisfy new customer needs. Identification of customer needs to be served by core competences is based upon analysis of the organization's competitive environment using the resource-based framework developed in Chapter 2. The remainder of this chapter considers the alternative strategic directions which an organization can pursue and the methods which can be employed in following these strategic directions.

Strategic directions

Igor Ansoff's product-market framework

The most commonly-used model for analysing the possible strategic directions which an organization can follow is the Ansoff matrix shown in Figure 8.4. This matrix shows potential areas where core competences and generic strategies can be deployed. There are four broad alternatives:

- *market penetration* – increasing market share in existing markets utilizing existing products;
- *market development* – entering new markets and segments using existing products;
- *product development* – developing new products to serve existing markets;
- *diversification* – developing new products to serve new markets.

Market penetration

The main aim of a market penetration strategy is to increase market share using existing products within existing markets. This may involve taking

Products

		Existing	New
Markets	**Existing**	Market penetration (increase market share)	Product development (new or improved products)
	New	Market development (new customers, new market segments or new countries for existing products)	Diversification (new products into new markets)

Figure 8.4 The Ansoff matrix (growth vector components). Adapted from Ansoff (1987).

steps to enhance existing core competences or build new ones. Such competence development may be intended to improve service or quality so as to enhance the reputation of the organization and differentiate it from its competitors. Equally, competence development may be centred on improving efficiency so as to reduce costs below those of competitors.

Mature or declining markets are more difficult to penetrate than those which are still in the growth phase. In the case of a declining market, the organization may also consider the possibility of *withdrawal* so as to redeploy resources to more lucrative markets (see the discussion of disposals and withdrawals in Chapter 11).

When a business's current market shows signs of saturation then it may wish to consider alternative directions for development.

Market development

Market development is based upon entry to new markets or to new segments of existing markets, employing existing products. Entering new markets is likely to be based upon leveraging existing competences but may also require the development of new competences (see the Key Concept on page 32). Entering new segments of existing markets may require the development of new competences which serve the particular need of customers in these segments.

Internationalization and globalization are commonly-used examples of market development. It is likely that an organization will need to build new competences when entering international markets to deal with linguistic, cultural, logistical and other potential problems.

The major risk of market development is that it centres on entry to markets of which the business may have only limited experience.

Product development

Product development centres on the development of new products for existing markets. As with the previous two growth directions, the intention is to attract new customers, retain existing ones and increase market share. Providing new products will be based upon exploiting existing competences but may also require that new competences are built (such as in product research).

Product development offers the advantage to a business of dealing with customer needs of which it has some experience because they are within its existing market. In a world of shortening product life cycles, product development has become an essential form of strategic development for many organizations.

Diversification

Diversification is business growth through new products and new markets. It is an appropriate option when current markets are saturated or when products are reaching the end of their life cycle. It can produce important synergies and can also help to spread risk by broadening the product and market portfolio. Diversification can take two main forms depending upon just *how different* the products and markets are to existing ones.

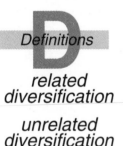

Definitions

related diversification

unrelated diversification

Related diversification is said to have occurred when the products and/or markets share some degree of commonality with existing ones. This 'closeness' can reduce the risk of diversification. In practice, related diversification usually means growth into similar industries or forward or backward in a business's existing supply chain.

Unrelated diversification is growth into product and market areas that are completely new and with which the business shares no commonality at all. It is sometimes referred to as *conglomerate* diversification.

Related diversification

Related diversification can follow three main patterns:

- *Vertical backward diversification* – an organization seeking to operate in markets from which it currently obtains its resources (i.e. extending the value chain in an upstream direction). A supermarket chain beginning to produce some of the products which it sells would be an example of this. The major potential benefits to an organization of upstream integration are greater control over supplies of resources.

- *Vertical forward diversification* – an organization seeking to operate in markets currently served by its customers or distributors (i.e. extending the value chain in an downstream direction). In this case an example would be a brewery establishing its own chain of off-licences where the off-licence has new markets and *some* new products. This form of diversification gives an organization closer contact with customers and can give significant marketing advantages.
- *Horizontal diversification* – involves an organization entering complementary or competing markets. An example of this would be an organization which previously manufactured only motor-cycles beginning to manufacture motor-cars (this being the strategy pursued by Honda). This should not be confused with horizontal integration which is the acquisition of a competitor.

Related diversification has the benefit of leveraging existing competences as well as requiring the building of some new competences. In other words, it draws upon existing organizational knowledge as well as requiring the building of some new skills and knowledge.

Unrelated diversification

Unrelated diversification carries greater risk than related diversification as it involves producing new products for markets with which the organization is unfamiliar. Businesses tend to take this option when they see serious restrictions on growth potential in their existing markets, and in related markets, or when they see significant opportunities for growth in new market areas. In addition, there are potential financial and risk-bearing economies of scale, opportunities to build on existing competences and the possibility of synergy.

Strategic development and risk

There are risks associated with all forms of strategic development. The risks are smallest when development is largely based upon existing core competences and when it takes place in existing markets. The risks are greatest when development requires entry to unrelated markets. Whether or not the risks are worth taking will depend upon the current position of the business and the state of its markets and products. Entry to new markets, whether related or unrelated, will depend upon the business's assessment of the opportunities in new markets compared with opportunities in its existing markets.

Summary

The essence of competitive advantage is the ability to outperform competitors. Whilst it is difficult to identify the source or sources of a business's competitive advantage precisely, it is possible to place potential sources of competitive advantage into broad categories which assist in the analysis of a business and in the formulation of its future strategies. Porter's generic strategy framework, modified to incorporate the concept of hybrid strategies, is useful in appraising the roles of differentiation, price and cost in achieving competitive advantage. The core competence and distinctive capability frameworks offer a means of evaluating the part played by a business's resources, competences, relationships, reputation, innovation and assets in delivering competitive edge. It is the way in which the business configures and manages its value adding activities which forms the link between core competences and generic strategies.

Core competences and generic strategies can be exploited in existing and new markets. The strategic direction of the business determines the nature of product and market development.

Review and Discuss

1 What is meant by the term 'competitive advantage'?
2 Explain Porter's generic strategy framework and discuss its strengths and weaknesses as an analytical framework.
3 Explain the contribution made by the 'hybrid strategy' concept to the generic strategy framework.
4 Explain the meaning of the term 'distinctive capability'.
5 Discuss the relationships between generic strategies, core competences and the value chain.
6 What factors will determine the strategic direction of a particular business and the methods of development that it employs?

References and further reading

Ansoff, I. (1987) *Corporate Strategy*. London: Penguin.

Cravens, D.W., Greenley, G., Piercy, N.F. and Slater S. (1997) Integrating contemporary strategic management perspectives. *Long Range Planning*, 30 No. 4, August, 493–506.

Cronshaw, M., Davis, E. and Kay, J. (1990) On being stuck in the middle or Good food costs less at Sainsbury's. Working paper, Centre for Business Strategy, London School of Business.

Grant, R.M. (1991) The resource based theory of competitive advantage: implications for strategy formulation. *California Management Review*, 33, Spring, 114–135.

Hall, R. (1992) The strategic analysis of intangible resources. *Strategic Management Journal*, 13, 135–144.

Hamel, G. and Prahalad, C.K. (1989) Strategic intent. *Harvard Business Review*, 67 No. 3.

Hamel, G. and Prahalad, C.K. (1994) *Competing for the Future.* Cambridge, MA: Harvard Business School Press.

Heene, A. and Sanchez, R. (eds) (1997) *Competence-Based Strategic Management.* New York: John Wiley.

Johnson G. and Scholes, K. (1997) *Exploring Corporate Strategy.* Hemel Hempstead, UK: Prentice Hall.

Kay, J. (1993) *Foundations of Corporate Success.* Oxford: Oxford University Press.

Kay, J. (1995) Learning to define the core business. *Financial Times*, December 1.

Miller, D. (1992) The generic strategy trap. *Journal of Business Strategy*, 13, No. 1, 37–42.

Mintzberg, H. (1991) *The Strategy Process – Concepts, Contexts, Cases.* Englewood Cliffs: Prentice Hall.

Mintzberg, H., Quinn, J.B. and Ghoshal, S. (1995) *The Strategy Process: Concepts, Contexts and Cases*, European Edition. Englewood Cliffs: Prentice Hall.

Porter, M.E. (1980) *Competitive Strategy: Techniques for Analysing Industries and Competitors.* New York: Free Press.

Porter, M.E. (1985) *Competitive Advantage.* New York: Free Press.

Prahalad, C.K. and Hamel, G. (1990) The core competence of the corporation. *Harvard Business Review.*

Stalk, G., Evans, P. and Shulmann, L.E. (1992) Competing on capabilities: the new rules of corporate strategy. *Harvard Business Review*, March/April, 57–69.

Case linkage

Questions for the Kwik Save Group plc case study.

1 Identify the generic strategy employed by Kwik Save plc.
2 Discuss the extent to which Kwik Save's generic strategy has been successful.
3 Discuss the ways in which the company has supported its generic strategies by internal organization and value chain linkages.
4 Identify the generic growth strategies (from the Ansoff matrix) that Kwik Save has used.

Questions for the Derwent Valley Foods case study.

1 Identify DVF's generic strategy.
2 In what ways do the internal activities support the generic strategy?

3 To what extent is the culture compatible with the generic strategy?
4 Comment upon the extent to which DVF's strategy has been successful.
5 What are DVF's key strengths?

Part IV

Strategic implementation and management

Introduction

The process of strategic implementation begins by taking the information gained from the strategic analysis. This information is then used as an input to the process of selecting the most appropriate strategic option. A model for this stage is discussed in Chapter 9 and a number of tools are described to assist in the process.

Once the most appropriate strategic option has been selected, an organization must consider a number of issues relating to actually putting the proposed strategy into action.

First, implementation involves reconfiguring the organization's resource base. Does it have the inputs it needs in terms of finance, employees, physical inputs (like stocks, land, buildings, etc.) and intellectual assets (like legal permissions) to carry out the strategy? If not, these will need to be obtained (Chapter 10).

Second, the organization will need to bring its structure and culture into such a position that they facilitate a successful outcome. It may be that structure and culture are (to begin with) not entirely appropriate. In such a situation, the organization's management will need to make any requisite changes (also Chapter 10).

Third, the implementation of strategy usually involves some internal changes – say of its culture or structure. The management of internal change can be the greatest management challenge in the strategic process and we address this matter in Chapter 10.

Fourth, implementation sometimes involves planning for growth or decline in the size of the business. Some strategies involve growth, and this can be achieved through either internal or external development, or, occasionally, through joint ventures. These, and planning for a reduction in size, are discussed in Chapter 11.

Fifth, successful implementation sometimes involves a significant change in the organization's approach to its customers. This brings into focus the issue of product quality. The operations function and the quality of output it produces is of strategic importance and is often a key area of consideration in strategic implementation (Chapter 12).

Sixth, one of the most important strategic issues that has a bearing upon business success is the extent to which the business is internationalized. In some markets such as those for petrochemicals, pharmaceuticals, air travel, banking and professional education, this is amongst the most important considerations. We consider international strategy in Chapter 13.

Seventh, strategic implementation increasingly necessitates a thorough investigation of how the strategy will impact upon the organization's internal and external stakeholders. The social impact of a business's activities (i.e. of its strategy) is sometimes a matter that requires detailed examination during implementation. We consider the social and ethical role of businesses in Chapter 14.

Finally, it is important to understand that the fact that a strategy is being undertaken doesn't mean that the organization's environment is not changing. It may be that there have been some changes in the internal or external environment since the previous strategic analysis was undertaken. Some of these changes may mean that the strategy currently being implemented is no longer appropriate. It is for this reason that the strategic process is ongoing – it never ends. At every stage of implementation, the business needs to continually re-evaluate its environments. Changes in any of these may necessitate a revision of the strategic selection and, accordingly, a modification of the process of implementation.

Chapter 9

Evaluation and selection of strategies

Introduction

Important decisions are never easy. In order to ensure that we make the right choice in any given situation, we must first of all be in possession of all relevant information. This is the purpose of the strategic analysis stage – to ensure that the management of a business is fully aware of the internal strengths and weaknesses, and of the external opportunities and threats.

The next stage in making an important decision is to be aware of *all* of the options available. The most obvious choice is not necessarily the right one. Following the generation of options, the next stage is to evaluate each option using consistently applied criteria. The purpose of evaluation is to ensure that all options are assessed with equal thoroughness. Finally, strategic selection involves actually making a decision based upon the evaluation of the options.

This chapter considers each of these stages in turn.

Objectives

After studying this chapter, students should be able to:

- describe the nature of strategic options;
- explain the key areas that strategic decisions concern;
- describe the four criteria that are applied to strategic options;
- understand the financial tools that can be used to evaluate strategic options;
- understand a number of other tools that can be used to evaluate strategic options;
- explain the limitations of an emergent approach to strategy when it comes to strategic evaluation and selection.

Identifying strategic options

The nature of strategic options

At the start of this chapter, we must remind ourselves of what makes a decision *strategic* in nature as opposed to one that is *operational*. We encountered these terms in Chapter 1 in the context of the nature of strategic objectives.

Strategic decisions are taken at the highest level of an organization. They concern decisions on how the whole organization will be positioned in respect to its product and resource markets, its competitors and its macro influences. Accordingly, the options at the strategic level are those that offer solutions to the 'big questions' in this regard.

Operational decisions are those that are concerned with how the internal parts of the organization should be configured and managed so that they best achieve the strategic objectives.

The 'big questions' that are considered in strategic selection usually concern three major areas, all of which are discussed in detail elsewhere in this text:

1   decisions on products and markets (see Chapter 5);
2   decisions on generic strategy and scope (see Chapter 8);
3   decisions on growth and development options (see Chapter 11).

In most cases, a business will need to make decisions continually on all of these matters. We should not lose sight of the fact that the strategic process is just that – a process. Strategic selection is no more of a 'once-and-for-all' activity than either strategic analysis or strategic implementation and management. For organizations that exist in rapidly changing environments, decisions on strategic options will be required on a continual basis, hence the importance of ensuring we have a good grasp of the issues that are discussed in this chapter.

Product and market decisions

The questions over *which products* and *which markets* are extremely important because they can determine not only the levels of profitability, but also the survival of the business itself.

There are a number of product and market decisions to be made.

Product and market categories

Firstly, decisions must be made about the categories of products that the business will offer. We encountered the major product classifications in Chapter 5, particularly those distinctions between:

● goods and/or services;

- consumer and/or industrial products;
- convenience, shopping and speciality products (Copeland, 1923).

For markets, the business will have to reach decisions on geographic coverage, international exposure and the benefits and risks that attend such options (see Chapter 13).

Product features

Secondly, decisions must be made on the features that the product will possess. The mix of product benefits that a product will possess will not only strongly affect costs, but also the position that the product will assume in the market. We encountered Kotler's (1997) five 'levels' of product features (or 'benefits') in Chapter 5 and the inclusion or 'leaving out' of any of these will have a strong bearing upon any proposed strategy.

Product and market portfolios

Thirdly, product and market decisions must include a consideration of portfolio. The extent to which the products and markets are focused or spread can be very important. A broad portfolio (presence in many product market sectors) offers the advantages of the ability to withstand a downturn in one sector and to exploit opportunities that arise in any of the areas in which the business operates. Conversely, a narrow portfolio enables the organization's management to be more focused and to develop expertise in its narrower field of operation.

Life cycle considerations

The final consideration to be made for products and markets concerns their life cycle positions. It is perhaps intuitively obvious to say that products or markets that are approaching late maturity or are in decline should be of particular concern, but there is also a need to produce new products or develop new markets on an ongoing basis.

Generic strategy decisions

Decisions over the organization's generic strategy are important not only because they define the organization's competitive position, but also because they will determine the way that the internal value chain activities are configured (see Chapter 2 and Chapter 8).

If the company elects to pursue a differentiation strategy, for example, the implications of this will be felt in all parts of the organization. The culture and structure will need to be configured in such a way that support the generic strategy and the product features and quality will also reflect it (see Chapter 12). Similarly, the way that the organization configures its resource base will need to support the strategy.

The same issues will be considered if a cost-driven strategy is chosen, although the way in which the internal activities are configured will be somewhat different.

Growth and development decisions

Unless the strategy choices include a 'no change' option, it is likely that the strategy will involve a change in the company's size. This may be a 'grow smaller' element, such as when the company has a presence in a declining market, but most growth strategies are 'grow bigger' in nature.

Two types of decisions are taken in this regard. The first decisions concern the generic growth direction that the organization will pursue (see Chapter 8). These strategies arise from Igor Ansoff's (Ansoff, 1987) framework and should not be confused with Porter's generic strategies (Porter, 1985). The second set of decisions concern the mechanism that the company will employ to pursue its generic growth strategy (see Chapter 11).

Ansoff's generic growth strategies concern whether growth will involve new or existing markets and products. The growth mechanisms can be either internal (organic) or external. Each growth option has its own benefits and risks and the strategy evaluation and selection stage will usually involve a full analysis of these.

Applying evaluation criteria

When considering which course of action to pursue, it is normally the case that a number of options present themselves to an organization's top management. In order to ensure that each option is fairly and equally assessed, a number of criteria are applied.

For each option, four criteria are applied – questions to ask of each option. In order to 'pass', the option must usually receive an affirmative answer to each one. The four criteria are:

1 Is the strategic option *suitable?*
2 Is the strategic option *feasible?*
3 Is the strategic option *acceptable?*
4 Will the strategic option enable the organization to *achieve competitive advantage?*

Suitability criterion

A strategic option is suitable if it will enable the organization to actually achieve its strategic objectives. If it will in any way fall short of achieving these objectives, then there is no point in pursuing it and the option should be discarded.

To give a simple example, the option of driving south out of Paris would be an *unsuitable* one if my objective is to reach London. If, however, one option was to drive north or even in a northerly direction, then we could accept the option as being suitable. Similarly, if an organization's objective is to spread market portfolio by gaining a presence in foreign markets, then the option of increasing the company's investment in its domestic home would clearly be unsuitable.

Feasibility criterion

A strategic option is feasible if it is *possible*. When evaluating options using this criteria, it is likely that the options will be feasible to varying degrees. Some will be completely unfeasible, others 'might be', whilst yet others are definitely feasible.

The extent to which an option is suitable will depend in large part upon the resource base that the organization has. A deficit in any of the key resource areas (physical resources, financial, human and intellectual) will present a problem at this stage of evaluation. If an option requires capital that is unavailable, human skills that are difficult to buy in, land or equipment that is equally difficult to obtain or a scarce intellectual resource, then it is likely to fail the feasibility criterion.

Acceptability criterion

A strategic option is acceptable if those who must agree to the strategy accept the option. This raises an obvious question – who are those who agree that the option is acceptable?

We encountered the concept of stakeholders in Chapter 1 and we shall return to it in more detail in Chapter 14. The extent that stakeholders can exert influence upon an organization's strategic decision-making rests upon the two variables, power and interest (see Chapter 1). Stakeholders that have the highest combination of both the ability to influence (power) and the willingness to influence (interest) will have the most *effective* influence. Where two or more stakeholder groups have comparable influence, the possibility of conflict over acceptability will be heightened. In most cases, the board of directors will be the most influential stakeholder.

Competitive advantage criterion

We learned in Chapter 1 that one of the key objectives in strategy is to create competitive advantage. This criterion asks a simple question of any strategic option: 'What is the point of pursuing an option if it isn't going to result in superior performance (compared with competitors) or higher than average profitability?' In other words, a strategic option would fail this test if it was likely to result in the business being only 'ordinary' or average with regard to the industry norm.

This is particularly important when considering product options. For example, if a new product option is forecast to receive an uncertain reception from the market, we might well ask what is the point of the launch at all. It would be unlikely to result in competitive advantage for the business.

Financial tools for evaluation

In the evaluation and selection stage, a number of 'tools' are available to managers that may assist in deciding upon the most appropriate option. Not all of them will be appropriate in every circumstance and some are more widely used than others. They are used to explore the implications of the options so that the decisions that are made are based upon the best possible information.

Accountants are usually very involved in strategic evaluation and selection because of their expertise in understanding the financial implications of the possible courses of action. There are two major areas of financial analysis: cash-flow forecasting and investment appraisal.

Cash-flow forecasting

One of the most straightforward financial tools is cash-flow analysis – sometimes called funds-flow analysis. Essentially, it involves a forecast of the expected income from an option, of the costs that will be incurred and, from this, the forecast net cash inflows or outflows. For most options, the forecast will be broken down into monthly 'chunks' and a profit and loss statement will be constructed for each month. If the same procedure is carried out for each option, the most favourable can be identified.

Investment appraisal

An investment, at its simplest, is some money put up for a project in the expectation that it will enable more money to be made in the future. The questions surrounding investment appraisal concern *how much* will the organization make against each investment option.

There is a strong time element to investment appraisal techniques because the returns on the investment may remain for several years or even decades. It is for this reason that a factor is often built in to the calculation to account for inflation.

The first and most obvious thing that accountants want to know about any investment is the *payback period*. This is the time taken to repay the investment – the shorter the better. If, for example, an investment of £1000 is expected to increase profits by £100 a month, then the payback period will be 10 months.

In practice, payback periods are rarely this short and it is this fact that makes investment appraisal calculations a bit more complicated. When the effects of inflation are taken into account, the returns on an investment can be eroded over time. Consequently, accountants include a factor to account for the effects of inflation, usually on a 'best-guess' basis.

Limitations of the financial tools

The limitations of the financial tools rest in the problem of the unpredictability of the future. We learned in Chapters 6 and 7 that the macro- and microenvironments can change – sometimes rapidly. Accordingly, the actual returns that an organization makes on an investment may not always be what was expected.

A similar limitation applies to forecasting the level of inflation for net present value calculations. In the major First World economies such as those in Western Europe, North America, Japan and Australia, the level of inflation has historically been relatively stable at between 2 per cent and 10 per cent, with an occasional 'shock' such as in the mid-1970s when in the UK it reached 24 per cent. In other parts of the world, however, problems with the supply of goods and the value of currency can lead to much higher inflation levels – sometimes exceeding 1000 per cent a year. A presumption of low and stable inflation will therefore tend to encourage investment rather than high and unpredictable inflation.

Other tools for evaluation

Financial evaluation of strategic options is very important, but for most organizations other tools can also provide useful information. These may require financial information as an input and so they should be seen not as 'instead of' financial analyses, but 'as well as'. They enrich the information, enabling management to select the best strategic option.

Cost–benefit analysis

Cost–benefit analysis applies to almost every area of life, not just strategic evaluation and selection. Each option will have a cost associated with it and will be expected to return certain benefits. If both of these can be quantified in financial terms, then the cost–benefit calculation will be relatively straightforward. The problem is that this is rarely the case.

The costs of pursuing one particular option will have a number of elements. Any financial investment costs will be easily quantifiable. Against this, the cost of not pursuing the next best option needs to be taken into account – the opportunity cost. There may also be a number of social and environmental costs which are much harder to attach a value to.

The same problems apply to the benefits. In addition to financial benefits, an organization may also take into account social benefits and others such as improved reputation or improved service. Intangible benefits are very difficult to attach a value to for a cost–benefit analysis as they can take a long time to work through in increased financial performance.

Key Concepts

Social costs and benefits

All organizations have an impact upon the societies that are in their locality or that are affected by their products or activities. Although the term *social* is a bit nebulous, it is generally taken to mean the effect on the condition of employment, social well-being, health, chemical emissions, pollution, aesthetic appearance (e.g. 'eyesores'), charitable societies, etc.

A strategic option will have an element of social cost and social benefit. We would describe a social cost as a deterioration in any of the above – an increase in unemployment, higher levels of emissions, pollution, declining salaries, etc. Conversely, a social benefit will result in an improvement in the condition of society – increasing employment, cleaner industry, better working conditions, etc.

Impact analysis

When a strategic option may be reasonably expected to have far-reaching consequences in either social or financial terms, an impact study may be appropriate. Essentially, this involves asking the question, 'If this option goes ahead, what will its impact be upon ...?'

The thing that might be impacted upon will depend upon the particular circumstances of the option. For a proposed development of a new nuclear power station, for example, the impact study would typically take into account the development's implications for local employment, local tourism, heath risk to employees and local residents, the reputation and appearance of the town or region, local flora and fauna, among other things.

In many cases, an impact study will be an intrinsic part of the cost–benefit calculation, and it suffers from the same limitations – that of evaluating the true value of each thing that may be impacted.

'What if?' and sensitivity analysis

The uncertainties of the future, as we have seen, make any prediction inexact. Whilst an organization can never be certain of any sequence of future events, 'what if?' analysis, and its variant, sensitivity analysis, can give an idea of how the outcome would be affected by a number of possible disruptions.

The development of computerized applications such as spreadsheets have made this activity easier than it used to be. A financial model on a spreadsheet that makes a number of assumptions such as revenue projections, cost forecasts, inflation rate, etc., can be modified to show instantly the effect of, say, a 10 per cent increase in costs or a higher-than-expected rate of inflation. This is designed to show how sensitive the cash flow is to its assumptions – hence the name.

Qualitative variables can also be analysed. If an option has a high dependency upon the availability of a key raw material or the oversight of a key manager, a 'what if?' study will show the effect that the loss or reduction in the key input would have.

Strategic evaluation in emergent strategies

In Chapter 1, we encountered the idea that business strategies can be either deliberate (or prescriptive) or emergent (we return to this concept in more detail in Chapter 15). This is to say that some strategies are planned in advance, often following a rational sequence of events – prescriptive strategies. Others are not planned in this way and are said to be emergent – they result from an organization's management following a consistent pattern of behaviour.

This distinction is important when it comes to strategic evaluation. Companies that employ the deliberate model are likely to use the criteria and the tools above whilst those that prefer the emergent model are very unlikely to do so explicitly. This is not to say, however, that the analytical process cannot form a part of an intelligent manager's intuitive thinking.

It is here that one of the potential limitations of emergent strategy becomes apparent. If an organization follows a deliberate process with its systematic and sequential events, then it can be more certain that all possible options have been identified and evaluated before the most appropriate one is selected. An intuitive emergent approach that relies upon patterns of behaviour cannot be certain that the best option is taken in all times of decision. It might get it right – but it might not.

Summary

The process of selecting the best strategy begins by generating all of the possible options. Then, each option is considered in turn using four overarching criteria – suitability, feasibility, acceptability and whether or not it will lead to competitive advantage. A number of financial and non-financial tools can be used to evaluate each option before the most favourable one is chosen. However, there are risks inherent in an emergent strategy approach when it comes to strategic evaluation.

Review and Discuss

1 Where does strategic evaluation and selection fit into the strategic process?
2 Describe the four criteria that can be used to evaluate strategic options.
3 Describe the benefits of cash-flow forecasting and investment appraisal.
4 What are the limitations of a cost–benefit analysis?
5 What is a social cost?
6 Describe the limitations that emergent strategies may have in the strategic evaluation stage.

References and further reading

Ansoff, I. (1987) *Corporate Strategy*. London: Penguin.
Copeland, M.T. (1923) Relation of consumers' buying habits to marketing methods. *Harvard Business Review*, 1 (April), 282–289.
Kotler, P. (1997), *Marketing Management Analysis, Planning, Implementation, and Control*, Ninth Edition. Englewood Cliffs: Prentice Hall.
Porter, M.E. (1985) *Competitive Advantage*. New York: Free Press.

Chapter 10

Strategic implementation

Introduction

Strategic implementation is all about what issues are considered to be necessary for the successful execution of strategy. In a prescriptive strategic process, strategic implementation would be carried out only after a company has gathered sufficient information on its internal and external environments (this being the purpose of strategic analysis) and after it has undertaken the process of strategy evaluation and selection (see Chapter 9).

In order successfully to carry out a strategy, a company must consider several key areas. Firstly, it must establish how the strategy will be resourced. Secondly, it should ask itself how well its current culture, structure and internal systems are able to meet the challenges of the strategy. Changes in any or all of these may become necessary. Finally, most strategies necessitate some degree of internal change and this process of change will need to be managed. This chapter discusses each of these matters in turn.

Objectives

After studying this chapter, students should be able to:

- describe where implementation fits into the strategic process;
- describe the role of resource planning in strategic implementation;
- explain how and why corporate culture plays an important part in implementation;
- understand the link between structure and strategy;
- describe the essentials of change management.

Implementation and the strategic process

Most people intuitively understand that a lot of information is required before any big decision is made. We wouldn't buy a house without a thorough survey and we would normally find out something about a company before we accepted a job with it. In the same way, a business would be risking a great deal if it were to pursue a strategic option without first carrying out a detailed analysis of its internal and external environments.

Put simply, successful strategy selection and implementation relies upon the presupposition that the organization has carried out a meaningful strategic analysis and is consequently aware of its internal strengths and weaknesses and its external opportunities and threats. Without being 'armed' with this information, the company cannot be certain that the chosen strategy would be the correct choice. The process leading to implementation is shown in Figure 10.1.

In order successfully to carry out (implement) a strategy, an organization will need to work out how to resource it. This means how it will obtain the requisite finance, human resources (usually in the form of appropriately skilled employees) and the plant, equipment and buildings. It should also reconfigure its culture and structure to 'fit' the proposed strategy. Finally, strategic implementation often means change inside the organization in order to achieve the agreed objectives. Change management is thus the third area to be considered in strategic implementation. This chapter will briefly consider each of these issues.

Resources and implementation
Resources – the key inputs

In the same way that people and animals need the inputs of air, food, warmth, etc., so also organizations need inputs in order to function normally. Economics textbooks would refer to these inputs as the *factors of production*. They fall into four broad categories:

1 physical resources (land, buildings, plant, equipment, etc.);
2 financial resources (share and loan capital required for development and expansion);
3 human resources (obtaining the requisite number of appropriately skilled employees);
4 intellectual or 'intangible' resources (non-physical inputs that may be necessary in some industries such as databases, legal permissions, brand or design registration, contacts, etc.; see Hall, 1992).

In most industries, competitors must obtain resource inputs in competitive markets. This means that they must compete with other businesses for the

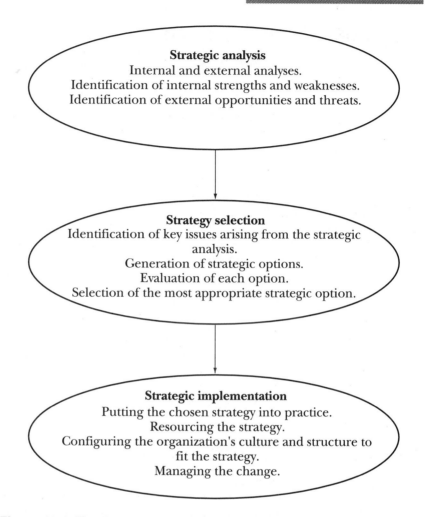

Figure 10.1 The linear-rational (prescriptive) strategic process.

best people, the cheapest finance, the best locations for development, etc. All of these inputs have a cost attached to them and so careful planning for resource requirement is usually a key calculation in strategic implementation.

Matching strategy with resources

Once a strategic option has been settled upon (following the strategic selection stage), management attention turns to evaluating the resource implications of the strategy. The extent to which the resource base needs to be adjusted will, of course, depend upon the degree of change that the proposed strategy entails.

Broadly speaking, resource planning falls into three categories (Johnson and Scholes, 1998). Firstly, some strategies, particularly those that are not particularly ambitious, require *few changes* in the resource base. They may require, for example, a *slight* increase in financing to fund modest expansion or the recruitment or retraining of some human resources to meet a skill shortage on one or two areas. Conversely, of course, a few-changes strategy may require the disposal of some assets or a slight reduction in the human resource base.

Secondly, some strategies require an *increase* in the resource base in order to facilitate a more substantial programme of growth. This usually entails two things: an internal reallocation of resources and the purchasing of fresh resource inputs from external suppliers. Internal reallocation entails reducing resource employment in one area of the business and moving it across to where it is needed, say by redeploying human resources or by selling some equipment to reinvest the money in the area of growth. New resources (from outside the organization) are obtained through the usual channels – from the job market, the real estate market, the financial markets and so on.

Thirdly, some strategies involve a *reduction* in the resource base in order to successfully manage decline. If an organization finds, after a resource audit, that it has too many resources (too many employees, too much land, etc.) then measures are put in place to carry out some reduction. Excess capital or physical resources can often be successfully reinvested in business areas which are in more buoyant markets whilst excess human resources must usually be released.

Key Concepts

Resource audit

An audit process can be used to make assessments of any or all of the resource inputs. In Chapter 3 we discussed in some depth the human resource audit, but the same procedures can be employed to audit financial, physical or intellectual resources.

The nature of an audit of any kind (including resource audits) is purposeful checking or testing. Resources are audited (or purposefully checked) for:

- *sufficiency* (is there enough for the purpose);
- *adequacy* (is the condition, location, state, or quality of the resource adequate for the purpose)
- *availability* (are the required resources available at the time and in the quantities required).

An audit of an organization's land and buildings (examples of physical resources) might take the form of assessing whether the floor area is *sufficient* for current needs and any planned expansion. This might be followed by an evaluation of its *adequacy* – its location relative to customers, etc., and its condition. Finally, if more is required or if development of the land or buildings is needed, *availability* is examined, either of additional property or of permissions for development.

Developing and controlling resources

In order to meet the resource requirements of a proposed strategy, resources are developed and then controlled to ensure they meet the needs of the strategy.

Financial planning

Financial planning takes the form of financing the proposed strategy (see Chapter 4 for a more detailed discussion of these issues). *Capital budgeting* concerns projecting the capital needs of a strategy. This is usually a relatively straightforward operation as costs can normally be forecast with some accuracy. Once the capital requirements are known, a plan is put in place to finance any shortfall. Whilst some strategies can be financed from retained profits (depending upon how much retained profit the company has), others are financed from external sources such as share (rights) issues, debt capital or the issuing of corporate bonds or debentures. The pros and cons of these approaches to financing are discussed in Chapter 4.

Human resource planning

Human resource planning (see Chapter 3) involves projecting the human capital required for the successful prosecution of the proposed strategy. It would typically take the form of forecasts of both the *numbers* of people required and the types of *skills and abilities* that will be in demand. If a shortfall in either of these is identified, the 'gap' will be filled by one or more of the following:

● training, retraining or staff development – to close the skills gap by developing existing employees;
● appointing new employees – entering the labour market and competing with other employers for the requisite number of appropriately skilled employees.

Physical resource planning

Physical resource planning is slightly more complex than financial and human resource planning. The reason for this is that so many inputs fall into this category. We include in this category land, buildings, location, plant, equipment and raw material stock.

Some physical resources are more easily obtained than others. Most stock, plant and equipment is relatively easily obtained, unless the requirement is very specialized. More problematic is obtaining location, land and buildings. Businesses that have requirements for key locations and buildings of particular specificity expose themselves to the possibility of having to settle for second best if they are unable effectively to compete in these particular resource markets.

One industry that exemplifies competition for physical resources is retailing. The location of a retail outlet will often be a key determinant in the success of the business. Successfully competing with other retailers for prime locations and the best buildings will consequently be of paramount importance, especially when these locations are in short supply.

Intellectual resource planning

Intellectual resources – inputs that cannot be seen and touched – can be the most important resource inputs of all (see Chapter 2). Some proposed strategies have a requirement for a legal permission, a database (say of key customers in a certain market segment), a patent registration or something similar.

It is the possession (or not) of key intellectual resources that often determines the success of strategy. Some business operations require a legal licence or permission, examples of these being energy production, arms, pharmaceuticals and construction. Others rely upon a particular information input such as a database, superior market knowledge or superior technical knowledge. We shall return to the theme of organizational learning in Chapter 15.

Culture and implementation

Culture suitability

We encountered the concept of culture in Chapter 3. Strategic implementation usually involves making an assessment of the suitability of a culture to undertake the strategy. In the same way that human personalities differ in their readiness to undertake certain courses of action, so also some organizational 'personalities' differ.

 In the context of implementation, culture is usually analysed for its suitability. If we consider human personalities, we can readily appreciate that not all personalities are equally suitable for all jobs or tasks.

Some people, for example, have a personality that is ready to embrace a new challenge and who take to change with vigour and excitement. They enjoy bungee jumping and parachute jumps. Other people prefer things not to change. They are conservative in nature and they would be likely to turn down the opportunity to engage in risky sports. These two personality types highlight the suitability contrasts that can exist.

In Chapter 3 we encountered two typologies of corporate culture. Handy (1993) identified four types of culture – power, role, task and person. Miles and Snow (1978) also identified four culture types by their reaction tendency, and this is probably the more useful typology in this context.

Miles and Snow's typology and cultural postures

Miles and Snow's (1978) typology divided culture types according to how they approach strategy. These distinctions are important as they tell us how each culture type will react to different strategic options.

A review of the Miles and Snow categories

Defender cultures are suitable for organizations that exist in relatively well-defined market areas and where improving the position in existing markets is the most appropriate strategic option (e.g. market penetration). The culture would feel uncomfortable with having to develop new markets or diversification. The values resident within defender cultures work well if markets are stable and relatively mature.

Prospector cultures, in contrast to defenders, are continually seeking out new product and market opportunities. Accordingly, they often create change and uncertainty. The cultural norms within the culture are consequently more able to develop new markets and products.

Analyser cultures exhibit features of both defenders and prospectors. They have developed a culture that is able to accommodate both stability (which defenders like) and instability (which prospectors have learned to adjust to). The culture can be formal in some circumstances and flexible and 'organic' in others.

Reactor cultures can sometimes lack strategic focus and are consequently sometimes accused of being 'blown around' by changes in their environments. They do not innovate and tend to emulate the successes of competitors.

The purpose of examining Miles and Snow's typology

It is evident that the ability of cultures to undertake different strategic courses of action varies. It is likely, for example, that defender cultures and those like them would be less able to undertake a programme of radical change than, say, those which exhibit prospector characteristics.

Cultural differences between *what is* and *what is required* for a strategy is one of the most important aspects of strategic implementation. Incongruities between the two present a challenge to management in respect of either changing the culture or compromising on strategic objectives such that cultural change is required to a lesser extent. We will return to the nature of change – including cultural change – later in this chapter.

Structure and implementation

What is structure?

Organizational structure refers to the 'shape' of the business. The importance of structure to strategic success is intuitively easy to grasp by using the structure of a human body as a metaphor. Some people are naturally large and may be a tad overweight whilst others are smaller, lithe and fit. The skeletal and muscle structure of people is a major determinant of their suitability for certain activities. People who are large and overweight are less suitable for ballet dancing but are more suitable as sumo wrestlers or as members of tug-of-war teams. Conversely, smaller and fitter people are better at running, rowing and competitive horse-racing.

Organizational structure tend to be described in terms of their 'height', their 'width' and their complexity. A fourth, related way of describing organizational structures is according to their method of division.

The 'height' of structures

Height refers to the number of layers that exist within the structure. It is perhaps intuitively obvious that larger organizations are higher than smaller ones. The guide to how high an organizational structure should be depends upon the complexity of the tasks that a proposed strategy entails. A small, single-site manufacturer will typically be involved in competing in one industry, sometimes with a single product type. This scenario is much less complex than a multinational chemical company that competes in many national markets, in several product types and with a high dependence on research and legal regulations.

Essentially, height facilitates the engagement of specialist managers in the middle of an organization who can oversee and direct the many activities that some large organizations are involved in. Not all organizations have this requirement and it would be more appropriate for such organizations to have a flatter structure (see Figure 10.2).

Tall and short structures

Tall structures, involving more layers of specialist managers, enable the organization to co-ordinate a wider range of activities across different product and market sectors. It is more difficult for senior management to control and is obviously more expensive in terms of management overhead.

Shorter structures involve few management layers and are suitable for smaller organizations that are engaged in few products or market structures. They are cheaper to operate and facilitate a greater degree of senior management control.

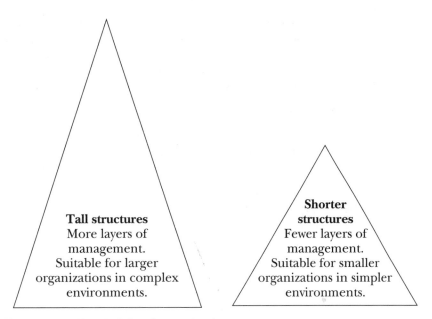

Figure 10.2 The height of organizations.

The 'width' of structures

The 'width' of organizational structures refers to the extent to which the organization is centralized or decentralized. A decentralized organizational structure is one in which the centre elects to devolve some degree of decision-making power to other parts of the organization. A centralized organization is one in which little or no power is devolved from the centre. In practice, a continuum exists between the two extremes along which the varying extents of decentralization can be visualized (see Figure 10.3).

As with the height of structures, there is a trade-off between the costs and benefits of width. The advantages of centralization are mainly concerned with the ability of the centre to maintain tighter direct control over the activities of the organization. This is usually more appropriate when the

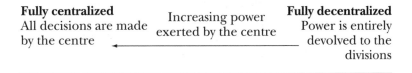

Figure 10.3 The centralization–decentralization continuum.

organization is smaller and engages in few product or market segments. Some degree of decentralization is advantageous when the organization operates in a number of markets and localized specialized knowledge is an important determinant of overall success.

Complexity of structure

The complexity of structure is usually taken to mean the extent to which the organization observes formal hierarchy in its reporting relationships. Strict hierarchy is not always an appropriate form of organization, especially when it cannot be automatically assumed that seniority guarantees superior management skill.

In some contexts, formal hierarchy is entirely appropriate in implementing strategy. In others, however, allowing employees to act with some degree of independence can in fact enable the organization to be more efficient. The use of matrix structures, for example, can result in the organization being able to carry out many more tasks than a formal hierarchical structure. Many companies go 'half way' in this regard by seconding employees into special task forces or cross-functional teams that are not part of the hierarchical structure, and which act semi-independently in pursuit of their brief.

Methods of divisionalization

The fourth and final way of understanding how structure fits into strategic implementation is by considering how the parts of the organization are to be divided. As with all of the other matters to be considered in structure, the method of division is entirely dependent upon the context of the company and its strategic position. It is a case of establishing the most appropriate divisional structure to meet the objectives of the proposed strategy.

Divisions are based upon the grouping together of people with a shared specialism. By acting together within their specialism, it is argued that synergies can be obtained both with and between divisions. There are four common methods of divisionalization:

1 by functional specialism (typically operations, HRM, marketing, finance, R&D);
2 by geographic concentration (where divisions are regionally located and have specialized knowledge of local market conditions);
3 by product specialism (where divisions, usually within multi-product companies, have detailed knowledge of their particular product area);
4 by customer focus (where the company orientates itself by divisions dedicated to serving particular customer types, for example retail customers, industrial customers).

Managing the changes in implementation

The need for change

At its simplest, strategy is all about change. In this chapter, we have encountered the importance of an organization's resource base, its culture and its structure. In order to bring about strategic repositioning (say in respect to products and markets), all of these may need to be changed.

Different organizations exhibit differing attitudes to change. We can draw a parallel here with different types of people. Some people are very conservative and configure their lives so as to minimize change. Such people will generally fear change and will resist it. Other people seem to get bored easily and are always looking for new challenges, new jobs, and so on. Organizations reflect this spectrum of attitudes. It is here that we encounter the concept of *inertia*.

Inertia – identifying barriers to change

Inertia is a term borrowed from physics. It refers to the force that needs to be exerted on a body to overcome its state in relation to its motion. If a body is stationary (i.e. at rest) then we would need to exert a force upon it to make it move. The size and shape of the body will have a large bearing upon its bearing – compare the inertia of a football to that of a train.

In the same way, different organizations present management with varying degrees of inertia. Some are easy to change and others are much more reluctant. The willingness to change may depend upon the culture of the organization, its size, its existing structure, its product and/or market positioning and even its age (i.e. how long it has existed in its present form).

For most purposes, we can say that resistance to change on the part of employees can be caused by one or more of the following attitudes.

Firstly, it may be that those affected by the change *lack an understanding* of the details. They may not have had the reasons for the change explained to them or they may not be aware of how they will personally be affected. This particular barrier can normally be overcome relatively easily by managment taking the requisite measures to close the information gap.

Secondly, there may be a *lack of trust* on the part of employees in respect to management.

Thirdly, employee inertia may be based upon *fear* – particularly in respect to their personal position or their social relationship. Those affected by the change may fear that the proposed changes will adversely affect their place in the structure or the relationships they enjoy in the organization.

Finally, some inertia is driven by *uncertainty* about the future. Attitudes to uncertainty vary significantly between people with some showing a much more adverse reaction to it than others.

Kurt Lewin's three-step model of understanding change

Lewin (1947) suggested that organizational change could be understood in terms of three consecutive processes: unfreezing, moving to a new level and then refreezing.

Unfreezing

Unfreezing involves introducing measures that will enable employees to abandon their current practices or cultural norms in preparation for the change. In many organizations, nothing has changed for many years and unfreezing is necessary as a 'shaking-up' phase. The impetus for unfreezing can come from either inside or outside the organization itself. Changing market conditions, for example, sometimes give employees warning that change will be imminent. A particular market crisis may precipitate the expectation amongst employees that change must happen as a result. Internally, a management shake-up, a profit warning or talk of restructuring may bring about similar expectations.

Moving to a new level

Moving to the new level involves bringing about the requisite change itself. The time period given over to this phase varies widely. Structural change can usually be brought about relatively quickly. Changes in internal systems sometimes take longer (such as the introduction of new quality or information systems), whilst changing culture can take years.

Refreezing

Refreezing is necessary to 'lock in' the changes and to prevent the organization from going back to its old ways. Again, we would usually take cultural changes to require more 'cementing in' than some other changes and some resolve might be required on the part of senior management.

Step and incremental change

The pace at which change happens can usually be divided into one of two categories – step and incremental (see Figure 10.4). There are two factors that determine which is the most appropriate (Quinn and Voyer, 1998):

1 How urgent the need for change is. A market crisis will typically bring about an urgent need for rapid change whereas preparing for the introduction of a new legal regulation in five years time will usually allow change to be brought about more slowly and perhaps more painlessly.
2 How much inertia is resident within the organization's culture. The time taken to unfreeze the inertia in some organizations will necessarily take longer than in others.

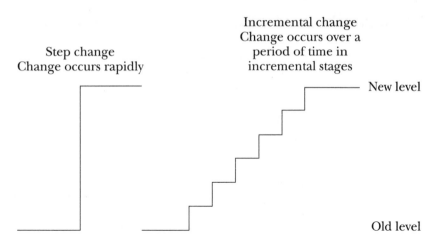

Figure 10.4 Step and incremental change.

Step change offers the advantage of 'getting it over with'. It enables the organization to respond quickly to changes in its environment and hence enables it to conform with new conditions without lagging behind. Its disadvantages include the 'pain' factor – it may require some coercion or force on the part of management, which in turn may damage employee–management relationships.

Incremental changes offer the advantage of a step-by-step approach to change. For organizations with high inertia, it enables management to gain acceptance before and during the change process, and, consequently, it tends to be more inclusive. The process is divided into a number of distinct phases and there may be periods of 'rest' between the phases. It would be an inappropriate technique to use in situations of rapid environmental change.

Models for managing change

The process of actually managing strategic change brings us to consider a number of managerial approaches and their appropriateness in various contexts. Writers in this area have tended towards two complementary approaches.

A range of managerial practices

Some writers have suggested that change can successfully be managed by employing a range of managerial practices. We can conceive of this approach as an 'if this doesn't work, try this' mechanism.

Most academics and managers have agreed that the process should begin with *education* and *communication*. The purpose if this is to inform those (usually internal) stakeholders who will be affected by the change. The message communicated will usually contain an explanation of the reasons for the change and an overview of its timescale and extent. In some organizational contexts, this procedure alone will be sufficient to overcome inertia and get the change process under way. In others, this will not be enough.

The next step will thus be to progress to *negotiation* and *participation*. Affected stakeholders will be invited to contribute to the process and to participate in its execution. It is thus hoped, by this process, that employees will be 'on board' – that they will feel some sense of ownership of the change. Some managers may introduce some degree of manipulation (of employees) in this stage, possibly by appealing to the emotional responses of employees or by over- or under-stating the reality of the changes in the environment.

Finally, if all else has failed to bring about the willing participation of the employees, management may be able to introduce some degree of *coercion*. This tactic is far from being appropriate in all contexts, but where it is possible, it can be used to significant effect. Coercion is the practice of forcing through change by exploiting the power asymmetry between executive management and 'rank and file' employees. It is usually only used as a last resort – it can have a very negative effect on management–employee relationships after the change.

A single change agent

Some texts refer to this approach as the 'champion of change' model. It is a change process that is managed from start to finish by a single individual. The individual (or change agent) may be a key manager within the organization or he may be brought in as a consultant for the duration of the process. The change agent approach offers a number of advantages.

Firstly, it provides a focus for the change in the form of a tangible person who becomes the personification of the process. A 'walking symbol' of change can act as a stimulus to change and can ensure that complacency is avoided.

Secondly, in many cases, the change agent will be engaged because he is an expert in his field. He may have overseen the same change process in many other organizations and so is well acquainted with the usual problems and how to solve them.

Thirdly, the appointment of a change agent sometimes means that senior management time need not be fully occupied with the change process. The responsibility for the change is delegated to the change agent and management thus gain the normal advantages of delegation. Accordingly, senior management are freed up to concentrate on developing future strategy.

Summary

The implementation of a selected strategy rests upon the successful management of a number of things. An organization must first ensure that sufficient resources are available and in place to implement the strategy. All deficits should be made good and resources, once acquired, need to be configured to support the key value-adding activities. The culture and structure need to be assessed for their suitability to undertake the strategy and must be changed as necessary. The management of change is an important part of managing the implementation of strategy.

Review and Discuss

1 Explain where implementation fits into the strategic process.
2 What is a resource audit?
3 What is involved in financial resource planning?
4 What is involved in human resource planning ?
5 Explain the importance of culture to implementation.
6 Explain the usefulness of Miles and Snow's typology to culture and implementation.
7 What are the advantages of centralization?
8 What are the advantages of decentralization?
9 Why is a strict hierarchy not always a suitable structural arrangement?
10 What are the four major methods of divisionalization?
11 What is inertia and how is it applied to organizational change?
12 Explain Lewin's three-step model of change.
13 Define and distinguish between step and incremental change.
14 What are the advantages of the change agent method of managing change?

References and further reading

Hall, R. (1992). The strategic analysis of intangible resources. *Strategic Management Journal*, 13, 135–144.

Handy, C.B. (1993) *Understanding Organizations*, Fourth Edition. London: Penguin.

Johnson, G. (1987) *Strategic Change and the Management Process*. Oxford: Blackwell.

Johnson, G. and Scholes, K. (1998) *Exploring Corporate Strategy*, Fifth Edition. Hemel Hempstead: Prentice-Hall.

Lewin, K. (1947) Feedback problems of social diagnosis and action: Part II-B of Frontiers in Group Dynamics. *Human Relations*, 1, 147–153.

Lewin, K. (1951). *Field Theory in Social Science*. New York: Harper & Brothers.

Miles, R.E. and Snow, C.C. (1978) *Organizational Strategy, Structure and Process.* New York: McGraw-Hill.

Moss Kanter, R. (1989). *The Change Masters: Innovation and Entrepreneurship in the American Corporation.* Englewood Cliffs, NJ: Simon & Schuster.

Pettigrew, A.M. (1988) *The Management of Strategic Change.* Oxford: Blackwell.

Quinn, J.B. and Voyer, J. (1998) Logical incrementalism: managing strategy formation. In Mintzberg, H., Quinn, J.B. and Ghoshal, S. (eds) *The Strategy Process.* Englewood Cliffs: Prentice Hall.

Quinn, J.B. (1980a) Managing strategic change. *Sloan Management Review,* Summer 1980, 3–20.

Quinn, J.B. (1980b) *Strategies for Change.* Homewood: Irwin.

Schein, E.H. (1985) *Organizational Culture and Leadership.* SF CAL: Jossey-Bass.

Stacey, R.D. (1993) *Strategic Management and Organizational Dynamics.* London: Pitman.

Williamson, O. (1975) *Markets and Hierarchies.* New York: Free Press.

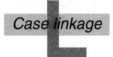

Case linkage

Questions for the Derwent Valley Foods case study.

1 Identify DVF's strategic objectives at the outset of the period of the case.
2 How did the objectives change as events progressed?
3 How did the company structure change over the period and why?
4 Discuss the extent to which the DVF culture helped or hindered the implementation of the strategy.

Questions for the Dansk Tyggegummi Fabrik A/S case study.

1 Explain how the structure of DTF changed as its strategy changed.
2 Has DTF become more or less decentralized over time? Comment upon the reasons for your answer.
3 From what we can tell about DTF's culture, comment upon its readiness to pursue its international strategy.
4 How well did DTF anticipate the differences between its domestic Danish culture and those in its international markets?

Chapter 11

Strategic development

Introduction

The decision as to which method of strategic development to adopt is critical to the success of competitive strategy. We encountered the idea of growth as one of the main business objectives in Chapter 1. Chapter 8 discussed the theory of development strategies and their contribution in achieving growth objectives. The theories developed in these earlier chapters underpin much of the discussion undertaken here. The variety of methods used for development will be considered, together with a critical appraisal of the success or failure of these methods.

The chapter briefly considers internal (or organic) growth, and then discusses the various mechanisms of external development. The growth in the popularity of mergers and acquisitions in terms of the number of such transactions is considered. Empirical research findings are presented that call into question the success of these approaches. The recent trend in collaborative arrangements such as the strategic alliance is discussed. Finally, the chapter looks at 'downsizing' strategies such as demergers.

Objectives

After studying this chapter, students should be able to:

- define and distinguish between internal and external business growth;
- describe the various types of merger and acquisition;
- explain the motivations behind mergers and acquisitions and the reasons why they succeed or fail;
- describe what a strategic alliance is and why organizations enter into them;
- explain what is meant by a disposal and describe why organizations pursue this pathway;
- understand the regulatory and legal frameworks that influence business growth.

Organic (internal) growth

The commonest mechanism of growth

Organic growth is the most straightforward mechanism of business growth. Most companies have used internal growth as their main method of growth at some time, and so its 'popularity' is obvious. The essential feature of organic growth is the reinvestment of previous years' profits in the existing business. By increasing capacity (by, say, the purchase of enlarged premises or more machines), the business takes on more employees to cope with the extra demand. In so doing, turnover increases and so does the capital (balance sheet) value of the business.

Organic growth is common during the early stages of corporate development as companies build markets and develop new products. However, large companies may use it alongside external growth to consolidate market position. The development of a new supermarket outlet is an example of internal growth. Earlier year's profits are channelled into the development and the company benefits from the increased market share and increased turnover.

Organic growth offers the advantage that it is usually a lower risk option than external growth. The fact that the increase in capacity remains fully under the control of the existing management means that the risks of dealing with other companies is avoided. Core competences can usually be exploited and existing expertise can be capitalized upon.

On the other hand, organic growth is usually a slower mechanism compared with external growth. The 'bolting on' of a new company by external growth is a faster route to growth than gradual growth by internal means.

Some large companies have reached their present size largely through successful year-on-year organic growth. Marks & Spencer, for example, have reached their present size largely through this method.

Key Concepts

Internal growth
Internal growth is expansion by means of the reinvestment of previous years' profits and loan capital in the existing business. This results in increased capacity, increased employment and ultimately, increased turnover.

Advantages: lower risk, within existing area of expertise, avoids high exposure to costs of alternative growth mechanisms (e.g. by debt servicing).

Disadvantages: slower than external growth, little scope for diversification, relies upon the skills of existing management in the business.

External mechanisms of growth – mergers and acquisitions (M&As)

Definitions

It is difficult to open the business press without encountering details of a proposed or progressing merger or acquisition. The term *merger* is however sometimes replaced in such text with the word *takeover* or *acquisition*. The same news story may use all three terms as though the words meant the same thing. For the purposes of a strategy text such as this, it is important to clarify the main terms generally used in connection with this process.

merger

In a *merger* the shareholders of the organizations come together, normally willingly, to share the resources of the enlarged (merged) organization, with shareholders from both sides of the merger becoming shareholders in the new organization.

acquisition

An *acquisition* is a 'marriage' of unequal partners with one organization buying and subsuming the other party. In such a transaction the share-holders of the target organization cease to be owners of the enlarged organization unless payment to the shareholders is paid partly in shares in the acquiring company. The shares in the smaller company are bought by the larger.

takeover

A *takeover* is technically the same as an acquisition, but the term is often taken to mean that the approach of the larger acquiring company is unwel-come from the point of view of the smaller target company. The term *hostile takeover* describes an offer for the shares of a target public limited company which the target's directors reject. If the shareholders then accept the offer (despite the recommendation of the directors) then the hostile takeover goes ahead.

Whichever of these routes is taken, the result is a larger and more finan-cially powerful company. The word *integration* is the collective term used to describe these growth mechanisms.

A brief history of M&As

The recent history of mergers and acquisitions in the UK is shown in Figures 11.1 and 11.2. These graphs show clearly that their popularity has changed over time. The early 1970s, late 1980s and mid to late 1990s were all periods of high levels of M&A activity. Figure 11.3 shows that the average value of M&As (usually defined by combined market value) increased from £5.24 billion in 1984 to £20.38 billion in 1989, a substantial increase which conceals the enormity of some of the mergers and acquisitions. The aborted merger between Glaxo Wellcome and SmithKline Beecham in 1998 would have produced a new company valued at over £100 billion. Some general

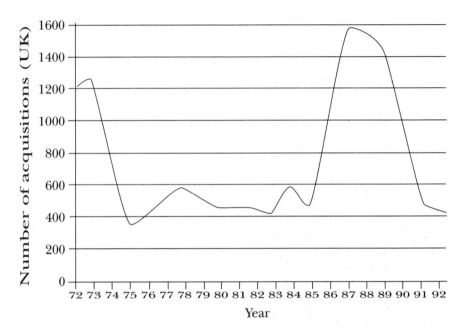

Figure 11.1 Total number of UK acquisitions. (*Source*: compiled from Central Statistical Office Bulletins (London, HMSO) from 1993.)

explanations can be suggested as to why these trends have occurred. Increased business internationalization, government attitudes towards industry structure and the buoyancy of the economy are the strongest influences.

Key Concepts

Combined market value

All public limited companies have a market value. Market value equals the number of shares on the stock market (the *share volume*) multiplied by the share price. It is taken to be a good indicator of the value of a company because it accounts for the company's asset value plus the 'goodwill' that the market attaches to the share. It follows that the combined market value of a merger or acquisition is the two companies' values added together. It is an indication of what the company will be valued at after the integration goes ahead.

Whilst the M&A process is a well-used mechanism in strategic development, recent history has shown that UK-based companies have used it

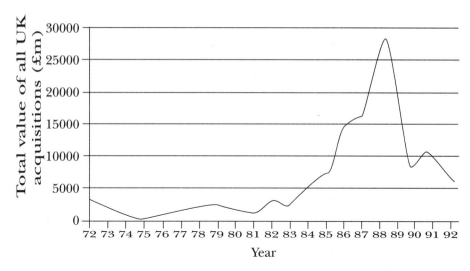

Figure 11.2 Total value of UK acquisitions. (*Source*: compiled from Central Statistical Office Bulletins (London, HMSO) from 1993.)

rather more than those based in mainland Europe. Only in the USA have companies used the mechanism to a similar extent. However, recent figures show increased merger and acquisition activity in the global economy generally as companies feel the need to increase in size to become more internationally competitive.

One of the consequences of M&A activity is that many of the well known 'names' of yesteryear have disappeared while some of today's best known companies are relatively young in their current form. Glaxo Wellcome plc, the leader in the world pharmaceutical industry, came about through the acquisition of Wellcome plc by Glaxo in 1995. Diageo, the giant food and drinks company, was formed by the merger between Guinness and Grand Metropolitan (hence becoming the 'beer and Burger King' company).

A common misunderstanding surrounding the integration process is that two organizations always come together in their entirety. In practice, many integrations are the result of one organization joining with a divested *part* of another. That is to say that one company has made a strategic decision to withdraw from an industry or market and in an attempt to maximize the value of the resources it no longer wants (i.e. an unwanted part of the previous company structure). The reasons why companies demerge and sell subsidiaries in non-core elements is addressed later in this chapter.

Explanations and motivations for M&As

There are a number of potential reasons for pursuing an external growth strategy. We have already encountered the overall objective of growth, but

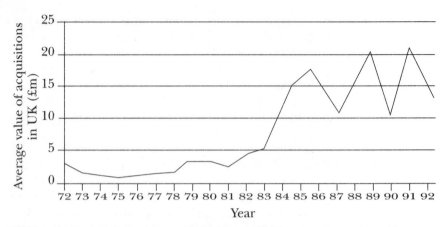

Figure 11.3 Average value of M&As in the UK by market value. (*Source*: compiled from Central Statistical Office Bulletins (London, HMSO) from 1993.)

growth is seldom a stand-alone objective. The question is, 'Why is growth a desired objective?' The following is a summary of these motivations:

● to *increase market share* in order to increase pricing power in an industry;
● to *enter a new market*, possibly to offset the effects of decline in current markets or to broaden market portfolio;
● to *reduce competition*, possibly by purchasing a competitor;
● to *gain control of valuable brand names* or pieces of intellectual property like patents;
● to gain preferential *access to distribution channels* (to gain factor inputs on preferential terms or to secure important supplies) by purchasing a supplier;
● to *broaden product range* in order to exploit more market opportunities and to spread risk;
● to *develop new products* for the market faster than internal R&D could do;
● to *gain access to new production or information technologies* in order to reduce costs, increase quality or increase product differentiation;
● to *gain economies of scale*, such as by increasing purchasing power so that inputs can be purchased at lower unit cost;
● to *make productive use of spare or underused resources*, such as finance that is sitting on deposit in a bank;
● to *'asset strip'* – the practice of breaking up an acquired company and recovering more than the price paid by selling the parts separately;
● to *enhance corporate reputation* (appropriate if the existing company name has been associated with an alleged misdemeanour).

The precise nature of the integration selected will depend upon the specific objectives being pursued. If, for example, market share is the most important objective, then it is likely that a company will seek a suitable horizontal integration. On the other hand, a vertical integration would be more appropriate if supply or distribution concerns are uppermost amongst a company's threats.

External growth is usually expensive and it therefore has significant financial resource implications, not to mention a sizeable legal bill. Accordingly, it is entered into for specific strategic purposes that cannot be served through the normal progression of organic development.

Synergy – the main objective of M&As

Overriding all other purposes served by integration is that of synergy. Synergy refers to the benefits that can be gained when organizations join forces rather than work apart. An integration can be said to be synergistic when *the whole is greater than the sum of the parts*. More popularly, synergy can be expressed as '2 + 2 = 5'. If the integration is to achieve synergy, the 'new' company must perform more efficiently than either of the two parties would had they remained separate.

On a simple level, we can conceptualize synergy using a human example. When two people work *together* performing a task like lifting heavy logs onto a lorry, they can achieve far more work than two people lifting logs separately. A rally team of two enables the team to win a race if they work together with one driving and one navigating. If the two were to work separately, then each person would have to drive and navigate at the same time.

Synergy is measured in terms of increased added value. Kay (1993) makes the point that, 'Value is added, and only added [in an integration] if distinctive capabilities or strategic assets are exploited more effectively. A merger adds no value if all that is acquired is a distinctive capability which is already fully exploited, as the price paid will reflect the competitive advantage held.' Accordingly, integrations that do not enable the 'new' organization to produce higher profits or consolidate a stronger market position are usually deemed to have been relatively unsuccessful. The next section describes why failures sometimes occur.

Potential problems with M&A – why do they sometimes go wrong?

The fact that mergers and acquisitions are undoubtedly popular as methods of business growth may lead us to conclude that they are always successful. In practice, this is not always true. A number of studies have analysed the performance of companies after integrations and the findings are not very encouraging (see for example Kay, 1993; Porter, 1985; Ravenscraft and Scherer, 1987).

These studies found that many corporate 'marriages' failed to work and ended in divorce. Of those that did survive, Kay (1993) found that when profitability before and after the integration were compared, a 'nil to negative effect' was achieved.

The main failure factors

There are a number of reasons why integrations do not work. We can summarize these 'failure factors' under six headings:

1 *lack of research* into the circumstances of the target company (and hence incomplete knowledge). Failure in this regard can result in some nasty surprises after the integration;
2 *cultural incompatibility* between the two parties;
3 *lack of communication* within and between the two parties;
4 *loss of key personnel* in the target company after the integration;
5 *paying too much for the acquired company* and hence over-exposing the acquiring company to financial risk;
6 *assuming that growth in a target company's market will continue indefinitely.* Market trends can fall as well as rise.

Government policy on integrations

Government policy on mergers may have contributed to some integration failures. Corporate growth can be restricted by government (which in the UK is represented by the Monopolies and Mergers Commission), as companies are only allowed to establish a certain market share. In the UK an integration which would result in the new organization controlling over 25 per cent of the market is generally subject to government scrutiny which often results in such a merger being blocked. Being prevented from expanding in a related area may force some companies to take the more risky route of diversification (acquiring a company making different products in different markets).

Success factors for M&A

History has shown that mergers and acquisitions work best when the initiator company follows a number of intuitively obvious 'rules'. They are designed to offset the failure factors we identified above.

First, success depends upon the *identification of a suitable 'target' candidate* with whom to merge or acquire. The emphasis on the word *suitable* is expanded upon below.

Second, a preparation for an approach should involve a detailed evaluation of the target company's *competitive position*. This would typically comprise a survey of its profitability, its market share, its product portfolio, its competitiveness in resource markets and so on.

Third, consideration should be given to the *compatibility of the two companies' management styles and culture.* Because integrations often involve the merging of the two boards of directors, it is usually important that the directors from the two companies are able to work together. In addition, the cultures, if not identical in character, should be able to be brought together successfully.

Fourth, there should be the possibility of a successful marriage between the two *corporate structures* (see the discussion of this in Chapter 10). If one is, for example, very tall and centralized and the other is shorter and decentralized, problems may occur in attempting to bring the two together.

Fifth, if the target company has key personnel (say a key manager or a distinctive research capability resident within a number of uniquely qualified scientists), then measures should be taken to ensure that these *key people are retained after the integration*. This can often be achieved by holding contractual talks with these people before the integration goes ahead.

Finally, the initiating company should ensure that the *price paid for the target* (of the valuation of its shares) *is realistic*. A key calculation of any investment is the return made on it and this is usually measured as the profit before interest and tax divided by the price paid for it. It follows that the return on investment (as a percentage) will depend upon the price paid for the target company. The valuation of a company is a complex accounting calculation which depends on the balance sheet value, the prospects and performance of the company, and the value of its intangible assets (such as its brands, patents, etc.)

Accordingly, the importance of detailed information-gathering before the integration cannot be over-emphasized.

External growth without M&A – strategic alliances

What are strategic alliances?

The term *strategic alliance* is used to describe a range of collaborative arrangements between two or more organizations. These agreements can vary from a very formalized agreement, which could see the creation of a new jointly owned limited company, to an informal arrangement for a short-term project.

The legal structure of the organization is not a barrier to co-operation. In recent years, for example, many government departments and quangos have entered into partnerships with public companies such as through the UK government's Private Finance Initiative. In the private sector, public limited companies have also employed this approach to further their particular strategic objectives such as when BT and Securicor got together in a highly formalized agreement to form Cellnet, the mobile phone company. The Channel Tunnel, in common with other large construction projects, was built by a consortium of several companies working together for the duration of the project.

Strategic alliances can therefore assume a number of different forms depending upon the structure, the mechanism of decision-making, the nature of the capital commitment and apportionment of profit. Some exist for a particular project only and are short-term in timescale whilst others are more permanent. The choice of arrangement will depend upon the specific objectives that the participants have at the time.

Types of strategic alliance

Focused and complex alliances

The degree of involvement between the joint venture partners can range between the focused and the complex.

Focused alliances are those which tend to focus on collaboration at one, or possibly two stages of the value chain. They may, for example, purchase as one in order to exert greater buying power on a supplier. Others may collaborate on product distribution or on technology.

More complex alliances are those which involves co-operation over a wide range of activities on the value chain. The relationship that existed between 1979 and 1994 between Honda from Japan and the British Rover Group was a complex alliance. Although the two companies remained legally separate, they co-operated in all of the primary value adding activities, including product design.

Consortia

The term *consortium* is often used when referring to an alliance that involves more than two organizations. Consortia are often created for time-limited projects such as civil engineering or construction developments. The Channel Tunnel was constructed by a number of construction companies in a consortium which was called Trans Manche Link (TML). TML was dissolved upon the completion of the project. Camelot, the UK National Lottery operator, is another example of a consortium (see the case study on Camelot in Part V of this book).

The form of alliance chosen by the parties will depend upon several factors. The complexity of the alliance will depend upon the objectives that the two parties are pursuing. Alliance partners tend to seek co-operation on the minimum number of areas that are needed in order to avoid over-exposure to the risk of one of the parties leaving abruptly or 'finding out too much'. The selection of partners for a consortium will depend upon matching the resource and skill requirement of the project with those organizations that are willing to contribute to the effort. Organizations with previous experience of projects of the type proposed will obviously be among the most in demand as consortium participants.

Motivations for forming strategic alliances

International competitive pressures

One of the major drivers towards the use of strategic alliances in corporate development is the growth in international market development. As organizations seek out new markets for their products, many recognize that they have skills or knowledge deficiencies where an in-depth knowledge of a foreign market is required. The need to develop local knowledge is increased if overseas production (with an overseas alliance partner) is being considered to meet market demands. While local knowledge can be hired (say through a local importing agent), it is often quicker and more reliable to seek assistance from an already established producing organization of the host country. It should also be noted that a legal requirement of many countries is that foreign organizations must have host partners before they can trade, making a joint venture an essential method of development.

Capital pooling

Whilst the globalization of markets may have encouraged some organizations to consider the use of alliances there are other factors that have encouraged companies to develop them further within national boundaries. The high capital requirements of many projects, in terms of both set-up costs, ongoing running cost and delays in profit generation, together with high levels of risk generally generated by such delays, are reasons for considering the use of alliances. The desire to gain economies of scale in areas such as research and development and the desire to secure access to markets are other reasons why companies choose alliances.

Successful alliances

The success of an alliance is attributed to a number of factors, some of which are similar to the factors present in a successful integration. Faulkner (1995) suggested the following critical success factors:

- complementary skills and capabilities of the partners;
- the degree of overlap between the parties' markets be kept to a minimum;
- a high level of autonomy, with strong leadership and commitment from the parent organizations (if appropriate);
- the need to build up trust and not to depend solely on the contractual framework of the relationship;
- recognition that the two partners may have different cultures.

Researchers in this area have noted that alliances seem to work best when the partners are from related industries (or the same industry) or when the objective of the alliance is the development of a new geographical region. Success is further enhanced when the parties are of a similar size and are as equally committed (in resource terms) to the alliance. Strict adherence to the initial objectives of the alliance can often limit its success, as modification of the original purpose may become necessary if the business environment changes. There is thus a need continually to reappraise the parameters of the agreement.

Brouthers *et al.* (1995) advanced a more succinct version of Faulkner's success factors in the '3 Cs' of successful alliances. The two parties should have:

- complementary skills;
- compatible goals;
- co-operative cultures.

Disposals

What are disposals?

We should not assume that business strategies are always designed to cause business growth. There are times when organizations may wish to become smaller. As with growth strategy, size reduction can be achieved by organic reduction (by winding down production of a product area), by divestment (the opposite of acquisition) or by demerger (the opposite of merger).

Demergers and divestments (which together are referred to as *disposals*) involve taking a part of a company and selling it off as a 'self-contained' unit with its own management, structure and employees in place. The unit may then be sold on to a single buyer (for whom it will be an acquisition) or it may be floated on the stock market as a public limited company.

Reasons for disposal

There are a number of reasons why a company may elect to dispose of a part of its structure. The most prominent reasons include:

1 under-performance of the part in question (e.g. poor profitability), possibly due to negative synergy;
2 a change in the strategic focus of the organization in which the candidate for disposal is no longer required;
3 the medium to long-term prospects for the disposal candidate are poor;
4 the disposal candidate is an unwanted acquisition (or an unwanted subsidiary of an acquired company that is otherwise wanted);
5 the need to raise capital from the disposal to reinvest in core areas or to increase liquidity in the selling company;

6 the belief that the disposal candidate would be more productive if it were removed from the seller's structure;

7 as a tactic to deflect a hostile takeover bid, particularly if the predatory company is primarily interested in acquiring the company to gain control over the disposal candidate;

8 as part of a programme of 'asset stripping' – the process of breaking a company up into its parts and selling them off for a sum greater than that paid for the whole.

Case Example

An example of asset-stripping – Hanson plc and the SCM Group
Hanson plc was a British-based company which, prior to its recent demerger, owned over 600 subsidiary companies all over the world. As one of the UK's biggest companies, Hanson's group turnover in the year to 1994 was over £11 billion and its strategy for many years had been to buy up 'sleepy' conglomerates and then dismantle the acquisitions by selling off each subsidiary separately in the hope that the total value of the disposals would exceed the price paid for the acquisition. One such acquisition illustrates this process of 'asset stripping' particularly well.

In January 1986, Hanson bought 100 per cent of the shares in the US-based SCM Group. At the time of the purchase, SCM was a group of 17 companies in a wide variety of industries including paint, chemicals, food, paper and typewriters. Hanson immediately set about recovering its investment in the SCM purchase by splitting it up and selling off its constituent companies separately. The chronology of events was as follows:

1986	Hanson bought SCM for $930 million;
1986	Hanson sold off former SCM companies for $935 million;
1987	Hanson sold off former SCM companies for $28 million;
1988	Hanson sold off former SCM companies for $266 million;
1989	Hanson sold off 52 per cent of the shares in one former SCM company for $309 million;
1990	Hanson sold off former SCM companies for $41 million.

The total receipts from the sales of former SCM companies to 1990 was thus $1,579 million ($1.579 billion). Compared with the purchase price of $930 million, Hanson made a cash surplus on the deal of $649 million. This in itself would have been a shrewd piece of business, but it didn't sell all of the SCM companies. The one company retained – SCM Chemicals, based in Baltimore – is the world's third largest supplier of an industrial chemical called titanium dioxide. This company alone is capable of generating over $350 million a year in pre-tax profits.
(*Source*: Hanson plc)

Shareholders and disposals

The most common method of corporate disposal is a 'private' transaction between two companies, which is intended to be of benefit to both parties. The seller gains the funds from the transaction, and is able to focus on its core areas. The buyer gains the product and market presence of the disposal, which, in turn, will be (we assume) to its strategic advantage.

Disposals are designed to create synergy to the shareholders in the same way as are integrations. We should not lose sight of the fact that business organizations are owned by shareholders and it is the role of company directors (as the shareholders' agents) to act in such a way that shareholder wealth is maximized. If this can be achieved by breaking a part of the company off, then this option will be pursued.

The value of disposals to shareholders can be illustrated by an example where a demerger was successful. As part of a strategic review in ICI plc (the British chemical multinational) in the early 1990s, the main board made the decision to focus on its core areas of speciality chemicals. This necessarily meant that parts of the company that did not fit into the realigned structure would be disposed of. Some parts, especially the bulk intermediates plants, were divested to competitors for whom the bulk business was within their core.

What was previously ICI pharmaceuticals division was not divested – the board decided that it should be demerged. The division was made into a stand-alone company which was called Zeneca plc, and it was then floated on the Stock Exchange with the proceeds from the flotation going to benefit the shareholders of ICI. The stock market welcomed the flotation of Zeneca as, it believed, it could now compete in the competitive pharmaceuticals industry without the 'encumbrance' of being a part of a widely diversified chemical group (ICI). In the months following the demerger, the value of ICI shares increased by over 75 per cent and Zeneca's share price increased by some 400 per cent.

Other methods of disposal

In addition to divestments and demergers, two other disposal methods are noteworthy.

Equity carve-outs

Equity carve-outs are similar to demergers insofar as the spin-off company is floated on the Stock Exchange. However, in this form of disposal, the selling company retains a shareholding in the disposal, with the balance of shares being offered to the stock market. In this respect, equity carve-outs can be seen as a semi-disposal – part of the disposal is kept, but not as a wholly-owned subsidiary.

The decision of the Thomson Corporation of Canada to float the Thomson travel group in 1998 is an example of such a policy. In this case the Thomson family retained 20 per cent of the new company's equity, in order to gain an ongoing return on the stock, albeit without strategic control over the company.

Management buy-outs

A management buy-out (MBO) is said to have occurred when a company which a parent company wishes to dispose of is sold to its current management. MBOs are often a mutually satisfactory outcome when the disposal candidate is unwanted by its parent but when it has the possibility of being run successfully when the existing management have the requisite commitment and skills.

The advantages of MBOs can be summarized as follows:

1 The selling parent successfully disposes of its non-core business and receives a suitable price for it which it can then re-invest in its main areas of activity.
2 The divested organization benefits from committed managers (who become its owners). When the management team finds itself personally in debt as a result of the buy-out (having had to find the money for the purchase), their motivation and commitment tends to be maximized. In some MBOs, some of the capital for the purchase is provided by venture capital companies.
3 If part of the MBO capital is met by the company's existing employees, the organization benefits from the commitment of people who have part-ownership, and who therefore share in the company's success through dividends on shares and through growth in the share price.

The regulatory framework of external growth

The purpose of regulation

Most governments have taken the view that there is some need to put in place a regulatory framework for external business growth because of the implications for competition in markets. There is a careful balance to be struck in this regard. Governments are usually keen to encourage business activity in their countries because of their beneficial effects upon employment, tax revenues, exports and standard of living. At the same time, it is generally true that the larger organizations become, the more difficult it is for smaller competitors to make headway against them in terms of pricing and market share. Regulation is therefore a matter of some discretion.

National and supranational regulators

In the UK, regulation arises from two sources – from the national level and from the European level. They have in common two areas of concern – company size and, more specifically, market share.

European Union regulation

Since Britain joined the European Community in 1973, it has been subject to EU regulations and directives. European competition regulations are provided for in the Treaty of Rome 1957 (the primary legislation of the European Union), in the form of two 'articles' that regulate integration between companies resident within two or more EU states. Both articles are designed to stimulate competition between companies in member states. They can be used by authorities within the EU to influence the behaviour of businesses that may seek to enter into integrations that may reduce competition in a market. One of these, Article 86, refers particularly to mergers and acquisitions.

Article 86 is designed to prohibit the abuse of a dominant market position (i.e. a high market share). It does not prohibit monopoly as such, but seeks to ensure that large businesses do not use their power against consumer and competitor interests. This indirectly acts against large companies seeking to acquire a high market share by integration.

The administrative part of the EU – the European Commission – has the responsibility to implement Article 86. It can prohibit mergers or acquisitions resulting in a combined national market share of 25 per cent or when the combined turnover in European Union markets exceeds a certain financial figure (which at 1998 was ECU 250 million). On a more operational level, the way that integrations are conducted is also regulated. Rules are in place regarding the transparency of approach (i.e. how it should be announced) and how shareholders should be informed of proposed integrations.

Integrations in the UK

Integrations between companies based in the UK are subject to possible scrutiny by the Office of Fair Trading (OFT) and the Monopolies and Mergers Commission (MMC). Their activity is governed by two major pieces of British legislation: the Fair Trading Act 1973 and, to a lesser extent, the Competition Act 1980.

The Fair Trading Act 1973 targets three areas in pursuit of maintaining healthy levels of competition in markets:

1 monopoly practices;
2 restrictive practices;
3 mergers and acquisitions.

Under its provisions to review mergers and acquisitions, this Act allows the government's regulatory bodies to review an integration if the combined market share exceeds 25 per cent. In this regard, it is in agreement with Article 86.

The OFT and the MMC

The two bodies in the UK that exist to regulate integrations activity are provided for under the terms of the above mentioned Acts of Parliament. Both act independently of the government under the instruction of the Secretary of State for Trade and Industry and exist in the legal form of quangos.

The Office of Fair Trading

The OFT was established in 1973 and is headed by the Director General of Fair Trading (DGFT) – an individual charged with, among other things, the enforcement of the terms of the Fair Trading Act. The OFT is also required to act as a central bureau which collects and publishes information on competition and anti-competitive practices in the UK.

The DGFT has six broad areas of responsibility: The first and most important of these is to collect information on business activities that are potentially harmful to competition or the public interest including mergers and acquisitions (the DGFT has the power to refer cases to other authorities for review).

In this regard, the OFT is able to review an integration when:

- two or more enterprises cease to be distinct;
- at least one of them is a UK or UK-controlled company;
- they have a combined market share of 25 per cent or assets to the value of £70 million (as at 1999).

In applying the above criteria the following factors need to be taken into account by the DGFT:

- the extent of competition within the UK in respect to the market in question;
- the level of efficiency of the companies intending to integrate;
- the impact the proposed integration will have on employment in both a national and regional context;
- the competitive position of UK companies on an international basis;
- the national strategic interest (rarely an important factor);
- the implications of the method of financing used to fund the merger (particularly in respect to the welfare of shareholders or the banking sector);
- the probability that a weak partner will be turned round by the acquirer.

The Monopolies and Mergers Commission

The role of the MMC is to look into proposed mergers and acquisitions when instructed so to do by the OFT or by the Secretary of State for Trade and Industry. It is headed by a full-time chairman to whom three part-time deputy chairmen report. This team then draws upon the expertise of specialist members from a range of backgrounds including business, finance, academia and trade unions. All of the members, including the chairman, are appointed by the Secretary of State. The MMC comprises a total of 31 members (as at 1995).

The MMC is unable to act on its own initiative, and its recommendations after an investigation are advisory only. The Secretary of State may elect to adopt or reject its findings.

The chairman describes MMC's role as follows.

We are required under the Fair Trading Act, in accordance with the public interest, to take into account all relevant considerations including:

- **maintaining and promoting effective competition;**
- **promoting the interests of consumers in terms of price, quality and range of goods and services;**
- **promoting efficiency and innovation and facilitating market entry;**
- **maintaining balanced distribution of industry and employment in the UK;**
- **promoting international competitiveness (i.e. the competitiveness of UK businesses in international markets).**

Summary

Organic growth is arguably the most common form of strategic development, as most organizations use it on an ongoing basis. It is therefore difficult to quantify the degree of internal development taking place at any time. The action which creates one organization from two is known as an integration.

Historically, UK companies have used integration to a greater extent than those from other European countries, though there has been a growth in its use throughout Europe in recent times. Evidence suggests that the volume of mergers increases as the economic cycle moves from recession to growth and the value of mergers whilst following that trend has also steadily increased over time.

Whilst there are many logical reasons for organizations to select this method of development, research evidence has suggested that its success rate is not particularly high. Integrations are unsuccessful for many reasons but mainly due to a lack of research into the target company and its environment.

Strategic alliances are relationships between businesses which are short of full merger. The various forms of alliance can range from informal to highly formalized agreements and their success often depends on the commitment of both parties to achieving the objectives of the alliance.

Disposals occur when parent companies wish to offload a part of its structure that is no longer in line with its core activity. They can take the form of divestments, demergers, equity carve-outs or management buy-outs.

Integrations are subject to a regulatory framework. UK-based companies are subject to both European and national regulations. In the UK, mergers and acquisitions are regulated by the Office of Fair Trading and the Monopoly and Mergers Commission.

Review and Discuss

1 Define and distinguish between internal and external business growth.
2 Define and distinguish between a merger and an acquisition.
3 Summarize the reasons why a business might seek to pursue external rather than internal growth.
4 Describe the reasons why mergers and acquisitions sometimes go wrong.
5 Explain the measures a business should take to increase the probability of success of a merger or acquisition.
6 What is a strategic alliance and how does it differ from a merger?
7 Why might an organization seek to form a strategic alliance?
8 What might a business do to ensure that its alliance is successful?
9 What is a disposal?
10 When might a business consider disposal?
11 Define and distinguish between MBOs, equity carve-outs and asset-stripping.
12 Summarize the EU regulations that apply to external business growth.
13 Summarize the UK regulations that apply to external business growth.
14 What is the role of the OFT and the MMC in the UK?

References and further reading

Ansoff, H. (1987) *Corporate Strategy*. London: Penguin.
Bishop, M., and Kay, J. (1993) *European Mergers and Merger Policy*. Oxford: Oxford University Press.
Brouthers, K.D., Brouthers, L. E. and Wilkinson, T. J. (1993) Strategic alliances: choose your partners. *Long Range Planning*, 28, No. 3, 18–25.
Faulkner, D. (1995) *Strategic Alliances: Cooperating to Compete*. New York: McGraw-Hill.
Firth, M. (1991) Corporate takeovers, stockholder returns and executive rewards. *Managerial and Decision Economics*, Vol. 12.
Franks, J. and Harris, R. (1989) Shareholders wealth effects of corporate

takeover: the UK experience 1955–85. *Journal of Financial Economics*, Vol. 23.

Geroski, P.A. and Vlassopoulos, A. (1990) Recent patterns of European merger activity. *Business Strategy Review*, Summer.

Glaister, K.W. and Buckley, P. (1994) UK international joint ventures: an analysis of patterns of activity and distribution. *British Journal of Management*, Vol. 5.

Haspeslagh, P. and Jemison, D. (1991) *Managing Acquisitions: Creating Value Through Corporate Renewal*. New York: Free Press.

Kay, J. (1993) *Foundations of Corporate Success*. Oxford: Oxford University Press.

Kitching, J. (1974) Why acquisitions are abortive. *Management Today*, Nov.

Meeks, G. (1977) *Disappointing Marriage: A Study of the Gains from Mergers*. Cambridge: Cambridge University Press.

Porter, M.E. (1980) *Competitive Strategy*. New York: Free Press.

Porter, M.E. (1985) *Competitive Advantage*. New York; Free Press.

Ravenscraft, D.J. and Scherer, F.M. (1987) *Mergers, Sell-offs and Economic Efficiency*. Washington, DC: Brooking Institution.

Shleifer, A. and Vishny, R. (1986) Large shareholders and corporate control. *Journal of Political Economy*, 94, 461–488.

Shleifer, A. and Vishny, R. (1991) Takeovers in the '60s and the '80s: evidence and implications. *Strategic Management Journal*, Vol. 12.

Sudarsanam, P.S. (1995) *The Essence of Mergers and Acquisitions*. Englewood Cliffs: Prentice Hall.

Walsh, J. and Ellwood, J. (1991) Mergers, acquisitions and the pruning of managerial deadwood. *Strategic Management Journal*, Vol. 12.

Case linkage

Questions for the Camelot case study.

1 Why do you think the bidders to operate the lottery were consortia and not single companies?
2 Explain what each of the partners on Camelot brought to the consortia in terms of expertise and knowledge.
3 Suggest why the government deemed it necessary to appoint an independent Lottery Regulator.

Questions for the Honda Rover case study.

1 Explain the logic behind the multiple mergers that occurred in the 1950s and 1960s to bring the BL Group into existence.
2 What advantages did Rover Group gain from the alliance with Honda?
3 What advantages did Honda gain?
4 Suggest reasons why both parties entered into the alliance warily at first.

5 How might Honda have avoided the disappointment of seeing the alliance dissolved in 1994?

6 Suggest reasons why the Land-Rover Discovery was badged as a Honda for sale in Japan and not sold as a Rover product.

7 Discuss the extent to which the alliance was a success for both parties.

Questions for the Dansk Tyggegummi Fabrik A/S case study.

1 Identify the growth mechanisms employed by DTF in the case.

2 Explain why DTF might have chosen to use joint ventures in some countries whilst directly investing in others.

3 Discuss the extent to which international competitive pressures may have contributed to DTF's expansion strategy.

Questions for the Homebase case study.

1 Suggest strategic reasons why Sainsbury accepted Ladbrokes' offer to purchase the Texas chain.

2 Identify the reasons why the integration process was so troubled, especially in respect to integrating the cultures.

3 What measures did Homebase put in place to improve the likelihood of success of any further growth strategies?

4 Comment upon the likelihood of success of the measures introduced after the Texas integration if a further large-scale acquisition was embarked upon.

Chapter 12

Quality, operations, performance and benchmarking

Introduction

The strategic development of many companies has been marked by a recognition that good quality in operations can contribute to competitive advantage. One approach in particular (Total Quality Management or TQM) is seen by many companies as an important part of this operational emphasis, especially for those that aim to be 'world class' organizations. In order to recognize the importance of quality, each of the world's major industrialized nations has its own Quality Award. These awards act as an important strategic tool and can assist in an organization's product and market positioning.

In this chapter we explain how this emphasis on quality management has come about and explore the main features demonstrated by those organizations which have successfully adopted a TQM philosophy. Key features of the quality award frameworks are also discussed. Finally the chapter goes on to explain the various types of operational benchmarking in common use and the benefits that each has to offer.

After studying this chapter, students should be able to:

- describe the main order-winning factors for business;
- define quality and Total Quality Management;
- explain how TQM evolved;
- explain the main principles of TQM;
- discuss the role of quality awards and prize schemes including the EFQM Business Excellence Model;
- describe and distinguish between enablers and results elements of the BEM;
- describe how such self-assessment frameworks are used and say what benefits they can bring to businesses;
- distinguish between the different types of benchmarking and explain the benefits of each.

Operational performance in 'winning' organizations

The performance objectives

All successful business organizations share a number of important objectives in respect to the 'operations' part of the value chain. The key to success in the most important part of the value adding process can be expressed in simple terms.

- *Do the right things right*, that is provide the goods or service which the customer wants, without mistakes. This means providing the product that the customer wants, right-first-time, every time.
- Do things *quickly*, giving the fastest possible turnaround for a customer, from placing an order to receiving the ordered goods.
- Be *reliable*, which is providing the customer with goods on time and keeping any delivery promises made.
- Be *flexible* and responsive to change – be able to deal with unexpected circumstances, or simply to deal with changes in customer requirements.
- Be *cheap* – provide products or services at competitive prices whilst still maintaining a profit. Or, in the case of non-profit making businesses, give best-value performance.

Operations and operations strategy

The operations function of an organization is at the centre of the value-adding process. It should not be confused with the 'operational level' as distinct from the 'strategic level' (see Chapter 1).

The operations function is that part of the organization that produces the output for which the organization is known. For a motor manufacturing company, the operations function comprises the chain of events from buying in the sheet steel to driving the finished car out of the factory. For a hospital, the operations function comprises the clinical departments, both medical and surgical, which are staffed by nurses, doctors and other paramedical employees.

It should be distinguished from all of those other parts of the organization that do not add value such as personnel and finance.

An operations strategy, like a human resource strategy or a marketing strategy, is a course of action put in train at the operational level (see Chapter 1) to help achieve an organization's corporate level strategies.

The customer's influence on quality and performance

The most important factors that impact on any organization's operations strategy are those set by the customers. The purpose of any operations function is to manage the value adding activities inside the business in such a way that customer requirements are met in full.

What 'matters' to the customer will, of course, vary from market to market. For each element of product or service that is of concern to a customer, organizations will have an internal response that facilitates the satisfaction of the customer concern. The most successful businesses are those that can most effectively configure their operations to meet the customer requirements. Table 12.1 gives some examples of this relationship.

Types of stock

Stocks are the physical goods that are bought in, converted and then sold to the customers in a manufacturing business. There are three types of stock, depending upon where they are along the production process:

- *Raw materials* (RMs) or purchased parts are stocks in their 'raw' state. RMs are those goods that are purchased, before they undergo any processing within the manufacturing process.

- *Work-in-progress* (WIP) is the name given to stocks that are actually being worked on in the manufacturing process.
- *Finished goods* (FG) stocks are those which have passed through the process and are ready for distribution to the customers.

What matters to customers in selecting a product purchase	How a business responds to the customer demand
Low price	Producing at low unit cost
High quality products	Building quality into processes and products
Fast delivery	Short manufacturing lead times, ex-FG stock (see Key Concept) or fast distribution
Product reliability	Building reliability into products and delivering dependable service
Innovative (leading edge technologies)	Keeping abreast of latest developments and emphasizing R&D
Wide product choice	Flexibility to change and wide product mix
Responsive to changes in customer requirements	Flexibility in volume and delivery, quick response times to change

Table 12.1 Factors affecting the operating performance characteristics of an organization.

The list in Table 12.1 is useful as a starting point to identifying the wide-ranging issues which must be addressed by manufacturing companies and service sector organizations in the quest to become leaders in their own markets. Many 'winning' organizations – those that have a competitive advantage in their industry – have arrived at the conclusion that one area of concern in operations is more important than any other: quality.

Quality

What is quality?

A number of academics and practitioners have attempted to provide a coherent definition of quality. That there are so many definitions is testimony to the fact that it is a complicated matter upon which to agree.

For a common product such as a car, we might think of quality as referring to reliability, build, safety features, etc. For a service such as plastering a wall, we would probably arrive at a different set of things to describe a 'quality' job, such as the finish of the surface, the flushness of the edges and the degree to which it is even. It is the fact that the quality criteria vary from product to product that makes forming a definition problematic.

Some of the most noted thinkers in the field have described quality in respect to 'excellence' or more accurately 'perceived excellence'. Although quality means many things to different people, in general we can consider quality as meeting customer needs or expectations. In Table 12.2, we summarize some of the most widely used definitions.

Quality 'guru'	Definition of quality
Deming	Quality should be aimed at meeting the needs of the consumer, present and future
Juran	Quality is fitness for the purpose for which the product is intended
Crosby	Quality is conformance to requirements (either customer requirements or the specification predetermined for it)
Oakland	Quality is meeting customer requirements

Table 12.2: Some definitions of quality.

Key Concepts

The quality 'gurus'

A quality guru is someone who has been recognized for his contribution to the management of quality within business and whose messages have led to major change in the way organizations operate. There are a number people who are highly regarded as major contributors in the field of quality management. The major thinkers in the area are described in Table 12.3.

Quality 'guru'	Main messages
W. Edwards Deming	Sometimes referred to as 'the father of TQM', Deming believed that bad management is responsible for more than 90 per cent of quality problems. He argued that quality improvement is achieved by continuous reduction in process variation using *statistical process control* and employee involvement. Later, Deming developed his 'System of Profound Knowledge' in which he stressed the need for the organizations to operate as a coherent system with everybody working together towards the overall aims. Good quality relies in large part upon an understanding of the nature of variation (statistical theory), careful planning and prediction based on experience. Finally, he stressed the importance of psychology, recognizing the relationships of extrinsic and extrinsic motivation factors in the workplace.
Joseph M. Juran	Proposed a general management approach with human elements. He believed that less than 20 per cent of qual-

ity problems are due to the workers themselves. He defined quality as 'fitness for use'. Juran recommended a project approach to improvements by setting targets, planning to achieve targets set, assigning responsibility, and rewarding results achieved.

Arman V. Feigenbaum   Proposed a systematic approach involving every employee and all functions. He emphasized the need for 'quality-mindedness' through employee participation. He made the point that expenditure on prevention costs would lead to an overall reduction in product failure costs.

Kaoru Ishikawa   Stressed the importance of statistical methods, using his 'seven tools of quality' for problem solving. He is also recognized for his contributions to the company-wide quality control movement, involving all staff at all levels through quality circles.

Genichi Taguchi   Developed the 'quality loss function' concerned with the optimization of products and processes prior to manufacture. His methods can be applied in the design phase of products or systems, or in production to optimize process variables.

Shigeo Shingo   Introduced a practical approach to achieve zero-defects. With careful design of products and tooling systems, he eliminated the need for sample inspection, through his system of mistake proofing known as 'Poka-Yoke'. He is also acknowledged for his work on fast tooling changeovers. Commonly known as SMED (single minute exchange of dies), this is one of the most important contributions to JIT (just in time) operating systems.

Philip B. Crosby   Crosby's 14-step approach to quality improvement sets out to achieve conformance to requirements through prevention not inspection. Believing that 'quality is 'free' and 'zero defects' should be the target, Crosby rejected statistically acceptable levels of quality. He believed in a 'top down' approach to quality management and proposed his four absolutes of quality:
- quality is defined as conformance to requirements;
- a system of prevention not appraisal;
- performance standard should be zero defects;
- the measurement of quality should be the financial cost of non-conformance.

Tom Peters   Peters' early work stressed the importance of visible leadership and encouraged MBWA (management by walking about) giving managers the opportunity to listen and solve problems through face-to-face contact with workers. His later work focused on customer orientation and he stressed that managers need to be 'obsessed' with quality, never accepting shoddy goods. He recognized that everyone needs to be trained in quality tools, and supported the use of cross-functional teams. He believed that organizations should overcome complacency by creating 'endless Hawthorne effects' (after the work of Elton Mayo) through the generation of new goals and environments. He also stressed the importance of the role of suppliers and customers in the quest for improvement.

Table 12.3 The quality 'gurus'.

Historical perspective of quality

Quality has been an issue for as long as business has been carried out. For traditional crafts such as blacksmiths, tailors, innkeepers, etc., it was the craftsmen themselves that were responsible for the price, delivery and degree of quality of their wares and services. Reputations were established on the quality of workmanship, which in turn led to more demand for their skills and higher levels of profitability and prosperity for the individual. The more successful 'masters' recruited apprentices and employed other tradesmen. Quality was assured informally and depended on the pride that each individual had in their own work. In Europe, crafts guilds were established which aimed to ensure that adequate training was given and that apprentices 'qualified' only when they were demonstrably capable of producing adequate standards of workmanship. Much of this pride in workmanship was lost during the industrial revolution in the late eighteenth century with the introduction of machinery and high volume manufacturing. However large-scale production methods brought about a need to ensure consistent reproduction of parts, manufactured to exacting specifications, and so the concept of *quality control* was born.

By the early 1900s Frederick W. Taylor introduced his ideas on scientific management. His methodology was to separate the planning (thinking) function from the physical work elements in production. By breaking down each job into smaller elements of work, he was able to train workers to perform simple mechanical tasks which comprised only a part of the total production process. High volume repeatability allowed gains in speed and efficiency, and this led to cheaper products. Quality control techniques enabled specially trained inspectors to test finished components against a predetermined specification. This enabled defective parts to be identified and then removed or reworked before they reached the customer.

The modern quality movement

It wasn't until after the Second World War during the 1950s that the modern quality movement began. The demand for goods and merchandise saw Western industrial nations producing higher volumes of product with a resulting decline in quality. In Japan, during the rebuilding of its industrial base, help was given through a number of management consultants. In particular the work of Dr W. Edwards Deming and Dr Joseph Juran led the Japanese to completely review the accepted views on quality management.

Statistical quality control techniques were introduced to reduce variation in the production processes. Much emphasis was placed on the way that quality was managed, rather than simply concentrating on only the technical issues. The focus shifted from one of quality inspection to one of preventing quality problems. Management began educating and involving all employees to look for ways to improve product quality and work methods. The Japanese developed a new culture of continuous improvement where everyone was encouraged to believe that they had two jobs – doing the work and improving the work. They called this approach *Kaizen*.

This new manufacturing philosophy gradually evolved and this led to the Japanese domination in manufacturing industries by the late 1970s. During the 1980s the rest of the world awoke to this transformation and the TQM movement was born.

Key Concepts

Kaizen

Kaizen is a culturally-embedded concept of continual improvement pioneered in Japanese companies. It concentrates on small gradual changes involving all employees in every area of business. According to Imai (1986) it is 'the single most important concept in Japanese management – the key to Japanese competitive success.' Kaizen is process-oriented change, involving operators continuously searching for better ways to do their job.

Some companies use 'kaizen teams' who take responsibility for identifying opportunities for improvement. Typically ideas for change will be investigated, tested and measured by the team. Any savings in job cycle time, even though it may only amount to a few seconds, will be introduced as the new standard method of production. Staff are encouraged to participate in kaizen teams and are given full training in problem-solving tools and techniques.

The kaizen process begins with examination of the work processes and operating practices, continuously looking for improvement opportunities. It is important that every employee strives for improvement and so an acceptance of kaizen by the organizational culture is an important element. Employees are empowered to experiment and make incremental changes and are sometimes provided with their own limited budgets for doing so. It is important that kaizen activities are actively supported by management who will usually provide additional resources if required, perhaps when ideas for change are complex, requiring technical expertise, extra finance or help in other ways.

Total quality management

What is TQM?

Today, TQM is a holistic approach, which provides awareness of the customer–supplier relationship and continuous improvement effort in all departments and functions. There has been much written on the subject of TQM, and the philosophy means many things to different people.

Some have used an external customer focus, aiming to ensure employee awareness of customer needs and an elimination of faulty goods or service. Others have focused on the tools of quality such as brainstorming, statistical tools, control charts etc., to encourage problem-solving and a right-first-time attitude. Many have used teamwork and 'empowerment' in an effort to develop a 'quality' culture, to improve staff motivation and establish an ongoing cycle of quality improvement.

There are as many approaches to TQM as there are consultants selling their own formula for success, but whatever the approach the following features of TQM are usually present:

- it is strongly led by senior management;
- it is customer oriented;
- it recognizes internal customers in the value chain and external customers;
- it represents a fundamental change away from *controlling* bad quality to *preventing* bad quality from happening – it *causes* good quality;
- it encourages a right-first-time approach to all activities;
- everybody is made responsible for quality;
- there is an emphasis on kaizen;
- training and quality 'tools' are introduced in support of the quality regime;
- employees are encouraged to look for ways for improving quality in their own areas, such as by process 'tightening';
- it introduces measurement systems to control waste.

Key Concepts

Waste
Waste describes any activity in an operations process that is not value adding. It costs money but does not create value commensurate with its cost.
Examples include:

1 process inefficiency (say as a result of bad design);
2 all materials handing activity (say from station to station in the process);
3 any stock that is not actually being processed (and to which value is therefore not being added). This includes all raw materials, all finished

goods and any work-in-progress that is queuing between production stages;

4 stocks that have failed a quality test, either in-process or at final QC;

5 machine 'down-time', that is production time lost through machines not being operable for any reason such as breakdown or through tooling up or tooling down between batches;

6 the time and stock involved in producing unsold or unsaleable stocks.

Oakland's model for total quality management

A number of frameworks for TQM have been developed. The earliest were proposed by academics trying to explain and rationalize the TQM concepts, to facilitate implementation by managers in industry. Many business consultants followed with their own ideas and a proliferation of TQM models ensued.

Oakland's framework

Professor John Oakland developed a relatively simple framework, which usefully described the main features of TQM (see Figure 12.1). According to Oakland (1993), '[TQM is] an approach to improving the competitiveness, effectiveness and flexibility of a whole organization.'

The role of processes

At the heart of Oakland's model are processes and customer supplier chains, in order to recognize the importance of meeting customer requirements. The term *customer* does not just refer to the end customer; it also recognizes that all organizations have chains of internal customers and suppliers. For example in a manufacturing plant, raw materials are received into stores from suppliers and are then fed into the first production process. Here the materials are worked on in some way and then passed on to the next department (the next internal customer) where they are worked on again. At each stage value is added until the final product is sold to the external customer. Each operator in the chain is therefore both a customer and a supplier, with each having the responsibility of meeting their respective customer's requirements. Failing to do so at any stage results in inferior quality and a need to correct or rework the work in process stock of the finished goods product. At every stage, the work process and the skills of the operator must be capable of doing the job correctly to the designed specification.

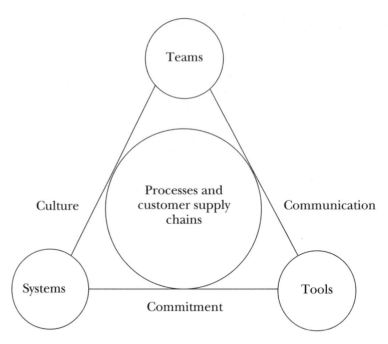

Figure 12.1 Oakland's model of TQM.

Quality systems

To achieve consistency in work processes a company must be organized so that the required standards are known and understood by all employees. This organization requires management systems to plan, monitor and control all activities. For many organizations this is achieved by setting out objectives through their quality policy and the use of a fully documented quality system such as ISO 9000. Using such a system ensures a consistent level of quality which, in turn, promotes customer confidence. In addition, such systems help the organization to manage internal and external operations in a cost-effective and efficient way.

Tools and techniques of quality

The quality system provides a framework for recording and dealing with quality problems. However, simply asking staff to take responsibility for solving their own quality problems is usually not enough. Employees often must be trained and educated so that they can identify problems and deal with them effectively. Many organizations now train staff in basic problem-solving tools and other quality techniques, encouraging them to become proactive in quality improvement activities.

Teams and the organization

Clear lines of authority and responsibility are important in most organizational structures (see Chapter 10). Just as important, however, is the need to ensure that departments and functions do not become so compartmentalized that barriers develop. In most modern manufacturing and service companies, work processes are complex in nature and are often beyond the control of any one individual. A team approach, therefore, offers a number of advantages.

The use of teams allows more complex problems to be solved because it brings together different skills and expertise. Interdepartmental teams can resolve issues that cross over functional boundaries and will also help reduce problems of internal politics. Teamworking can also help develop skills and knowledge and is often more satisfying for the individuals involved – improving morale, participation and decision-making.

Commitment, culture and communication

Achieving right-first-time quality requires a dedicated, well-motivated and loyal workforce who have been educated and trained to do the job properly. This requires leadership, policy setting, careful planning and the provision of appropriate resources at every level in the company. Senior managers must demonstrate their own commitment and the 'quality message' must be communicated and understood by everyone in the organization. Development of a TQM culture usually takes many years and must be demonstrated from senior management level down through the whole organization.

Quality award and assessment frameworks

Recognition for quality

The realization that quality is a key determinant of the competitive position of a business has brought about a number of methods of recognition. Accordingly, every First World economy has its own government-sponsored award to recognize those organizations that have achieved high quality and to stimulate others to follow the same path.

In the UK, for example, one such initiative emerged from the DTI (The Department of Trade and Industry). The 'Managing in the 90s' programme offered comprehensive assistance to industry across all aspects of business improvement. The support was directed at improving the full range of business activities ranging from innovation and design of products, selection and development of suppliers, the management of quality, processes, efficiency and reliability.

Demonstration of high quality and world-class performance has become an important marketing requirement for any organization wishing to compete in global markets. To recognize achievement, a number of prize and assessment frameworks have been developed and adopted by various countries. These frameworks are all based on the philosophy of TQM and have much in common. The high profile and publicity gained by the winners of these internationally-recognized awards give organizations significant marketing opportunities.

Three of the major frameworks in use today are:

- the Deming Prize (Japan);
- the Malcolm Baldrige Award (USA);
- the EFQM European Quality Award.

These frameworks have continued to evolve and are now being adopted by countries worldwide in similar forms. The primary use of the frameworks is as a self-assessment tool by which companies can critically review their own activities against a comprehensive set of criteria. Typically an organization prepares a detailed written submission of strengths and weaknesses for all aspects of its operations and business performance. For the best companies (those which demonstrate the highest levels of achievement), the submission can be used to judge them for the award. More importantly, and for most organizations, any weaknesses they have identified can be prioritized and developed into an action plan for business improvement.

The Deming Prize

In recognition of his work in Japan, the Union of Japanese Scientists and Engineers (JUSE) introduced the Deming Prize in 1951. The prize has several categories including prizes for individuals, small companies and factories. Hundreds of companies apply for the Deming Prize each year. Each applicant must submit a detailed account of quality practices and methods and from these submissions a shortlist of companies is selected for site visits and assessment. Past winners of the Deming Prize include Toyota Motor Company and NEC IC Microcomputer Systems.

The Malcolm Baldrige award

In 1987 the United States of America recognized that productivity and competitiveness were declining, and introduced its own quality award. The Malcolm Baldrige Award was designed to operate in a similar manner to the Deming Prize with the specific aim of stimulating American companies to improve quality and productivity. It was believed that by recognizing the achievements of the best organizations, other companies could learn from them. The award process provides guidelines for business, industrial, governmental and other enterprises to self-assess their own quality improvement efforts. Examination is based on a rigorous set of criteria that call upon organizations to demonstrate how they are improving competitiveness and show the results achieved.

The winners announced by President Clinton for 1997 were 3M Dental Products Division and Solectron Corporation (manufacturing sector); and Merrill Lynch Credit Corporation and Xerox Business Services (service sector). Past winners of the Malcolm Baldrige National Quality Award have generously shared their quality management strategies with other organizations. In doing so, they have raised awareness of the importance of quality to US national competitiveness, thus encouraging many other organizations to improvement efforts. Some of the more well known past winners include Armstrong World Industries Building Products Operations (1995); Eastman Chemical Company (1993); The Ritz-Carlton Hotel Company (1992); Cadillac Motor Car Company (1990); IBM Rochester – AS/400 Division (1990); Xerox Corporation – Business Products & Systems (1989); Milliken & Company (1989); Motorola Inc. (1988).

The European Foundation for Quality Management (EFQM)

The EFQM model

Following the success of the Deming Prize and the Malcolm Baldrige Award, fourteen leading European organizations, supported by the European Commission, formed the Brussels-based European Foundation for Quality Management (EFQM) in 1988. By 1999, membership of the EFQM had grown to over 600 members from across Europe and in most sectors of commercial and not-for-profit activity. The mission of the EFQM is to promote self-assessment as a key process to drive business improvement. The model, often referred to as 'The Business Excellence Model' (BEM), is shown in Figure 12.2.

The EFQM model is based on the following premise:

Customer satisfaction, people (employee) satisfaction and impact on society are achieved through leadership driving policy and strategy, people management, resources and processes, leading ultimately to excellence in business results. (EFQM, 1997)

The model contains nine elements, each of which contains a number of sub-criteria. The elements comprise five *enablers*, so called because they refer to *how* the organization sets up to do business, and four *results* elements, which refer to *what* the organization achieves by following the model. The self-assessment model can be used by all types and sizes of organization. Published guidelines are specifically written (by the EFQM) for manufacturers, service companies, public sector organizations and also for SMEs (small and medium enterprises).

The EFQM model offers a rigorous and structured approach to business improvements based on hard facts and supported evidence. Careful assessment against each of the criteria in Figure 12.2 allows an organization to calculate an overall score from a total possible 1000 points. This score can then be viewed as a benchmark for comparisons with other organizations. However, for many companies the score in itself is regarded as less important than the actual process of self-assessment. Self-assessment helps the organization work through the application of TQM and helps integrate many separate improvement activities into normal business operations.

One of the most powerful attractions of the model is its use as a diagnostic tool. It forces the compilation of a comprehensive list of 'areas for improvement'. These AFIs form the basis for a company-wide plan of improvement activities, which can be prioritized to yield best results. Improvements can be measured and revisited year after year to observe progress. Benchmarking both internally and externally provides a powerful method of setting realistic improvement targets, and is referred to constantly within the model. Because of its importance, benchmarking will be discussed in more detail later in this chapter.

To understand how TQM impacts holistically on the practices and performance of an organization we now turn to examine the BEM in more detail.

The enabler criteria

The first five criteria of the EFQM-BEM are devoted to examining how the organization sets itself out to manufacture goods or provide services to customers.

Leadership – how the behaviour and actions of the executive team and all other leaders inspire, support and promote a culture of TQM

This first element looks for visible demonstration of commitment to TQM by all managers within the organization. Managers must be 'role model' leaders, who have clear values based on the principles of TQM. They should define priorities and be personally involved in improvement activities, providing appropriate resources. They should be involved with customers and suppliers, and promote partnerships and joint improvement 'win–win' activities. Managers should also usually recognize individual and team achievements, both internally with employees and externally with customers

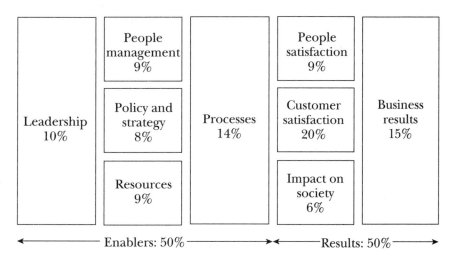

Figure 12.2 The EFQM business excellence model.

and suppliers. Leadership should promote the TQM ethos and ensure common direction and alignment of the business's aims and objectives.

Policy and strategy – how the organization formulates, deploys, reviews and turns strategy into plans and actions

Policy and strategy for any company must be based on comprehensive and relevant information (this being the purpose of strategic analysis). It is usually important to understand customers' needs and to exploit, as far as possible, the strengths of suppliers. If policies are going to work efficiently, the views of employees may also be taken into account. In addition external views may also be considered relating to the social, environmental, economic, technological and legal issues. To ensure competitiveness the organization needs to review performance and use benchmarking to compare with the competition.

Exactly *how* the organization develops its policy and strategy are important. They must demonstrate consistency. They must show a balance between short and long term business requirements, whilst ensuring that competitive advantages are achieved. The policy and strategy must be used to plan the activities of the business to ensure that objectives are aligned and effectively communicated at all levels. Finally, strategy must be reviewed regularly and updated.

People management – how the organization releases the full potential of its people

The organization needs to demonstrate how the human resources plan aligns with policy and strategy and that the capabilities of the employees are managed and developed. The organization should encourage individual and team participation in improvement activities and empower staff to take action. In so doing, people can be recognized and appropriately rewarded. The BEM calls for effective vertical and horizontal employee communications. Finally, this criterion examines how people are cared for in terms of health and safety, the work environment, and even social facilities.

Resources – how the organization manages resources effectively and efficiently

In the context of this criterion, resources refer to all of the inputs employed by the company, other than the human resources already covered above. These include: the financial resources; information resources; suppliers and materials; buildings, plant and equipment; technology and intellectual property.

The BEM calls for good management showing positive trends in all appropriate financial measures such as cash flow, profitability, assets, shareholder value, etc. The organization needs to show also that it manages information resources to support its quality strategy. Supplier relationships must be continuously developed to improve the external linkages from the value chain. Inventory (stock management) should optimize stock levels and reduce or recycle waste where appropriate, thus conserving global non-renewable resources. Good utilization and careful maintenance of all physical assets such as buildings, plant and equipment must be demonstrated. The company must also show how it identifies, evaluates and then exploits technology to gain competitive advantage.

Processes – how the organization identifies, manages, reviews and improves its operational processes

In the past, organizations have structured themselves according to business functions, with each individual manager striving for departmental efficiency (see Chapter 10). In recent years the trend has been to consider the organization more holistically, striving for wider organizational efficiency, recognizing the importance of internal customer–supplier relationships. This element of the BEM requires companies to show that key processes have been identified and that they understand how they impact on the success of the business. Each key process must be systematically measured and managed to established standards, such as through formal systems (e.g. ISO 9000). Constantly striving to be more competitive requires regular reviews of processes and actual performance levels. The best-quality companies talk to their customers and suppliers, and proactively involve them in the design of future activities. The use of Best Practice Benchmarking helps identify innovation and new technologies and leads to improvements (see later in this chapter).

The results criteria

The remaining four criteria of the BEM are devoted to examining what the organization is actually achieving. To achieve a high score, a company must demonstrate strongly positive trends over at least five years in business results and profitability. Measures must also be in place showing strong satisfaction trends from customers, suppliers, employees and the wider community.

Customer satisfaction – what the organization is achieving in relation to the satisfaction of its external customers

This criterion carries more emphasis than any other element of the model (20 per cent of the overall total points), which reflects the importance placed on satisfying the customer. It seeks to gauge how well the organization satisfies the customer with regard to its products. Organizations are required to present targets, results and trends, and show how they compare with competitors.

People satisfaction – what the organization is achieving in relation to the satisfaction of its employees

Just as satisfying the external customer is important, employee morale is also a vital ingredient. Here, staff perception may be sought through satisfaction surveys, appraisals, etc. Training and development should lead to clear career progression in line with the organization's values and strategy. Developing a 'learning organization' culture can help and many organizations have found the application of the Investors in People (IiP) standard very useful.

Impact on society – what the organization is achieving in satisfying the needs and the expectations of the local, national and international community at large (as appropriate)

This part of the model seeks out how well the organization satisfies the needs of society as a whole. For example, equal opportunity practices, impact on local and national economies, and relationships with relevant authorities. Also the extent to which the company has involvement in the community, giving support to education and training, or perhaps providing sport and leisure facilities. Taking care of the environment and the prevention of pollution are also important areas where a company can demonstrate that they have a sense of real corporate citizenship (see Chapter 14).

Business results – what the organization is achieving in relation to its planned business objectives and in satisfying the needs and expectations of everyone with a financial interest or stake in the organization

The financial measures of the organization's performance are perhaps the most obvious area where it can demonstrate positive results. Particularly important here are the performance ratios we encountered in Chapter 4 such as *return on sales* or *return on capital employed*. Other financial measures may also be appropriate depending upon the organization's particular circumstances. For a public sector organization, for example, value-for-money measures are likely to be more important than profit measures.

Scoring against the model

A total possible theoretical score available against the criteria of the model is 1000 points, although typically award winning (world class) companies score around 700 points. The BEM is scored using a number of dimensions.

Each of the enablers is examined on:
- *approach* – looks for soundly based systematic prevention-based systems, which have been regularly reviewed and refined. High scores are indicative of approaches used by 'role-model' organizations;
- *deployment* – evaluates the extent to which the approaches are used across the business. High scores indicate full integration into all activities.

Each of the results is examined on:
- *results* – looks for excellence in the results of the business. High scores are indicative of strongly positive trends and sustained high performance over at least five years;
- *scope* – evaluates how far the results achieved extend into all areas and facets of the organization.

Benchmarking

What is benchmarking?

One of the key features established within any of the above frameworks is the importance of *benchmarking*. Superior performers in most industries regularly review themselves against the competition and other best-in-class companies to remain at the top. A report, *Fit for the Future*, published by the Confederation of British Industry (CBI) examined the strengths of UK companies. The report concludes, 'The most powerful process any company can adopt and which delivers immediate, measurable and sustainable productivity improvements is the transfer of Best Practice' (CBI, 1997).

This is the key to successful benchmarking – for an organization to analyse its own performance and then compare performance in several areas against competitors. If, for example, one competitor in an industry enjoys a lower rate of waste or higher quality than others, questions can be asked as to what the superior company has done to bring about the superior performance. By using benchmarking in this way, 'best practice' procedures can be emulated and performance improved in the lower performers.

Successful benchmarking usually rests upon the premise that competitors in an industry are willing, to some extent, to share, collaborate or make information available upon their performance and processes.

Types of benchmarking

In recent years the interest in benchmarking has grown. What started out as a relatively simple concept has grown increasingly complicated. Benchmarking has proved to be a profitable source of income for management consultants who have developed and published many different approaches and methodologies. For any organization just beginning to benchmark, reading the literature will confirm that there are many types of benchmarking in existence. Where do they start? Which form of benchmarking is best?

Here, we will consider the different types under three broad headings: metric, diagnostic and process benchmarking. A simple way is to view them along a continuum as shown in Figure 12.3.

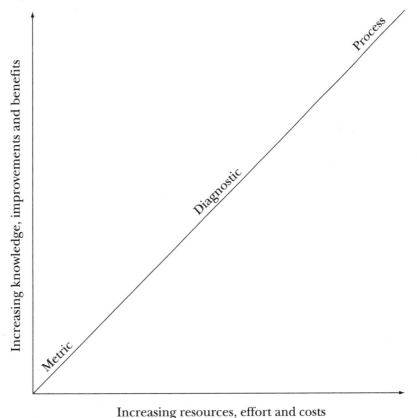

Figure 12.3 Types of benchmarking.

From Figure 12.3, we can see that there is an increase in effort, resources and costs as we move from metric benchmarking through to full process benchmarking. At the lower end, metric benchmarking can provide an indication of relative performance and perhaps identify leading competitors, but it is unlikely to yield any real ideas on how to change. At best it will only help define performance gaps.

Moving up, diagnostic benchmarking requires a little more effort but in return will identify areas of strength and more detail on areas of weakness for the organization. Done correctly, it will also help prioritize which processes should be targeted for improvement activities.

Process benchmarking requires considerably more resource, effort and time, but organizations successfully completing the process will be rewarded with many benefits of transferred best practice.

Metric benchmarking

Many organizations, both in manufacturing and in service-based sectors, use metric benchmarking as a means of direct comparison both internally and externally with other organizations. Metrics are performance indicators used as comparative measures. There are many published forms of metric data with which simple comparisons can be drawn. For example, league tables such as those published by government agencies or public sector organizations such as (in the UK) the NHS. Another example is the university league tables published by the *Financial Times*. In the manufacturing sector examples include the publication of *Manufacturing Winners* by the DTI *et al.* (1995), or the *Management Today*/Cranfield University 'Britain's Best Factories Award'.

Metric benchmarking is often used by companies to make inter-site comparisons using key performance indicators such as product costs, staffing levels, resources per unit produced, waste or rework levels, stock turns, etc. They are useful provided that each site is measured in the same way using like-with-like comparisons. Perhaps the biggest disadvantage of metric benchmarking is that even when it shows a performance gap between two companies, it does not explain how better performance can be achieved.

Diagnostic benchmarking

Made in Europe, a report written by IBM Consultants and London Business School (Hanson *et al.*, 1994), introduced an approach which measures and compares businesses on world class scales. The tool used, PROBE (PROmoting Business Excellence), has led the way in what is now referred to as diagnostic benchmarking.

This study compared hundreds of manufacturing organizations across Europe, examining the relationship between practice and performance.

The research found that good practice correlated strongly with performance. The tool has been followed by a number of similar instruments, some of which have been designed for particular industry sectors.

Researchers in Newcastle Business School at the University of Northumbria developed one such instrument, called PILOT. It was a questionnaire-based survey instrument based on PROBE, which asked around 50 questions on practice and performance measures, suitable for both manufacturing and service sector organizations.

On completion of the questionnaire, the participating organizations received feedback showing them how they compared against other organizations in the area. Like the PROBE analysis, the PILOT study found that good practice correlated strongly with business performance.

Process benchmarking

By far the most involved form of benchmarking, process benchmarking is where the most substantial benefits can be found. The focus is on any key business processes which have been identified as an area for improvement.

Fundamental to the success of process benchmarking is the recognition that many organizations have functions which use generically similar business processes regardless of sector or industry type. Thus one main advantage of process benchmarking is that businesses need not restrict themselves to observing practices in companies who are considered direct competition. Most business organizations, for example, issue invoices, collect payables (debts), appoint new people, etc. and these can be benchmarked regardless of industry.

Benchmarking activities can be widened to include partners from different sectors and this can enable completely new ways of working to be identified. This can lead to significant improvements in operating efficiency across industrial sectors.

Process benchmarking can be divided into four stages.

1 Understanding the nature and complexity of the business processes which are to be benchmarked. This requires careful process mapping and measurement of process metrics.
2 Identifying potential and willing benchmarking partners – not always a straightforward task as some corporate cultures resist 'opening up' to outside organizations.
3 Data collection and measurement. It is important to ensure that processes are compared on a like-with-like basis.
4 Implementation of change and transfer of best practice for a given process. This is not always easy because cultural, demographic or technological barriers may present unforeseen problems.

Summary

The quality movement has moved from simple inspection into a culture of customer orientation, continuous improvement and prevention based systems. TQM is a holistic approach to business activity which results in satisfying customers, employees and the wider society through strong leadership, strategy, well-motivated staff and efficient processes.

The main quality award and self-assessment frameworks for TQM demonstrate the approaches being used today in the drive for world class status.

Best practice benchmarking is a powerful technique for any company wishing to identify, prioritize and transfer improvements into their operations.

Review and Discuss

1 Explain the links between operations strategy and competitive advantage.
2 Describe the main definitions of quality.
3 Why is kaizen important in TQM?
4 Explain how the approach to quality management has changed over the years.
5 What are the key features of TQM?
6 What benefits might an organization expect to gain from using the BEM?
7 Describe the BEM and briefly discuss each of the nine elements.
8 Describe the main types of benchmarking and discuss the main advantages of each.

References and further reading

CBI (1997) *Fit for the Future: How Competitive is British Manufacturing?* London: Confederation of British Industry. Foreword.

Department of Trade and Industry (1995) *Manufacturing Winners: Creating a World-Class Manufacturing Base in the UK.* London: Department of Trade and Industry.

EFQM (1997) *Self Assessment – Guidelines for Companies.* Brussels: European Foundation for Quality Management.

Hanson, P., Voss, C., Blackmon, K. and Oak, B. (1994) *Made in Europe: A Four Nations Best Practice Study.* London: IBM Consultancy Group and London Business School.

Imai, M. (1986) *Kaizen: The Key to Japan's Competitive Success.* New York: McGraw Hill.

Oakland, J.S. (1993) *Total Quality Management,* Second Edition. Oxford: Butterworth-Heinemann.

PILOT is a benchmarking survey tool developed by Newcastle Business

School as part of the Regional Competitiveness Project. The project lasted three years (1996–1998) and was 50 per cent funded through the European Regional Development Fund and led by the Northern Development Company.

Case linkage

Questions for the Honda Rover case study.

1 Which elements of British Leyland in the 1970s might have caused its customers to lose confidence in its products?
2 How did Honda's involvement in the joint venture increase the quality of Rover's products?
3 Why do you think that Honda's products were considered to be 'higher quality' than Rover's in the 1970s?

Chapter 13

International and global strategies

Introduction

One of the most important considerations in the implementation of strategy is the extent to which the organization's activities are spread across geographical regions. Some businesses are entirely domestically based, others operate in many countries, and others still operate in almost all regions of the world. This chapter is concerned with a discussion of the key issues surrounding the *why* and *how* questions: why do organizations expand in this way and how do they go about it? The *why* questions are covered in a discussion of the factors that drive increased internationalization. The *how* questions are answered in a discussion of the market entry options.

Objectives

After studying this chapter, students should be able to:

- define and distinguish between internationalization and globalization;
- explain the factors that drive globalization;
- describe and demonstrate the application of Yip's framework for analysing the extent of globalization in an industry and market;
- explain the major global strategy alternatives;
- describe the international market entry strategies.

Internationalization and globalization

What is the difference?

Business has been international since the days of the ancient Egyptians, Phoenicians and Greeks. Merchants travelled the known world to sell products manufactured in their home country and to return with products from other countries. Initially, international business simply took the form of exporting and importing. The term *international* describes any business which carries out some of its activities across national boundaries.

Globalization, on the other hand, is more than simply internationalization. A large multinational company is not necessarily a global business. In order for a business to become global in its operations, we would usually expect a number of important characteristics to be in place.

Firstly, global organizations take advantage of the increasing trend towards a convergence of customer needs and wants across international borders (e.g. for fast foods, soft drinks, consumer electronics; see Levitt, 1983).

Secondly, global organizations compete in industries that are globalized. In some sectors, successful competition necessitates a presence in almost every part of the world in order to effectively compete in its global market.

Thirdly, global organizations can – and do – locate their value-adding activities in those places in the world where the greatest competitive advantages can be made. This might mean, for example, shifting production to a low-cost region or moving design to a country with skilled labour in the key skill area.

Finally, global organizations are able to integrate and co-ordinate their international activities between countries. The mentality of 'home base, foreign interests' that has been so prevalent amongst traditional multinational companies is eroded in the culture of global businesses. They have learned to effectively manage and control the various parts of the business across national borders and despite local cultural differences.

The development of an organization's global strategy, therefore, will be concerned with global competences, global marketing and global configuration and co-ordination of its value-adding activities (see our discussion of value adding in Chapter 2).

Multinational and transnational companies

Both multinational and transnational companies share the feature in that they are usually large and they have direct investments in one or more foreign countries. The foreign investments may be part-shareholdings, but are more usually wholly-owned subsidiaries.

The difference is in the degree to which the foreign investments are co-ordinated. We tend to think of a transnational company as one that has a high degree of co-ordination in its international interests. It will usually have a strategic centre which manages the global operation such that all parts act in accordance with a centrally-managed strategic purpose.

The term multinational company is usually taken to mean an international company whose foreign interests are not co-ordinated from a strategic centre.

Globalization of markets and industries

Levitt and market homogenization

It was Levitt (1983) who first argued that changes in technology, societies, economies and politics are producing a 'global village'. By this he meant that consumer needs in many previously separate national markets were becoming increasingly similar throughout the world. Developments in transport have not only made it easier to move products and materials between countries but they have also resulted in a huge increase in the amount that people travel around the world. Such travel educates people to the products available in other countries and, on their return home, they often wish to have access to products and services from overseas. This trend has been reinforced by changes in information technology, particularly those related to cinema and television, which have been important in some aspects of cultural convergence. The development of the WTO (World Trade Organization) and its predecessor, GATT (the General Agreement on Tariffs and Trade), has resulted in huge reductions in the barriers to trade between countries since the Second World War. Rising income levels throughout many parts of the world have also given economic impetus to the development of global markets.

It is not only markets which are in many cases becoming more global. Industries are also becoming more global. The value chains of businesses in many industries span the globe. In the case of the fashion house, Yves Saint Laurent, design and marketing are concentrated in France while products are mainly manufactured in the Far East. Organizations concentrate certain of their activities in locations where they hope to obtain cost, quality or other advantages. Other activities, like distribution, are also often dispersed around the world. The way that a business configures its activities across national borders can be an important source of competitive advantage. The spread of an organization's value-adding activities around the world also means that there are important advantages to be gained from effective integration and co-ordination of activities.

Porter and multi-domesticity

Porter (1990) argues that industries can be either global or *multi-domestic*. Multi-domestic industries are those where competition in each nation is essentially independent. He gives the example of consumer banking where a bank's domestic reputation and resources in one nation have tended to have little effect on its success in other countries. The international banking industry is, Porter agues, essentially a collection of domestic industries.

Global industries are those in which competition is global. The consumer electronics industry is a good example where companies like Philips, Sony and Panasonic compete in almost all countries of the world. The implication would appear to be that businesses should adopt a global strategy in global industries and a multi-local strategy in multi-domestic markets. Yet the situation is not as simple as this. Even markets like consumer banking are becoming more global.

It is also the case that the degree of globalization of an industry or market may not be uniform. In other words some aspects of an industry or market may be indicative of globalization while others may be indicative of localization. The degree of globalization of an industry can be assessed using Yip's globalization driver framework (1992). This is a more useful framework than Porter's because it makes it possible to evaluate both the overall degree of globalization of an industry and which features of the industry are more or less global in nature.

Globalization drivers

Yip's framework

Yip (1992) argues that it is not simply the case that industries are 'global' or 'not global', rather that they can be global in some respects and not in others. Yip's globalization driver framework makes it possible to identify which aspects of an industry are global and which aspects differ locally. Analysis using this framework can play an important role in shaping the global strategy of a business. A global strategy, according to Yip, will be global in many respects but may also include features which are locally oriented.

Yip argues that, 'To achieve the benefits of globalization, the managers of a worldwide business need to recognize when industry conditions provide the opportunity to use global strategy levers.' Table 13.1 shows a breakdown of the globalization drivers.

Yip identifies four drivers (see Figure 13.1) which determine the nature and extent of globalization in an industry. These are:

- market drivers;
- cost drivers;
- government drivers;
- competitive drivers.

We will consider each of these drivers in turn.

Market globalization drivers

The degree of globalization of a market will depend upon the extent to which there are common customer needs, global customers, global distribution channels, transferable marketing and lead countries. It is not simply

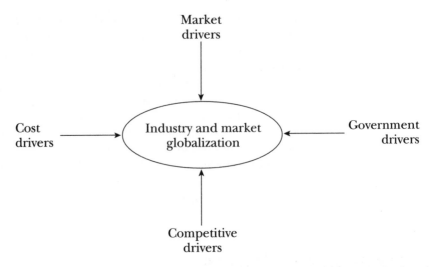

Figure 13.1 A framework describing drivers for internationalization (adapted from Yip, 1992).

a case of a market being global or not global. Managers must seek to establish which, if any, aspects of their market are global.

Common customer needs

Probably the single most important market globalization driver is the extent to which customers in different countries share the same need or want for

Market globalization drivers	Cost globalization drivers
• common customer needs	• global scale economies
• global customers	• steep experience curve effect
• global distribution channels	• sourcing efficiencies
• transferable marketing techniques	• favourable logistics
• presence in lead countries	• differences in country costs (including exchange rates
	• high product development costs
	• fast changing technology
Government globalization drivers	Competitive globalization drivers
• favourable trade policies	• high exports and imports
• compatible technical standards	• competitors from different continents
• common marketing regulations	• interdependence of countries
• government owned competitors and customers;	• competitors globalized
• host government concerns	

Table 13.1 A summary of the globalization drivers.

a product. The extent of shared need will depend upon cultural, economic, climatic, legal and other similarities and differences. There are numerous examples of markets where customer needs are becoming more similar. Examples include motor vehicles, soft drinks, fast food, consumer electronics and computers. The importance of McDonald's, Burger King and Pizza Hut in fast food, of Coca-Cola and Pepsi Cola in soft drinks and of Sony and Panasonic in consumer electronics are all illustrative of converging customer needs in certain markets. Levitt (1983) refers to this similarity of tastes and preference as increasing *market homogenization* – all markets demanding the same products, regardless of their domestic culture and traditional preferences.

Global customers and channels

Global customers purchase products or services in a co-ordinated way from the best global sources. Yip identifies two types of global customers:

1 *national global customers* – customers who seek the best suppliers in the world and then use the product or service in one country, e.g. national defence purchasers who try to source the highest specification weapons and other military hardware from around the world for use by the domestic armed forces;
2 *multinational global customers* – they similarly seek the best suppliers in the world but then use the product or service obtained in many countries, e.g. transnational corporations source components for their products globally to ensure optimal quality standards.

Examples of markets with global customers include automobile components, advertising (advertising agencies) and electronics. Nissan, for example, manufacture motor cars in a number of different locations around the world including Japan, the United Kingdom and Spain but source many components for all of these locations globally. Businesses serving global customers must 'be present in all the customers' major markets' (Yip, 1992).

Alongside global customers there are sometimes global, or more often regional, distribution channels which serve the global customers. Global customers and channels will contribute towards the development of a global market.

Transferable marketing

Transferable marketing describes the extent to which elements of the marketing mix like brand names and promotions can be used globally without local adaptations. Clearly, when adaptation is not required it is indicative of a global market. In this way brands like McDonald's, Coca-Cola and Nike are used globally. Yet advertising for Nike can be both global and locally adapted according to the popularity of different sports in different parts of the world. If marketing is transferable it will favour a global market.

Lead countries

When, as Porter (1990) found, there are certain countries which lead in particular industries, then 'it becomes critical for global competitors to participate in these lead countries in order to be exposed to the sources of innovation.' Lead countries are those that are ahead in product and/or process innovation in their industry. These lead countries help to produce global standards and hence global industries and markets. Japan, for example, has leadership in the consumer electronics industry and leads developments within it, whilst the USA is the lead country in microcomputer and Internet software.

Cost globalization drivers

The potential to reduce costs by global configuration of value-adding activities is an important spur towards the globalization of certain industries. If there are substantial cost advantages to be obtained then an industry will tend to be global.

Global scale economies

When an organization serves a global market then it is able to gain much greater economies of scale than if it serves only domestic or regional markets. Similarly, serving global markets also gives considerable potential for economies of scope. Thus businesses like Procter and Gamble and Unilever who produce household products like detergents gain huge economies of scope in research, product development and marketing.

Key Concepts

Economies of scale and scope
Economies of scale describe the benefits that are gained when increasing volume results in lower unit costs. Although economies of scale can arise in all parts of the value chain, the idea is probably best understood by illustrating it using purchasing as an example. An individual purchasing one single item will pay more per item than a large company buying many of the same item. It is said that the purchaser who is able to purchase in bulk (because of the size and structure of the buyer) enjoys scale economies over smaller organizations who buy in at lower volumes.

Economy of scope is a concept that describes the benefits that can arise in one product or market area as a result of activity in another. For example, research into material properties for the benefit of the NASA space programme (one area of scope) has resulted in advances in other areas such as fabrics, non-stick pans and coatings for aircraft. Organizations who invest heavily in research and development (such as pharmaceutical companies) are amongst those who are always seeking economies of scope – seeking to use breakthroughs in one area to benefit another.

Steep experience curve effect

When there is a steep learning curve in production and marketing, businesses serving global markets will tend to obtain the greatest benefits. In many high tech and service industries there are steep learning curves yielding the greatest benefits to global businesses.

Learning curve

The idea of the learning curve has been used in many areas of life – not just in business. It describes the rate at which an individual or an organization learns to perform a particular task. The gradient of the beginning of the curve is referred to as its 'steepness' and is the most important part. The steeper this first part, the quicker the task is being learned. The general shape of a learning curve is described as *exponential* because the gradient usually decreases along its length as the time taken to perform the task decreases as those performing the task become more accomplished at it.

When a lecturer sits down to mark a batch of exam papers, he must first familiarize himself with the questions and the answers that are expected. Having done that, the first paper will take the longest of all to mark. When the lecturer has internalized all of the questions and answers, the time taken to mark each paper will reduce until the last few papers take the shortest time of all (see Figure 13.2).

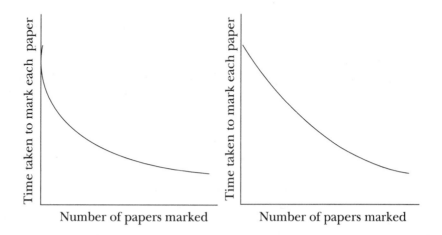

Figure 13.2(a) Steep learning curve – a fast learner.

Figure 13.2(b) Shallow learning curve – a slow learner.

Sourcing efficiencies

If there are efficiency gains to be made by centralized sourcing carried out globally then this will drive an industry towards globalization. Businesses like those in sports apparel and fashion clothing benefit from global sourcing to obtain lowest prices and highest quality standards.

Favourable logistics

If transportation costs comprise a relatively high proportion of sales value, there will be every incentive to concentrate production in few, large facilities. If transport costs are relatively small, such as with consumer electronic goods, production can be located in several (or many) locations which are chosen on the basis of other cost criteria such as land or labour costs.

Differences in country costs

Production costs (materials, labour, etc.) vary from country to country which, like favourable logistics, can stimulate globalization. Thus, countries with lower production costs will tend to attract businesses to locate activities in the country. Many Asian countries have been chosen as centres for production because of their favourable cost conditions. Although countries like Thailand have suffered in some respects because of the devaluation of their currency in 1997–98, from the point of view of being chosen as centres for production, they have benefited.

Fast-changing technology and high product development costs

Product life cycles are shortening as the pace of technological change increases. At the same time research and development costs are increasing in many industries. Such product development costs can only be recouped by high sales in global markets. Domestic markets simply do not yield the volumes of sales required to cover high R&D costs. Thus industries like pharmaceuticals and automobiles face very rapidly changing technology and hypercompetition, together with high development costs. As a consequence they must operate in global markets so as to ensure the volumes of sales necessary to recoup these costs.

Government globalization drivers

Since the Second World War many governments have taken individual and collective action to reduce barriers to global trade.

Favourable trade policies

The World Trade Organization and its predecessor, the General Agreement on Tariffs and Trade, have done much to reduce barriers to trade which have, in the past, hindered globalization of many industries. Although there are still significant barriers to trade in certain areas, the movement towards freedom of trade has been substantial, thus favouring globalization. The growth of customs unions and 'single markets' such as the European Union and the North American Free Trade Area (NAFTA) have also made an important contribution in this regard.

Compatible technical standards and common marketing regulations

Many of the differences in technical standards between countries which hindered globalization in the past have been reduced. For example, telecommunications standards, which have traditionally differed between countries, are increasingly being superseded by international standards. Similarly standards are converging in the pharmaceutical, airline and computing industries which makes it easier to produce globally-accepted products.

There remain important differences in advertising regulations between countries, with the UK regulations among the strictest. Generally, however, these differences are being eroded and this is expected to favour greater globalization.

Government-owned competitors and customers

Government-owned competitors, which often enjoy state subsidies, can act as a stimulus to globalization as they frequently compete with other global competitors, thus being forced to become more efficient and global market oriented. On the other hand, government-owned customers tend to favour domestic suppliers which can act as a barrier to globalization. The privatization of many state-owned businesses in many European countries has reduced this barrier to globalization.

Host government concerns

The attitudes and policies of host government concerns can either hinder or favour globalization. In certain circumstances, host governments may favour the entry of global businesses into domestic industries and markets which will assist globalization. For example, the UK government has, in recent years, done much to attract inward investment by Japanese and Korean companies. The more governments that espouse such policies, the greater will be globalization of an industry. In other cases, host governments will seek to protect industries which they see as strategically important and will attempt to prevent foreign businesses from entry.

Competitive globalization drivers

The greater the strength of the competitive drivers the greater will be the tendency for an industry to globalize. Global competition in an industry will become more intense when:

● there is a high level of import and export activity between countries;

- the competitors in the industry are widely spread (they will often be on different continents);
- the economies of the countries involved are interdependent;
- competitors in the industry are already globalized.

High exports and imports

The higher the level of exports and imports of products and services the greater will be the pressure for globalization of an industry.

Competitors from different continents

The more countries that are represented in an industry and the more widely spread they are, the greater the likelihood of globalization.

Interdependence of countries

If national economies are already relatively interdependent, then this will act as a stimulus for increased globalization. Such interdependence may arise through, for example, multiple trading links in other industries, through being a part of a single market or through being in a shared political alliance

Competitors globalized

If a competitor is already globalized and employing a global strategy then there will be pressure on other businesses in the industry to globalize as well. Globalization in the automotive industry is high because of the pressure on organizations to compete globally. An automobile manufacturer will struggle to survive if it only serves domestic markets.

Using the globalization driver framework

Yip's globalization driver framework provides an extremely useful tool for analysing the degree of globalization of an industry or market. Equally, it makes possible an understanding of which particular aspects of an industry or market are global and which aspects are localized. Each of the drivers must be analysed for the industry and market under consideration and the results of the analysis will play an important role in assisting managers to form the global strategy of their organization. The results will help to determine which features of the strategy are globally standardized and which features are locally adapted.

There are several models which explain the basis of global strategy. This chapter explains the frameworks developed by Porter (1986 and 1990) and Yip (1992). Porter focuses on adapting the generic strategy framework to global conditions and the role of configuration and co-ordination of value activities in securing global competitive advantage. Yip develops the concept of 'Total Global Strategy' based upon his globalization driver framework.

Although these are the models considered in this chapter, interested readers should consider reading the work of Bartlett and Ghoshal (1987 and 1989), Prahalad and Hamel (1986).

Porter's global generic strategies

We learned in Chapter 8 that Porter (1980) argued that competitive advantage rests upon a business selecting and adopting one of the three generic strategies (differentiation, cost leadership or focus) to modify the five competitive forces in its favour so as to earn higher profits than the industry average. In 1986 Porter extended the generic strategy framework to global business. The model suggests that a business operating in international markets has five strategy alternatives (see Figure 13.3). The five strategic postures are defined according to their position in respect to two intersecting continua: the extent to which the industry is globalized (or country-centred horizontal axis) and the breadth of the segments served by the competitors in an industry (which, put simply, means the number of different customer groups served by an industry).

The five strategic postures are:

1 *Global cost leadership* – the business seeks to be the lowest cost producer of a product globally. Globalization provides the opportunity for high volume sales and greater economies of scale and scope than domestic competitors.
2 *Global differentiation* – the business seeks to differentiate products and services globally, often on the basis of a global brand name.
3 *Global segmentation* – this is the global variant of a focus strategy when a single market segment is targeted on a worldwide basis employing either cost leadership or differentiation.
4 *Protected markets* – a business the identifies national markets where its particular business is favoured or protected by the host government.
5 *National responsiveness* – the business adapts its strategy to meet the distinctive needs of local markets (i.e. not a global strategy). Suitable for purely domestic businesses.

The model suffers from similar flaws to those discussed in Chapter 8 relating to the generic strategy framework. As in the case of the conventional understanding of generic strategy, it is possible for a business to pursue a hybrid international strategy. Nissan, for example, concentrates not only on cost control but also on ensuring that it differentiates its products on the basis of their reliability.

Porter's global strategy – configuration and co-ordination of internal activities

One of Porter's most important contributions to understanding global strategy is his work on the global value chain (1986 and 1990). Porter makes the case that global competitive advantage depends upon configuring and co-ordinating the activities of a business in a unique way on a worldwide basis. To put it another way, competitive advantage results from the global scope

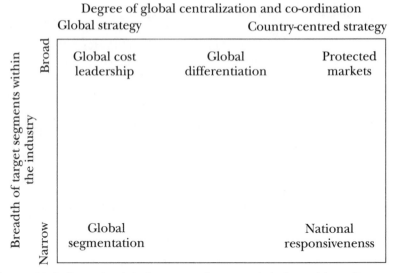

Figure 13.3 Porter's global strategy framework (adapted from Porter,

of an organization's activities and the effectiveness with which it co-ordinates them. Porter (1986, 1990) argues that global competitive advantage depends upon two sets of decisions.

1 *Configuration of value-adding activities* – managers must decide in which nations they will carry out each of the activities in the value chain of their business. Configuration can be broad (involving many countries) of narrow (few countries or just one).

2 *Co-ordination of value-adding activities* – managers must decide the most effective way of co-ordinating value-adding activities which are carried out in different parts of the world.

Configuration and co-ordination present four broad alternatives illustrated in Figure 13.4. In the case of configuration, an organization can choose to disperse its activities to a range of locations around the world or it may choose to concentrate key activities in locations which present certain advantages. Many businesses concentrate the manufacture of their products in countries where costs are low but skill levels are good. Many clothing manufacturers manufacture their products in the Far East where labour costs are low but tailoring standards are high. An organization can decide to co-ordinate its worldwide activities or to manage them locally in each part of the world. The latter approach misses the opportunity for global management economies of scale. For Porter, the 'purest global strategy' is when an organization concentrates key activities in locations giving competitive advantages and co-ordinates activities on a global basis. In the long term, according to Porter, organizations should move towards 'purest global strategy' as far as is practicable.

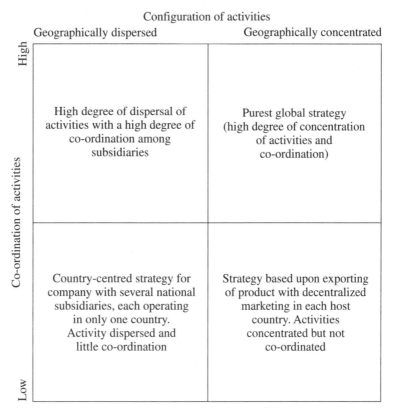

Figure 13.4 Configuration and co-ordination for international strategy (adapted from Porter, 1986)

'Total global strategy'

Yip's stages in total global strategy

Yip (1992) argues that successful global strategy must be based upon a comprehensive analysis of the globalization drivers we encountered above. Managers of a global business must, he contends, evaluate the globalization drivers for their industry and market and must formulate their global strategy on the basis of this analysis. If, for example, they find that customer demand is largely homogeneous for their product then they can produce a largely standardized product for sale throughout the world. If, on the other hand, they find that there are few cost advantages of global concentration of manufacturing because of unfavourable logistics or adverse economies of scale, they may choose to disperse their manufacturing activities around the world to be close to their customers in different parts of the world. Thus the 'total global strategy' of an organization can be a mix of standardization and local adaptation as market and industry conditions dictate.

Yip goes on to identify three stages in developing a 'total global strategy':

1 *Developing a core strategy* – this will, in effect, involve building core competences and generic or hybrid strategy which can potentially give global competitive advantage (see Chapter 8).
2 *Internationalizing the core strategy* – this will be the stage at which the core competences and generic strategy are introduced to international markets and when the organization begins to locate its value-adding activities in locations where competitive advantages like low cost, access to materials or skills are available. This will include choice of which markets the business will enter and the means by which it will enter them.
3 *Globalizing the international strategy* – this stage is based upon co-ordinating and integrating the core competences and strategy on a global basis. It will also include deciding which elements of the strategy are to be standardized and which are to be locally adapted on the basis of the strength of the globalization drivers in the industry and market.

Key strategic decisions

Once a business has developed core competences and strategies which can potentially be exploited globally, the decisions must be made as to where and how to employ them. Initial moves into overseas markets will involve market development, as such markets and segments can be regarded as new to the business. The initial market development may then be followed by product development and, perhaps, diversification (see Chapter 8).

When a business enters international and global markets it will be necessary to build new competences, alongside those which have brought about domestic competitive advantage. These new competences could well be in the areas of global sourcing and logistics, and global management.

The globalization of a business does not happen overnight. It may well involve entry to key countries with the largest markets first, followed by entry to less important countries later. In the initial stages of globalization the key decisions are usually as follows:

1 Which countries are to be entered first?
2 In which countries are value-adding activities to be located?
3 Which market development strategies are to be employed to gain entry to chosen overseas markets?

Market entry decisions

Decision criteria

The decision as to which countries and markets are to be entered first will be based upon a number of important factors:

- *The potential size of the market* – is the market for the product in the country likely to be significant? This will, in turn, be determined by the factors following.
- *Economic factors* – are income levels adequate to ensure that significant numbers of people are likely to be able to afford the product?
- *Cultural and linguistic factors* – is the culture of the country likely to favour acceptance of the product to be offered?
- *Political factors* – what are the factors which may limit entry to markets in the host country?
- *Technological factors* – are levels of technology adequate to support provision of the product in the host market and are technological standards compatible?

To begin with, a business will choose to enter markets in those countries where the above conditions are most favourable.

Location of value-adding activities

Managers must determine within which countries they will locate key value-adding activities of their business. They will seek to gain cost, skill and resource advantages. In other words, they will attempt to locate activities in countries where there are production advantages to be gained.

Such advantages depend upon:

- *wage levels* – low wage levels will assist in low production costs;
- *skill levels* – there must be suitably skilled labour available;
- *availability of materials* – suitable materials must be accessible;
- *infrastructure* – transport and communications must be favourable to the logistics of the business.

The existence of these conditions within a country will, in turn, depend upon:

- *economic factors* – level of economic development, wage levels, exchange rate conditions;
- *social factors* – attitudes to work, levels of education and training;
- *political factors* – legislation favouring investment, etc.;

- *technological factors* – levels of technology and transport and communications infrastructure of the country.

Market development methods

Once decisions have been made as to which countries' markets are to be entered and where value-adding activities are to be located, the task for management becomes the determination of which method of development to employ to enter another country. Broadly speaking a business can choose either *internal* or *external methods* for development of overseas markets (see Chapter 11). Internal methods are usually slower, but tend to entail lower risk. External methods involve the business developing relationships with other businesses. Internal methods of development include direct exporting, overseas manufacturing, local assembly and establishing overseas subsidiaries. External methods include joint ventures and alliances, mergers and acquisitions, franchising and licensing. The choice of method will depend upon a number of factors:

- the size of the investment required or the amount of investment capital available;
- knowledge of the country to be entered and potential risk involved (e.g. of political instability);
- revenue and cash flow forecasts and expectations;
- operating cost considerations;
- control considerations (some investment options will have implications for the parent to control activity in the host country).

Internal development methods

Internal methods are based upon the organization exploiting its own resources and competences and involve the organization carrying out some of its activities overseas. This may be exporting its products or setting up some form of production facilities abroad. The advantages of internal methods of development are that they maximize future revenue from sales abroad and they make possible a high degree of control over overseas activities. On the other hand, they can involve significant risk if knowledge of the host country and its markets are limited, and they may require considerable direct investment from the business.

The major internal methods of development overseas are direct exporting and development of an overseas facility.

Direct exporting

Direct exporting is the transfer of goods (or services) across national borders from the home production facility. Such exporting may simply be shipping a product or, as sales increase, a sales offices may be set up overseas. Exporting, at its simplest, is the marketing abroad of a product made in an organization's home country.

To avoid some of the pitfalls of direct exporting (like lack of local knowledge and access to distribution channels) many exporting businesses make use of local agents or distribute their products through locally based retailers (known as a *piggyback* distribution arrangement).

Overseas production or assembly

Organizations may choose to manufacture or assemble their product overseas. There are a number of reasons for direct investment. Transport costs for the finished product may be so high as to discourage exporting or the business wishes to take advantage of local cost advantages. In some industries, direct investment may be an appropriate option to circumvent import restrictions put in place by host governments.

Internal development may involve establishing a foreign subsidiary of the business. This is the case when it is favourable for the parent company to have total control of its overseas operations, decision-making and profits. Such a subsidiary may carry out the full range of activities of the parent business or it may be only a manufacturing or marketing subsidiary.

External development methods

External methods of development involve the organization entering into relationships with businesses in a host country. External development methods can take the form of alliances or joint ventures, mergers or acquisitions, or franchises (see Chapter 11 for a discussion of these topics). Such methods have the advantages of providing local knowledge, potentially reducing risks, and reducing investment costs (except in the case of mergers or acquisitions). The major disadvantages (again except in the case of mergers and acquisitions) are reduced revenues and reduced control of activities as optimal income is traded off against the advantage of lower financial exposure.

International alliances and joint ventures

Alliances and joint ventures allow a business to draw upon the skills, local knowledge, resources and competences of a locally based company. They reduce the risks of entry to overseas markets by providing local knowledge and they help reduce investment costs. The Honda–Rover alliance (1979–94) provided Rover with access to Honda's technology and reputation and gave Honda access to the European market via Rover's inside knowledge and production facilities (see the Honda Rover case study in Part V of this book).

International mergers and acquisitions

A business may use mergers or acquisitions to enter overseas markets. Such mergers and acquisitions give a business access to the knowledge, resources and competences of a business based in the host country, thus reducing some of the risks of market entry.

International franchising and licensing

A franchise is an arrangement under which a franchisor supplies a franchisee with a tried-and-tested brand name, products and expertise in return for the payment of a proportion of profits or sales. The major advantage to the franchisor is that the risk, investment and operating costs of entering overseas markets are reduced considerably. At the same time the franchisee can contribute their local knowledge whilst also benefiting from the lower risks associated with an established business idea. Much of Burger King's expansion overseas has come through franchise development.

Licensing is similar to franchising but involves a producer transferring certain rights to a licensee for the sole use in a host country of its established brand, recipe, registered design or similar piece of intellectual property. The licensee pays the licensor a royalty for the use of the intellectual property and, as with franchising, gains from the established market position of the brand. Licensing is widely used in brewing and in some scientific industries.

Summary

The focus of global strategy is the attainment of global competitive advantage. Many industries and markets are becoming increasingly global, partly as a result of external factors but also as a result of the strategies of businesses themselves. Global strategy, like domestic strategy, is centred on the core competences of the business itself but it is equally dependent upon an understanding of which aspects of the organization's industry and market are global and which require local adaptation. Yip's (1992) globalization driver framework provides managers with an essential set of tools for beginning to understand the nature and extent of globalization in their particular industry and markets. Porter (1986 and 1990) provides insight into the importance of global configuration and co-ordination of value-adding activities in achieving and sustaining competitive advantage while Yip (1992) develops the concept of 'total global strategy' to explain how a worldwide approach to strategy can be developed. Finally, the methods by which organizations can develop global strategy in other countries have been explained.

It is to be remembered that the global business environment is particularly dynamic and that global strategy will have to be constantly adjusted and adapted as circumstances change if competitive advantage is to be sustained and developed. The use of the frameworks developed in this chapter make it possible for managers constantly to monitor and analyse their global environment and to develop global strategy accordingly.

1 What does the term 'globalization' mean?
2 Distinguish between globalization and internationalization.
3 Explain each of Yip's globalization drivers.
4 Explain how Porter develops the generic strategy framework to apply to global strategy. What does the concept of a 'global hybrid strategy' add to the framework?
5 Explain the importance of configuration and co-ordination of value-adding activities to global strategy.
6 Discuss the ways in which a business may develop a 'total global strategy'.
7 Distinguish between international franchising and licensing.
8 Discuss the advantages and disadvantages of different market entry methods. Explain why Burger King may have chosen its particular approach.

References and further reading

Bartlett, C. and Ghoshal, S. (1987) Managing across borders: new organizational responses. *Sloan Management Review*, Fall, 45–53.

Bartlett, C. and Ghoshal, S. (1989) *Managing Across Borders: The Transnational Solution.* Cambridge, MA: Harvard Business School Press.

Douglas, S.P. and Wind, Y. (1987) The myth of globalization. *Columbia Journal of World Business*, Winter, 19–29.

Doz, Y. (1986) *Strategic Management in Multinational Companies.* Pergamon Press.

Hamel, G. and Prahalad, C.K. (1985) Do you really have a global strategy? *Harvard Business Review*, July/August.

Heene, A. and Sanchez, R. (eds) (1997) *Competence-Based Strategic Management.* New York: John Wiley.

Henzler, H. and Rall, W. (1986) Facing up to the globalization challenge. *McKinsey Quarterly*, Winter.

Levitt, T. (1983) The globalization of markets. *Harvard Business Review*, May/June.

Mintzberg, H., Quinn, J.B. and Ghoshal, S. (1995) *The Strategy Process: Concepts, Contexts and Cases*, European Edition. Englewood Cliffs, NJ: Prentice Hall.

Porter, M.E. (1980) *Competitive Strategy: Techniques for Analysing Industries and Competitors.* New York: Free Press.

Porter, M.E. (1985) *Competitive Advantage.* New York: Free Press.

Porter, M.E. (1986a) *Competition in Global Business.* Cambridge, MA: Harvard University Press.

Porter, M.E. (1986b) Changing patterns of international competition. *California Management Review*, 28, No. 2, Winter, 9–40.

Porter, M.E. (1990) *The Competitive Advantage of Nations*. New York: Free Press.

Prahalad, C.K. and Doz, Y.L. (1986) *The Multinational Mission: Balancing Local Demands and Global Vision*. New York: Free Press.

Prahalad, C.K. and Hamel, G. (1990) The core competence of the corporation. *Harvard Business Review*, 79–91.

Yip, G.S. (1992) *Total Global Strategy – Managing for Worldwide Competitive Advantage*. Englewood Cliffs, NJ: Prentice Hall.

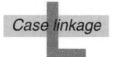
Case linkage

Questions for the Dansk Tyggegummi Fabrik A/S case study.

1 Identify the international entry strategies employed by DTF.
2 Suggest reasons why DTF made a direct investment in Russia (initially with the packaging plant) whilst pursuing alliances in some other countries.
3 Suggest reasons why DTF increased its investment in Russia with its production plant in Novgorod.
4 To what extent are the markets for DTF's products homogenized?
5 In what ways did DTF modify its marketing activities to account for regional and national differences?
6 To what extent was DTF's marketing in the UK successful?

Questions for the Honda Rover case study.

1 Describe some of the factors that led to the internationalization of the motor industry.
2 Why did some companies opt for direct investment whilst others chose joint ventures.
3 How might Honda have reduced the risk of the joint venture falling apart in 1994?

Chapter 14

Social responsibility and business ethics

Introduction

Business ethics is one of the most argued-about areas of business research. Almost every possible position is reflected in the literature. This chapter aims to set out an impartial discussion of the subject beginning with an introduction to the issues surrounding the debate about the relationships between business and society. The stockholder and stakeholder positions are discussed. The stakeholder position is presented as a kind of social contract and the ways in which stakeholders are classified are discussed. The debate is explored further using Donaldson and Preston's (1995) framework for understanding the stakeholder debate. The nature of stakeholder concerns are presented using Campbell's (1997) taxonomy and the strategic postures that business can adopt with respect to social concerns are outlined. Finally, the ways in which businesses discharge their social responsibility are discussed.

Objectives

After studying this chapter, students should be able to:

- understand the stockholder and stakeholder positions as descriptors of the business relationship to society;
- describe the ways in which stakeholders have been classified;
- describe the instrumental and normative approaches to the stakeholder relationship;
- explain the environmental and ethical concerns of stakeholders;
- describe the strategic postures that businesses can adopt in respect to social issues;
- discuss the mechanisms by which businesses discharge their social responsibilities.

Business and its relationship to society

Introduction

Any regular reader of the news will be aware of a trend over recent years towards an increasing awareness of the behaviour of business in respect to what have become known as 'ethical' or 'social' issues. Alleged 'bad' behaviour such as irresponsible environmental behaviour, the way that employees are treated, suspect product safety and responses to accidents like oil-spills are often reported and discussed in some depth in the press and on television.

Events such as these raise an important strategic question: 'What is the precise nature of a business's relationship to society?' The traditional 'economic theory of the firm' posits the notion that businesses exist primarily to make profits for their owners. Some writers in this field have taken the view that the only moral behaviour of business is that which is dedicated to maximizing profits for its shareholders (see for example Friedman, 1970). Others have adopted the diametrically opposite position – that businesses have a moral obligation to those constituencies from which they directly or indirectly benefit (see for example Clarkson, 1995; Evan and Freeman, 1993; Freeman, 1994). This area of argument has been called the stakeholder–stockholder debate.

The stockholder position

The stockholder position on business's relationship to society argues that businesses exist primarily for their owners (usually shareholders). Accordingly, any business behaviour that renders profit performance suboptimal is not only theft from shareholders but will also, eventually, lead to a level of business performance that will harm all of the stakeholders (employees, suppliers, etc.).

In what has become a well known (some would say infamous) article, in 1970 the Nobel Laureate Professor Milton Friedman contended that 'the moral obligation of business is to increase its profits.' Friedman argues that the one and only obligation of company directors (who are the legal agents of shareholders' financial interests) is to act in such a way as to maximize the financial rate of return on the owners' shares. The capitalist system upon which the Western economies is based rests in large part upon the presupposition that investments made in shares (e.g. in pension funds and unit trusts) will perform well. The profitable performance of shares lies in an increase in the shares' value and in the rate of dividend per share – objectives that can only be served by financial profits.

Proponents of stockholder theory argue that because the only moral duty of directors is to maximize shareholder wealth then the activities of business beyond profit-making are actually of no concern of other stakeholders. The intellectual pedigree of this view of social responsibility can be traced back over two hundred years.

The classical economic philosophy of Adam Smith (Smith, 1776) concerns the maximization of benefit to society through the economic mechanism whereby all individuals and businesses act freely in their own economic best interests. Smith's 'invisible hand' principle shows how, when each individual and business is free of external influence to make economic decisions, then ultimately everybody in society will benefit. Profitable businesses both stimulate economic growth in the macroeconomy and increase employment. Increased rates of employment, in turn, stimulate spending power in the economy and, hence, businesses further increase their profits. If this virtuous cycle can be maintained, then society becomes prosperous and the net effect is very positive.

Example

> **Stockholder theory and my car**
> I own a car and the state in which I keep it is none of your business. You may think that my car is dirty, that it is unfashionable, slow and badly maintained but your opinion matters not because the car is mine. I paid for it and risked my hard-earned money in buying it. The only purpose of the car is to serve me. You are welcome to express your opinion on my car, but I am at liberty to reject that opinion.

The stakeholder position

The stakeholder position posits that organizations, like individual people, are citizens of society. Citizenship carries with it certain *rights*, from which we benefit, but also certain *obligations*. Evidently, we enjoy the benefits of society, such as civil peace, freedom of molestation under the rule of law, the right to own and enjoy our property and so on. In return, we accept our obligations – both legal and social. Legally, we collectively agree to obey the law, to pay our taxes and to respect authority. Socially, most of us accept that society works best when we accord each other certain basic civilities. We apologize when we bump into somebody in a corridor, we sympathize with and comfort those going through hard times and we celebrate with each other when one of us gets good news.

In other words, there is a reciprocation package. If we wish to continue to enjoy the benefits of citizenship, then we must, in exchange, also accept our responsibilities. Turning to business, it is obvious that businesses enjoy certain benefits from society. They gain finance capital and employees from society and they rely on the continuing support of customers, local communities, suppliers and others. The stakeholder view of the business–society relationship argues that because businesses benefit from the goodwill of society, they owe certain duties in return.

The implications of this proposition are far-reaching. In essence, stakeholder theory argues that shareholders are neither the sole owners of a business nor the sole beneficiaries of its activities. Whilst shareholders are undeniably one stakeholder group, they are far from being the only group who expect to benefit from business activity and, accordingly, are just one of those groups who have a legitimate right to influence a company's strategic objectives.

Example

Stakeholder theory and my car
Although I own a car and it exists in large part to serve me, you have a legitimate right to comment upon its condition. Your right to express your opinion and my responsibility to hear your views rest upon certain key observations. Firstly, you may have to look at it and a dirty and rusty car may offend your conditioned sensibilities. Secondly, if my car is badly maintained, it may represent a potential hazard to you or your family. The brakes may fail as you are crossing the road, or the steering may fail resulting in my crashing into you. Thirdly, you may need a lift in my car and the internal mess and smell may soil your clothes or be in some other way offensive to you. All in all, although the car is legally mine by ownership, I take your concerns into account in my keeping of the car and modify my behaviour accordingly.

One way of conceptualizing stakeholder theory is as a *social contract*. Under a social contract, social institutions (such as governments or businesses) can only continue to enjoy social legitimacy if they continually modify their policies and activities to accord with societal opinion. We can readily appreciate that this must be the case for a democratically elected government as political parties seeking office offer policies that they feel will accord with the electorate's aspirations. If, during a government's term of office, policy objectives diverge from those of the electorate, the probability that they will be removed from office at the next election is increased.

Key Concepts

Social contract
Social contract theory posits the notion that any social institution exists alongside its constituencies via a social contract. The concept is a very old one but successive thinkers since the seventeenth century have modified our understanding of it. The English philosophers Thomas Hobbes

(1588–1679) and John Locke (1632–1704) developed the theory to explain the relationship between a government and the people over which it governs. In the twentieth century, the theory was modified to help to explain the relationship between powerful business organizations and the stakeholders that they can influence (see for example Rawls, 1971; Donaldson, 1982).

The essence of the theory is one of reciprocal responsibility. The constituency agrees to accept the authority of the powerful institution whilst the institution agrees to act in the best interests of its constituencies. If either party breaks the terms of the contract, then, it is argued, the nature of the contract is destroyed.

In respect to the business–stakeholder relationship, a social contract is said to exist between a powerful business organization and those groups in society upon whom it relies. The stakeholders (in effect) agree to support the activities of the organization (say as employees, customers, etc.) as long as the organization acts in a manner that is acceptable to the stakeholders.

The problem is, of course, that businesses are not subject to election by their constituents. Accordingly, according to social contract theory, businesses act in such a way so as to accord with their stakeholders' concerns

Ways of classifying stakeholders

We encountered the idea of stakeholders in Chapter 1 where we defined a stakeholder as *any person or party that can affect or be affected by the activities and policies of an organization.*

However, given the broad range of parties that are included in most definitions of 'stakeholder', there are bound to be difficulties in formulating strategy if all stakeholder opinions are to be treated with equal weight. Who could honestly argue, for example, that the owner of a local bar should or does have the same influence over strategy as the chief executive or a majority shareholder? It seems, therefore, that not all stakeholders are equal. A number of ways of classifying stakeholders have been advanced and these are examined in the next part of the chapter.

Criteria for distinguishing between stakeholders

In addition to the power–interest map, other writers in the literature have attempted to classify stakeholders according to criteria based on how stakeholders relate to the organization's activities.

Narrow and wide stakeholders

Evan and Freeman (1993) classified stakeholders as *narrow* and *wide* where the criteria for selection into each category is the extent to which stakeholders are affected by the organization's policies and strategies. Narrow stakeholders (those that are the most affected by the organization's policies) will usually include shareholders, management, employees, suppliers and customers that are dependent on the organization's output. Wider stakeholders (those less affected) may typically include government, less-dependent customers, the wider community (as opposed to local communities) and other peripheral groups. The Evans and Freeman model may lead us to conclude that an organization has a higher degree of responsibility and accountability to its narrower stakeholders. It may be excused for paying less attention to the concerns of its wider stakeholders.

Primary and secondary stakeholders

Clarkson (1995) drew a distinction between *primary* and *secondary* stakeholders. According to Clarkson, 'A primary stakeholder group is one without whose continuing participation the corporation cannot survive as a going concern.' Hence, whereas Evans and Freeman view stakeholders as *being* (or not being) *influenced by* an organization, Clarkson sees the important distinction as being between those that *influence* an organization and those that do not. For most organizations, primary stakeholders (those most vital to an organization) will include government (through its tax and legislative influence), customers and suppliers. Secondary stakeholders (those without whose 'continuing participation' the company can probably still exist) will therefore include communities and, in some cases, the management of the organization itself.

Active and passive stakeholders

Mahoney (1994) divides stakeholders between those that are *active* and those that are *passive*. Active stakeholders are those that seek to participate in the organization's activities. These stakeholders may or may not be actually a part of the organization's formal structure. Management and employees obviously fall into this active category but some parties from outside an organization may also fall into this category such as regulators (in the case of UK privatized utilities) and environmental pressure groups. Passive stakeholders, in contrast, are those that do not normally seek to participate in an organization's policy-making. This is not to say that passive stakeholders are any less interested nor any less powerful, but that they do not seek to take an active part in the organization's strategy. Passive stakeholders will normally include most shareholders, government and local communities.

Descriptions of the organization–stakeholder relationship

Donaldson and Preston's framework

Whatever model of stakeholder model one finds most appealing, we turn now to the question as to *why* organizations do or do not take account of stakeholder concerns in their strategy formulation and implementation. A parallel can be drawn between the ways in which organizations view their stakeholders and the ways in which individual people consider (or do not consider) the views of other people. Some people are intensely concerned about others' opinions of them whilst other people seem to have little or no regard for others' concerns. Furthermore, the reasons *why* individuals care about others' concerns will also vary.

In attempting to address this issue, Donaldson and Preston (1995) drew a distinction between two motivations describing *why* organizations accede to stakeholder concerns. They describe these two contrasting motivations as the *instrumental* and the *normative*.

The instrumental view of stakeholders

The *instrumental* view of stakeholder relations suggests that organizations take stakeholder opinions into account only insofar as they are consistent with other, more important, economic objectives (e.g. profit maximization). Accordingly, it may be that a business modifies its objectives in the light of environmental concerns *but only* because acquiescence to stakeholder opinion is the best way of optimizing profit or achieving other business success. If the loyalty or commitment of an important primary or active stakeholder group is threatened, it is likely that the organization will modify its objectives because not to do so would threaten to reduce its economic performance (e.g. profitability). It follows from the instrumental stakeholder approach that an organization's values are guided by its stakeholders' opinions – it may not have any inherent moral values of its own except for the overriding profit motive.

Example

The instrumental view and my car
Given that I now accept your legitimate right to offer your opinion on the state of my car, I take a moment of quiet reflection to examine my motives. I come to the honest opinion that the reason why I accede to your observations is because your opinions are important to me, but this, in turn, is because of your ability to influence another of my key objectives. It so happens that your dad is the vice-chancellor of the

University of Northumbria which just happens to be the institution at which I am employed. The outcome is that I do take your views into account in my management of my car, but *only because* I think that you may say nice things about me to your eminent father, which may, in turn, hasten my promotion to Principal Lecturer.

The normative view of stakeholders

The *normative* view of stakeholder theory differs from the instrumental view because it describes not *what is*, but what *should be*. The most commonly cited moral framework used in describing that which *should be* is derived from the philosophy of the German ethical thinker Immanuel Kant (1724–1804). Kant's moral philosophy centred around the notion of civil duties which, Kant argued, are important in maintaining and increasing the net good in society. According to Kant, we each have a moral duty to each other in respect of taking account of each others' concerns and opinions. Not to do so will result in the atrophy of social cohesion and will ultimately lead to everybody being (morally and possibly economically) worse off.

Extending this argument to stakeholder theory, the normative view argues that organizations should accommodate stakeholder concerns not because of what the organization can 'get out of it' for its own profit, but because it observes its moral duty to each stakeholder. The normative view sees stakeholders as ends in themselves and not as merely instrumental to the achievement of other ends.

Example

The normative view and my car
Given that I now accept your legitimate right to offer your opinion on the state of my car, I take a moment of quiet reflection to examine my motives. You are not the offspring of the vice-chancellor of the University of Northumbria, in fact you are not important in any way whatsoever. You have nothing to offer me in exchange for my acknowledgement of your opinions on my car. Nevertheless, it is my conviction that, because you are a human being, then you are, by virtue of that fact, worthy of listening to. I hear your opinions on the state of my car simply because you are a moral end-in-yourself. In other words, I care what you think because I see you and your concerns as inherently worthy of my attention.

Stakeholder concerns

The social concerns of stakeholders

If it can be coherently argued that organizations do (for whatever reason) have some degree of responsibility to their constituencies, then we now turn to the issues that are most frequently raised as being areas of concern. It has been noted (Campbell, 1997) that the most frequently mentioned stakeholder concerns can be divided into two broad categories:

1 concerns over the organization's attitude towards the *natural environment*; and
2 concerns over the *ethical behaviour* of organizations.

In describing how these broad categories are linked and subdivided, a framework (or taxonomy) has been developed (Table 14.1).

All of the above areas (environmental and ethical concerns) are matters for which organizations are (according to stakeholder theory proponents) accountable. Given that different stakeholders have raised these matters as being of concern, then all of them are part of the portfolio of issues for which organizations are, in part, responsible to society.

Strategic postures in social responsibility

The term *social responsibility* describes the persuasion that organizations are not free to act as though these concerns (above) did not exist. However, it is evident that not all organizations espouse the same attitudes in respect to social and environmental concern. Four general degrees of responsiveness have been identified – organizations that are:

- socially obstructive;
- socially obligative;
- socially responsive;
- socially contributive.

Socially obstructive organizations

Some businesses are actively *socially obstructive*. This description can be applied to organizations that actively resist any pressures or attempts to modify pure business objectives in the light of social concern. Such organizations may resist attempts to make them abide even to the minimum legal standards of behaviour – behaviour which may be followed by denial and an attempt to keep 'interfering' bodies out of their business. Some have

Key area	Subsidiary concerns	Examples of personal opinion areas
Environmental concern	Concern over the state of natural resources	• Energy resources and conservation • Mineral resources and conservation • Extinction and over-fishing
	Concern over the way in which business activities affect environmental pollution	• Global warming ('greenhouse' effect) • Ozone layer depletion • Health concerns (e.g. skin cancer, asthma) • Industrial emissions (into rivers, etc.) • Rubbish and waste (land-fill, nuclear, etc.) • 'Acid' rain (from coal power station emissions)
Ethical concern	Concern arising over the asymmetric nature of markets	• Third World debt and its repayment terms (to First World banks) • Fair-trade' between rich First World companies and poorer Third World producers. • Multinational companies' alleged 'exploitation' of weaker Third World economies
	Concern arising over the business's alleged responsibility to society	• Community involvement • Marketing practices (e.g. corporate sponsorships and advertising) • Animal 'cruelty' issues • Product health and safety • Compensation and reparations (e.g. drugs, oil spills)
	Concern arising from the internal and industry activities of the business	• Employment practices (employment rate of minorities, disabled people, women, etc.) • Health and safety in the workplace (over and above the legal minimum) • Treatment of suppliers, customers and other stakeholders (e.g. days taken to pay smaller creditors)

Table 14.1 A taxonomy of concern (after Campbell, 1997, p. 429).

argued that tobacco manufacturers fall into this category as in order to protect their sales of cigarettes, they may effectively deny that tobacco causes as much harm as some health professionals have suggested may be the case. Such companies would presumably argue that it would not be in their strategic interests to respond to stakeholder concerns.

Socially obligative organizations

Some businesses observe no more than their minimum *social obligations*. This description can be applied to organizations that are prepared to abide by whatever restrictions are placed upon them by governments, in other words, the legal minimum. They are unwilling to give credence to any pressure or lobby groups which, in the opinion of the organization, do not have any statutory influence over them.

Socially responsive organizations

The third group are those that are *socially responsive*. These organizations submit to minimum legal standards for corporate behaviour towards society and the environment, but go further than socially obligative organizations. The difference is that socially responsive organizations will do more to address people's concerns if pressurized to do so by stakeholders such as pressure groups.

Socially contributive organizations

The final group are those organizations which seek to make a *social contribution*. This description can be applied to organizations that willingly do all they reasonably can to extend their social and environmental involvement. In this sense, such organizations seek to make a positive contribution to the communities they serve, to help protect the natural environment and to avoid any unethical business practices. Some social contribution organizations may exist primarily for the purpose of promoting social responsibility and ethical business practice.

Mechanisms of social responsibility discharge

Given the extent to which organizations vary in their postures towards social responsibility, it is not surprising that a range of mechanisms have been adopted to express such responsibility. Essentially, this section is concerned with answering the question, 'How do organizations express their concerns over social issues?'

The answer is that there are a number of mechanisms by which organizations discharge their responsibility to society (or their alleged responsibility). The most frequently adopted mechanisms are:

- modifying the mission statement or other explicit declaration;
- adopting prescriptive codes of conduct;
- issuing publicly available reports on the social impact of business activity or including social information in regular corporate reports;
- issuing a separate social audit of the organization in addition to the mandatory financial statements.

We will consider these matters briefly in turn.

Modified mission statements

In Chapter 1 we learned that some organizations publish a mission state-ment as a vehicle by which stakeholders can be informed about what are the most important strategic objectives of the enterprise. Accordingly, it can generally be assumed that if an issue is mentioned specifically in a mission statement, then the organization considers it to be of strategic importance. Hence, a mention of a social or ethical concern in the statement is a good indication to stakeholders that the issue is to given very high promi-nence.

One enthusiastic adopter of this mechanism is Body Shop plc, the retailer of 'cruelty-free' cosmetics and health products. Its mission state-ment begins with the words, 'To dedicate our business to the pursuit of social and environmental change,' and continues, 'To passionately cam-paign for the protection of the environment, human and civil rights, and against animal testing within the cosmetics and toiletries industry.'

Body Shop's explicit statement is, however, rare. Most adopters of revised mission statements are much less direct. They may, for example, contain a clause stating that they will be fair to employees, pay their suppliers on time or make a contribution (albeit undefined) to the community.

Ethical 'codes of conduct'

Some organizations go a step further than modifying their mission state-ment by issuing a code of business ethics. This is a document which codifies how the organization intends to act towards its stakeholders. Many of the UK's largest companies have issued such a document, including British Airways, Barclays and Lloyds Banks, Whitbread, British Aerospace, Phillips Petroleum includes some leading business people. The Institute recom-mends that organizations issue statements in respect of ethical practice regarding:

● relations with customers;
● relations with shareholders and other investors;
● relations with employees;
● relations with suppliers;
● relations with the government and the local community;
● the environment;
● taxation;
● relations with competitors;
● issues relating to international business;
● behaviour in relation to mergers and take-overs;

- ethical issues concerning directors and managers;
- compliance and verification.

Corporate social reporting

Social reporting is the practice wherein a company voluntarily informs its stakeholders of its behaviour in respect to ethical and social concerns. The point here is that organizations have no legal obligations to make such disclosures but they nevertheless do. The disclosures may be of a social or environmental nature and, it has been argued, are designed to legitimize the organization's behaviour in the eyes of potentially critical stakeholders (see for example Guthrie and Parker, 1989; Gray *et al.*, 1995).

Social reporting disclosures can be carried in a number of company-produced documents. The practice is more established amongst larger companies who have more complex stakeholder relationships than smaller ones. Whilst the annual report remains the primary vehicle for social disclosure for most companies, some companies produce separate environmental or social reports (see next section). These are non-mandatory documents that set out in more detail how the company has behaved in respect to environmental or social concerns over the past year.

Social accounts

Like other forms of social disclosure, the production of social accounts is entirely voluntary. Social accounts are designed to report on the company's impacts (through its activities) on each of its social constituencies. Accordingly, those who prepare these statements must go to some length to find out and, if possible, quantify the extent to which the company has benefited or detracted from its stakeholders.

In order to add credibility to the social accounts, some companies have them independently audited in the same manner as their financial statements are. Audits have tended to be carried out by specialized consultancy groups, but the larger financial auditors are gradually picking up on social audit as demand for the service grows.

Social accounts are, however, relatively new to the world of business ethics. Early adopters included several alternative trading organizations (ATOs – businesses which exist to pursue ethical purposes like 'fair' Third World trade), but growth in the practice is expected amongst more mainstream businesses.

Summary

This chapter has introduced the areas of debate within the subject of business ethics and social responsibility. It discussed the stockholder and stakeholder positions and the stakeholder position is explored in some detail. The nature of stakeholder concerns was discussed and the ways in which companies can respond to social and ethical issues were explained.

Review and Discuss

1 Describe the stockholder position of a business's relationship to society.
2 What is a stakeholder?
3 Explain what is meant by a social contract.
4 Describe three ways in which stakeholders can be classified.
5 Define and distinguish between the instrumental and normative understandings of the stakeholder relationship.
6 Describe the four positions that organizations can adopt in respect to their social responsibility.
7 What are social accounts?
8 What is corporate social reporting?

References and further reading

Campbell, D. J. (1997). *Organizations and the Business Environment.* Oxford: Butterworth-Heinemann.

Clarkson, M.B.E. (1995) A stakeholder framework for analysing and evaluating corporate social performance. *Academy of Management Review*, 20, No. 1, 92–117.

Donaldson, T. and Preston, L. E. (1995) The stakeholder theory of the corporation: concepts, evidence and implications. *Academy of Management Review*, 20, No. 1, 65–91.

Donaldson, T. (1982) *Corporate Morality.* Englewood Cliffs, NJ: Prentice-Hall.

Evan, W.M. and Freeman, R.E. (1993) A stakeholder theory of the modern corporation: Kantian capitalism. In Cryssides, G.D. and Kaler, J.H. (eds) *An Introduction to Business Ethics.* Englewood Cliffs: Prentice-Hall, 254–266.

Freeman, R.E. (1994). The politics of stakeholder theory: some future directions. *Business Ethics Quarterly*, 4, No. 4, 409–421.

Friedman, M. (1970). The social responsibility of business is to increase its profits. *New York Times Magazine*, 13 Sept, 7–13.

Gray, R., Kouhy, R. and Lavers, S. (1995) Corporate social and environmental reporting. A review of the literature and a longitudinal study of UK disclosures. *Accounting, Auditing and Accountability Journal*, 8, No. 2, 47–77.

Guthrie, J.E. and Parker, L.D. (1989) Corporate social reporting: a rebuttal of legitimacy theory. *Accounting and Business Research*, 9, No. 76, 343–352.

Mahoney, J. (1994) Stakeholder responsibilities: turning the ethical tables. *Business Ethics – A European Review*, 3, No. 4, 212–218.

Rawls, J. (1971) *A Theory of Justice.* Cambridge, MA: Harvard University Press.

Smith, A. (1776) (Glasgow Edition, 2 vols, 1982) *An Inquiry into the Nature & Causes of The Wealth of Nations.* Glasgow: Liberty Fund.

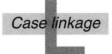
Case linkage

Questions for the Ben & Jerry's case study.

1 Identify the stakeholders that Ben & Jerry's and Häagen Dazs had in common at the time of the controversy.
2 Which of Donaldson and Preston's view of stakeholders did Häagen Dazs have at the time of the confrontation? Provide evidence from the case for your answer.
3 Which of Donaldson and Preston's view of stakeholders did Ben & Jerry's have in the case? Provide evidence from the case for your answer.
4 Comment upon the ethical behaviour of the two 'sides' of the Pillsbury dough boy campaign. Which side, if either, was right?

Chapter 15

Strategic management – present and future trends

Introduction

Strategic management is a comparatively young discipline, if indeed it can be called a discipline when it is in fact a multi- and interdisciplinary field of study. Strategists draw heavily upon disciplines as diverse as organization theory and behaviour, human resource management, economics, accounting and finance, and marketing as well as attempting to formulate their own theories and analytical frameworks. The future of strategic management will undoubtedly be longer than its past. For this reason, the theories, tools and techniques employed in strategic management in many cases are far from fully formulated. The subject will continue to evolve and the sophistication of its methods and methodology will develop and improve over time.

At the heart of strategic management is the desire to explain why certain businesses achieve competitive advantage through superior performance. The view in the 1980s was that competitive advantage was based upon the competitive positioning of the organization in its environment based upon highly systematic planning (Argenti, 1965; Porter, 1980, 1985). In the 1990s this view has been challenged by strategists who believe that in a turbulent business environment, strategy can be developed incrementally and that competitive advantage depends upon the ability of the business to build core competences which cannot be easily replicated by competitors (Prahalad and Hamel, 1990, 1994; Heene and Sanchez, 1997; Kay, 1993). This chapter, intended to be a summary of the book, serves the dual purpose of identifying the origins of strategic management before considering recent developments which will shape its future.

Objectives

After studying this chapter, students should be able to:

- outline the development of strategic management as an academic discipline;
- explain and explore the planned/prescriptive approach to strategic management;
- explain and explore the emergent/incremental approach to strategic management;
- explain and explore the competitive positioning approach to strategic management;
- explain and explore the resource/core competence approach to strategic management;
- identify likely developments in strategic management, namely collaborative advantage and knowledge management.

Themes in strategic management

The 'big' controversies

The developing nature of strategy as a coherent academic discipline is reflected in two related debates revolving around what constitutes the most appropriate approach to strategic management (see Figure 15.1). There is some disagreement among strategists on the best way of understanding the determinants of competitive advantage. Some writers advocate an approach to strategic management which is *planned* or *prescriptive* (sometimes called *deliberate*) while others argue that it is better to evolve strategy incrementally (the *emergent* approach to strategy – see the Key Concept on page 7). A parallel debate centres upon whether competitive advantage stems primarily from the competitive position of the business in its industry or from business specific core competences. These themes are explored in the following sections of this chapter.

The debate surrounding the development of strategic management can be summarized under two broad headings:

1 the planned/prescriptive versus emergent/incremental controversy;
2 the competitive positioning versus resource/core competence-based strategy controversy.

We discussed the first of these debates in Chapter 1 and the second in Chapter 7. Here, we summarize the main features of these approaches and briefly explore their advantages and disadvantages (see Table 15.1). The arguments are discussed below.

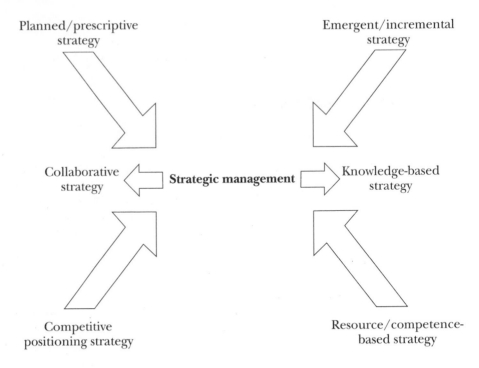

Planned/prescriptive
strategy

Emergent/incremental
strategy

Collaborative
strategy

Strategic management

Knowledge-based
strategy

Competitive
positioning strategy

Resource/competence-
based strategy

Figure 15.1 The development of strategic management.

The prescriptive versus emergent strategy debate

Planned or prescriptive strategy

The planned or prescriptive approach views the formulation and implementation of strategic management as a logical, rational and systematic
process. After analysis of the business and its environment, strategists must
set well-defined corporate and business objectives and formulate, select and
implement strategies which will allow objectives to be achieved. Such an
approach has been criticized on the grounds that there is often a major dis-
crepancy between planned and realized strategies (Mintzberg, 1987). It is
also argued that the increasing turbulence and chaos of the business environment makes highly prescriptive planning a nonsense. Rigid plans prevent the flexibility which is required in an environment of volatile change.
Being over-prescriptive, it is argued, also stifles the creativity which often
underpins successful strategy.

On the other hand, it is argued that systematic planning makes it possible to organize complex activities and information, unite business objectives, set targets against which performance can be evaluated and generally

increases the degree of control which can be exercised over the operation of the business. The planned or prescriptive approach is often linked to the *competitive positioning* approach (see later in this chapter).

Emergent or incremental strategy

The emergent or incremental view of strategy adopts the position that strategy must be evolved incrementally over time. This view is based upon the premise that businesses are complex social organizations operating in rapidly changing environments. Under such circumstances, strategy will tend to evolve as a result of the interaction between stakeholder groups and between the business and its environment. It is argued that an emergent approach has the advantages of increased organizational flexibility. It can form a basis in organizational learning and can provide an internal culture for managers to think and act creatively rather than have to act within the rigid framework of deliberate strategy . The danger is that an emergent approach may result in a lack of purpose in strategy and it can make it difficult to evaluate performance (because if an organization has no explicit objective, performance against it cannot be measured).

To counter the criticisms of emergent strategy, Quinn (1978) and Quinn and Voyer (1994) see a role for some planning in the context of emergent strategy, advocating 'purposeful incrementalism'. This approach places a strong emphasis on *organizational learning* (see later in this chapter).

The competitive positioning versus resource/core competence debate

Competitive positioning

This school of thought dominated strategic management in the 1980s and still had considerable significance in the 1990s. Although the approach has been widely criticized in the 1990s, the analytical frameworks devised by Porter in the 1980s (1980, 1985) are still widely used by both managers and academics. The major strength of the approach lies in the ready applicability of these frameworks to analysis of the business and its environment. The approach to strategy is essentially 'outside-in' (McKiernan, 1997) to establish a competitive position for the business in its environment which results in it outperforming its rivals.

In terms of procedure, the process of analysing competitive position begins with the *five forces framework*. This is used to analyse the nature of competition in the organization's industry. This is followed by selection of the appropriate *generic strategy* together with *value chain analysis* to ensure

Approach	Theory	Advantages	Criticisms
Prescriptive or planning strategy	Strategic management is a highly formalized planning process. Business objectives are set and strategies are formulated and implemented to achieve them.	Clear objectives provide focus for the business. Objectives can be translated into targets against which performance can be measured and monitored. Resources can be allocated to specific objectives and efficiency can be judged. The approach is logical and rational.	There are often major discrepancies between planned and realized strategy. Rigid planning in a dynamic and turbulent business environment can be unproductive. Prescriptions can stifle creativity. Rigid adherence to plans may mean missed business opportunities.
Emergent or incremental strategy	Strategy emerges and develops incrementally over time in the absence of rigid planning.	Emergent strategy increases flexibility in a turbulent environment allowing the business to respond to threats and exploit opportunities. Changing stakeholder interactions can mean that strategy is often, of necessity, emergent.	There is a danger of 'strategic drift' as objectives lack clarity. It is more difficult to evaluate performance as targets are less well defined.
Competitive positioning approach to strategy	Competitive advantage results from an organization's position in respect to its industry. The business analyses the strength of the competitive forces in its industry and selects an appropriate generic strategy. The business configures its value adding activities to support this generic strategy. The approach to strategy is 'outside-in'.	Well developed analytical frameworks like Porter's five forces, value chain and generic strategies. Structured approach helps to simplify the complexity of business and the business environment. Good for identifying opportunities and threats in the environment.	Neglects the importance of business-specific competences as opposed to industry-wide factors. Some of the analytical frameworks (e.g. generic strategies) have been widely criticized.
Resource or competence-based approach to strategy	Organizations must identify and build core competences or distinctive capabilities which can be leveraged in a number of markets. The approach to strategy is 'inside-out'.	The approach emphasizes the importance of the individual business in acquiring competitive advantage. Strategic intent, vision and creativity are emphasized.	Analytical frameworks are in their infancy and are currently poorly developed. The importance of the environment in determining competitive advantage is underestimated.

Table 15.1 Approaches to strategic management.

that the business configures its value adding activities in such a way as to support a strategy based on either differentiation or cost leadership.

In the 1990s, this approach was criticized for its overemphasis of the role of the *industry* in determining profitability and its underestimation of the importance of the individual business (Rumelt, 1990). Porter's frameworks have also been criticized as being too static although Porter argues that they must be applied repeatedly to take account of the dynamism of the environment. The reality is that without Porter's work, strategic management would be devoid of many of its most practical and applicable analytical tools.

Resource or core competence-based strategy

The 1990s witnessed the rise of what is known as *resource* or *core competence-based* strategic management (Prahalad and Hamel, 1990; Heene and Sanchez, 1997; Kay, 1993). The major difference to the competitive positioning approach is that the importance of the individual business in achieving competitive advantage is emphasized rather than the industry. The approach is therefore 'inside-out'. Although this approach came to prominence in the 1990s, its origins lie in the work of Penrose (1959) who emphasized the importance of the business and its resources in determining its performance. Interest in the approach was revived by Prahalad and Hamel's 1990 work 'The core competence of the corporation'. A core competence is some combination of resources, skills, knowledge and technology which distinguishes an organization from its competitors in the eyes of customers. This distinctiveness results in competitive advantage.

The approach also emphasizes organizational learning, knowledge management and collaborative business networks as sources of competitive advantage (Sanchez and Heene, 1997; Demarest, 1997).

The resource/core competence approach has focused the search for competitive advantage on the individual business but its critics argue that it lacks the well developed analytical frameworks of the competitive positioning school and, perhaps, understates the potential importance of the business environment in determining success or failure.

Towards an integrated approach to strategy

Similarities and differences between the approaches

The prescriptive and competitive positioning approaches are often seen as related to each other because they both adopt a highly structured view of strategic management. Similarly, the emergent and competence-based approaches are often linked to each other because of their shared focus on organizational knowledge and learning.

On the other hand, the prescriptive and emergent approaches are often presented as being diametrically opposed, as are the competitive position-ing and competence-based approaches. The reality is that the approaches are in many ways complementary as they present different perspectives of the same situation.

Mintzberg *et al.* (1995) argue that the competence-based and competitive positioning approaches ought be seen as 'complementary, representing two different forms of analysis both of which must be brought to bear for improving the quality of strategic thinking and analysis.' Similarly, Quinn and Voyer (1994) recognize that within logical incrementalism 'formal planning techniques do serve some essential functions.'

Acknowledging the contribution of each approach

The point is that each approach has its merits. By acknowledging the con-tribution of each approach, managers can arrive at an enriched method of understanding the complex area of strategic management. The contribu-tion of each approach to an integrated understanding is summarized as:

- *planned/prescriptive* – a degree of planning is necessary to provide focus for the strategy of the organization and to assist in the evaluation of per-formance;
- *emergent/incremental* – plans must always be flexible to allow organizations to learn and adapt to changes in the environment;
- *competitive positioning* – emphasizes the importance of the environment and provides useful tools for analysing the business in the context of its industry;
- *resource/competence-based* – focuses on the importance of the business and assists in identifying company-specific sources of competitive advantage.

Accordingly, we suggest that strategy must be both inward and outward looking, planned and emergent. By adopting this synthesis, a broader understanding of competitive advantage can be gained.

The future of strategic management thinking

This book has discussed the 'state of the art' in strategic thinking at the time of publication. In attempting to predict the areas that will focus the minds of academics in the near future, two central areas of interest are prominent – *collaborative advantage* and *knowledge management*.

Collaboration and competitive behaviour in industries

In recent years, considerable research and theorization has focused on the extent to which collaboration between businesses (as opposed to competi-tion) may contribute towards the attainment of competitive advantage

(Contractor and Lorange, 1988; Hamel, Doz and Prahalad, 1989; Quinn, Dooley and Paquette, 1990; Reeve, 1990; Davidow and Malone, 1992; Heene and Sauchez, 1997.)

Collaboration in non-core activities

The competence-based approach suggests that businesses should concentrate upon developing core competences so as to achieve competitive advantage. Any activities which are not seen as core can be outsourced to other organizations for whom those activities are core. Most networks centre on a focal business whose strategy drives the operation of the network. Quinn *et al.* (1990) suggest that such are the changes in service technologies that they now 'provide sufficient scale economies, flexibility, efficiency and specialization potentials that outside vendors [sellers] can supply many important corporate functions at greatly enhanced value and lower cost. Thus many of those functions should be outsourced.'

Rather than abandoning control to outside vendors it is sometimes best to form some sort of alliance or network with them. Collaborative networks potentially provide several advantages by:

- allowing businesses to concentrate on their core competences and core activities;
- allowing businesses to pool core competences, thus creating synergy between them;
- reducing bureaucracy and allowing flatter organizational structures;
- increasing efficiency and reducing costs;
- improving flexibility and responsiveness;
- making it difficult for competitors to imitate.

The formation of a collaborative network will involve:

- identifying the core competences of the organization;
- identifying and focusing upon activities which are critical to the core competence of the organization and outsourcing those which are not;
- achieving the internal and external linkages in the value/supply chain which are necessary for effective co-ordination of activities and which enhance responsiveness.

Collaboration can be:

- *horizontal* – partners are at the same stage of the value system and are often competitors;
- *vertical* – partners are at different stages of the value system (this includes collaboration with suppliers, distributors, and customers).

Collaboration can provide benefits including the linking of core competences (of the two parties in the relationship), access to resources and technology, risk reduction, greater control over supplies, better access to customers and reduced competition. Collaboration, however, can create problems which include conflicting objectives between the participating businesses, cultural differences, changing requirements among the partners and co-ordination and integration problems.

Virtual organizations

Developments in information and communications technology (ICT) have greatly increased the potential for collaboration between businesses by making it much easier to integrate and co-ordinate network activities. These changes in technology have made possible the development of 'virtual' organizations. A virtual organization is a network of linked businesses who co-ordinate and integrate their activities so effectively that they give the appearance of a single business organization.

There is considerable potential for such virtual organizations to enhance competitive advantage. ICT linkages greatly increase flexibility and efficiency, and make it difficult for competitors to replicate the activities of the network. Linkages to suppliers and customers are greatly improved as are flows of the information required for strategic decision-taking. The net result is that the virtual corporation is more flexible, more responsive and better able than its non-virtual rivals to compete on the bases of time and customer satisfaction.

Organizational learning and knowledge management

Closely related to the rational/logical approaches to strategy (such as the prescriptive and competitive positioning schools of thought) is the notion that organizations must continually learn both about themselves and their environment. At the same time – and here this point is in agreement with the core competence approach – it is widely acknowledged that organizational knowledge underpins many core competences. Accordingly, organizational learning and knowledge management have been the subject of considerable recent research and theorization (see for example Argyris, 1992; Grant, 1997; Demarest, 1997). Grant (1997) argues that 'the knowledge-based view represents a confluence of a number of streams of research, the most prominent being "resource-based theory" and "epistemology".'

Explicit and implicit knowledge

Organizational learning and knowledge management are concerned with the creation, development and dissemination of knowledge within an organization. This 'knowledge' can be either explicit or implicit:

- *Explicit knowledge* is knowledge whose meaning is clearly stated, details of which can be recorded and stored (such as important formulations, procedures, ways of acting, etc.).
- *Implicit or tacit knowledge* (Demarest, 1997) is often unstated, based upon individual experience and difficult to record and store. Implicit knowl-

edge is often a vital source of core competence and competitive advantage as it is most difficult for competitors to emulate (such as experience in a given sector, an understanding of a particular technology or the multiple contact networks that have been built up over many years by managers and sales people).

Both forms of knowledge begin as individual knowledge but, to improve performance substantially, they must be transformed into organizational knowledge. This is a particularly difficult transformation for implicit knowledge. It is the role of knowledge management to ensure that individual learning becomes organizational learning.

Types of organizational learning

Argyris (1978, 1992) argues that organizations must develop 'double loop learning'. In other words, learning is not just a case of learning how to solve an immediate problem but must also aim at developing principles which will inform and determine future behaviour. It must also result in the ability to generalize from specific learning. Such learning takes place when individual solutions are reached and then generalized to apply in other circumstances.

Senge (1990) identifies two types of learning found in leading organizations: 'adaptive learning' and 'generative learning'. Adaptive learning centres on changing in response to developments in the business environment. Such adaptation is often necessary for business survival. Generative learning is, on the other hand, about building new competences or identifying or creating opportunities for leveraging existing competences in new competitive arenas. For example, Marks & Spencer's entry into financial services was based upon leveraging its existing competences in retailing and adding new competences, based upon learning about the nature of financial services, initially through its store card operations.

The keys to successful knowledge management

Knowledge management incorporates organizational learning but it is also concerned with the management of existing stocks of knowledge. Effective knowledge management must overcome (based on Demarest, 1997):

- barriers to learning and knowledge creation;
- difficulties in storing and sharing knowledge (particularly tacit knowledge);
- difficulties in valuing and measuring knowledge.

Knowledge management is, therefore, primarily concerned with the creation of new knowledge, storage and sharing of knowledge and the control of knowledge. Knowledge management is an important element in building core competences which must be distinctive and difficult to imitate.

The often intangible nature of knowledge tends to make it distinctive and difficult to copy. In the case of a company like Microsoft, it is evident that its core competences are largely knowledge based. Quinn (1992) argues that 'most successful enterprises today can be considered intelligent enterprises' as they focus on building knowledge-based core competences. Similarly, Grant (1997) points out that 'companies such as Dow Chemical, Anderson Consulting, Polaroid and Skania are developing corporate-wide systems to track, access, exploit and create organizational knowledge.' Within such organizations, questioning and creativity are encouraged, as are trust, teamwork and sharing. At the same time, they have created infra-structures which support learning, which assist in the storage and con-trolled diffusion of knowledge, and which co-ordinate its application in creating and supporting core competences.

There is some way to go in understanding the role of knowledge and its management in strategy. It is likely that significant developments will take place in this area in the new millennium.

Summary

Strategic management is fundamentally concerned with understanding the nature of competitive advantage and the means by which it is acquired and sustained. This chapter has explored the major approaches adopted by strategists seeking to better understand the factors which underpin com-petitive advantage, allowing certain organizations to outperform their com-petitors. The different approaches should not be regarded as mutually exclusive, but rather they provide alternative methods for better under-standing the means by which strategy is formulated and implemented. A degree of planning of strategy is required but, equally, strategy might also emerge incrementally. Heracleous (1998) argues that 'strategic thinking' (which is distinctive and creative) is required in the formulation of new strategies while 'strategic planning' (which is analytical and conventional) is needed successfully to implement new strategy.

Future developments in strategic management are likely to centre on the role of collaborative networks and knowledge management in producing competitive advantage. The discipline is in its adolescence and, as with all adolescents, it is difficult to predict what will happen next!

Review and Discuss

1 Explain the differences between the planned/prescriptive approach and the emergent/incremental approach to strategic management.
2 Discuss the view that the competitive positioning and resource/com-petence-based approaches to strategic management are mutually exclusive.
3 Explain how collaboration between businesses can contribute to the acquisition of competitive advantage.

4 What is 'knowledge management'? How can knowledge be an important source of competitive advantage?
5 What do you see as the likely major developments in strategic management in the future?

References and further reading

Ansoff, I. (1987) *Corporate Strategy*. London: Penguin.
Argenti, J. (1965) *Corporate Planning*. Allen and Unwin.
Argyris, C. (1977) Double loop learning in organizations. *Harvard Business Review*, September–October, 115–125.
Argyris, C. and Schon, D. (1978) *Organization Learning: A Theory of Action Perspective*. Reading, MA: Addison Wesley.
Argyris, C. (1992) *On Organizational Learning*. London; Blackwell.
Contractor, F. and Lorange, P. (1988) Why should firms co-operate? In *Co-operative Strategies in International Business*, Lexington Books.
Cravens, D.W., Greenley, G., Piercy, N.F. and Slater S. (1997) Integrating contemporary strategic management perspectives. *Long Range Planning*, 30, No. 4 August, 493–506.
Davidow, W.H. and Malone, M.S. (1992) *Structuring and Revitalizing the Corporation for the 21st Century – The Virtual Corporation*. London: Harper Business.
Demarest, M. (1997) Understanding knowledge management. *Long Range Planning*, 30 (3), 374–384.
Grant, R.M. (1991) The resource based theory of competitive advantage: implications for strategy formulation. *California Management Review*, 33, Spring, 114–135.
Grant, R.M. (1997) The knowledge-based view of the firm: implications for management practice. *Long Range Planning*, 30 (3), 450–454.
Hamel, G., Doz, Y. and Prahalad, C.K. (1989) Collaborate with your competitors and win. *Harvard Business Review*, January–February.
Hamel, G. and Prahalad, C.K. (1989) Strategic intent. *Harvard Business Review*, 67 (3).
Hamel, G. and Prahalad, C.K. (1994) *Competing for the Future*. Cambridge, MA: Harvard Business School Press.
Heene, A. and Sanchez, R. (eds) (1997) *Competence-Based Strategic Management*. London: John Wiley.
Heracleous, L. (1998) Strategic thinking or strategic planning. *Long Range Planning*, 30 (3).
Kay, J. (1993) *Foundations of Corporate Success*. Oxford: Oxford University Press.
Kay, J. (1995) Learning to define the core business. *Financial Times*, December 1.

McKiernan, P. (1997) Strategy past; strategy futures. *Long Range Planning*, 30 (5), October.

Mintzberg, H. (1987) Crafting strategy. *Harvard Business Review*, July–August.

Mintzberg, H. (1991) *The Strategy Process – Concepts, Contexts, Cases.* Englewood Cliffs: Prentice Hall.

Mintzberg, H., Quinn, J.B. and Ghoshal, S. (1995) *The Strategy Process: Concepts, Contexts and Cases,* European Edition. Englewood Cliffs: Prentice Hall.

Penrose, E. (1959) *The Theory of the Growth of the Firm.* Oxford: Oxford University Press.

Porter, M.E. (1980) *Competitive Strategy: Techniques for Analysing Industries and Competitors.* New York: The Free Press.

Porter, M.E. (1985) *Competitive Advantage,* New York: The Free Press

Prahalad, C.K. and Hamel, G. (1990) The core competence of the corporation. *Harvard Business Review,* 79–91.

Quinn, J.B. (1978) Strategic change; logical incrementalism. *Sloan Management Review,* Fall.

Quinn, J.B. (1992) *The Intelligent Enterprise.* New York: Free Press.

Quinn, J.B. and Voyer J. (1994) *The Strategy Process.* Englewood Cliffs: Prentice Hall.

Reve, T. (1990) The firm as a nexus of internal and external contracts. In Aoki, M., Gustafsson, M. and Williamson, O.E. (eds) *The Firm as a Nexus of Treaties.* London: Sage.

Rumelt, R. (1991) How much does industry matter? *Strategic Management Journal,* March.

Sanchez, R. and Heene, A. (eds) (1997) *Strategic Learning and Knowledge Management.* New York: Wiley.

Senge, P. (1990) Building learning organizations. *Sloan Management Review,* Fall.

Part V

The case studies and scenarios

Ben & Jerry's Homemade Ice Cream Inc.
'A new corporate concept of linked prosperity'

The beginning

Ben Cohen and Jerry Greenfield became friends at school in the late 1960s in Burlington, Vermont in the North Eastern United States. Their reputation as the two 'odd' eccentrics at school led them to form a strong friendship that would last for many decades.

When they left school, both Ben and Jerry became 'hippies' – social dropouts who lived an alternative and unconventional lifestyle. They both grew their hair and a beard and together with their dog, Malcolm, they moved in together as flatmates. One of the interests they shared was in food and as they discussed various ways of making a living, they concluded that the two most exciting areas of fast food at the time were bagels and ice cream.

Having established that the equipment needed to bake bagels would cost $40,000, the two men enrolled on an ice cream making correspondence course for the cost of $5 each.

In 1978, having developed some basic ice cream recipes, Ben and Jerry set up a shop in a renovated petrol station in Burlington with a capital investment of $12,000 ($4000 of which was borrowed). From the outset, Ben and Jerry wanted to produce a premium product and the fact that it was made from 'fresh Vermont milk and cream' was stressed. The outlet was called 'Ben & Jerry's Homemade Ice Cream' and to give the shop a unique and welcoming character, they employed a piano player to play blues in the background.

Initially, the shop was a success amongst Burlington locals, many of whom had known the men when they were growing up. The staff that Ben and Jerry employed were encouraged to take the same 'hippie-ish' view of business activity as the owners ('every day was a party'), but the major competitive advantage arose from the uniqueness of the product. Whereas the majority of ice cream products were traditionally flavoured, Ben and Jerry introduced unusual flavours with 'chunks' to make the textures more interesting, such as fruit, chocolate, nuts, toffee and similar sweets. 'Chunky' ice cream became the prominent feature of the new organization's image.

During the summer of 1978, customer numbers grew as the reputation of the shop and the ice cream grew. It was when the winter set in at the end of the year that the troubles began. Over-the-counter ice cream sales dried up and Ben and Jerry realized they would have to find other outlets for their products if they were to avoid bankruptcy.

They persuaded a number of local grocers in Vermont to stock the product in one-pint tubs, but it soon transpired that a broader customer base would be needed. Having approached a number of national supermarket chains, Ben Cohen learned that the size of the business, not to mention his appearance and attitude to business, made the buyers reluctant to take stock from him. He was advised that he ought to seek to sell the ice cream to large independent ice cream distributors in neighbouring states who would then sell the product on to the major retail multiples. It was then that Ben and Jerry encountered a problem.

The Pillsbury confrontation

Ben approached the Dari-Farms corporation with a view to have it distribute Ben & Jerry's ice cream throughout the New England states. Dennis Silva, the company vice-president, agreed to take some of Ben & Jerry's stock despite Ben's unconventional approach to business. In order to increase distribution further, Ben also approached Paul's Distributors where its chairman, Chuck Green, also agreed to act as a Ben & Jerry distributor.

The market leader in the super-premium ice cream segment at the time was Häagen Dazs which was then owned by the large US-based Pillsbury Corporation. Pillsbury turned over $4 billion a year and had extensive food interests in addition to Häagen Dazs including Green Giant (vegetables) and Burger King, the fast food outlet.

Kevin Hurley, president of the Häagen Dazs subsidiary of Pillsbury, was the son-in-law of the company's founder, Reuben Matthus. Matthus had started Häagen Dazs in 1959 in New York. He came up with the Danish-sounding name in the belief that it conjured up a feeling in the consumer of an exotic European brand. By 1984 when the confrontation with Ben & Jerry's took place, Häagen Dazs held a 70 per cent share of the super-premium ice cream market.

When Hurley discovered that both Dari-Farms and Paul's were distributing Ben & Jerry's as well as Häagen Dazs, he rang both Dennis Silva and Chuck Green. Although Ben & Jerry's still had a tiny share of the market compared with Häagen Dazs, Hurley was determined that the distributors he used were not going to help a competitor.

'We didn't say to the distributor, "You can't carry Ben & Jerry's. We're asking you to make a choice,"' said Hurley. 'We just told them [Silva and Green] that they couldn't sell Ben & Jerry's *and* Häagen Dazs.' This 'it's us or them' ultimatum took the two distributors by surprise and it presented a distressing dilemma.

'We were just stunned at this comment coming from Häagen Dazs, this huge company where we were selling trailer loads of ice cream versus this minuscule amount of Ben & Jerry's we were selling,' said Chuck Green of Paul's Distribution. 'They had drawn this line in the sand saying that we had to make a decision.'

When Ben and Jerry heard of Hurley's threat, they arranged a meeting with the distributors to discuss the situation. In view of the potential of Ben & Jerry's, neither distributor wanted to stop taking their products, but at the same time, the thought of having Häagen Dazs withdraw their supply could prove very damaging indeed. The three parties agreed that they would need legal representation if they were to take on the might of Pillsbury and they chose Howie Fuguet, a business lawyer who had spent his professional life defending large organizations.

Like Ben and Jerry, Howie was an eccentric. He was said to have cared little for his appearance and had holes in his shoes. He agreed that Pillsbury had behaved in a curious way and sent off a letter to Pillsbury setting out the nature of Ben & Jerry's grievance. Protesting that Hurley had acted unfairly, Howie wrote to the Board of Pillsbury.

'It would be wishful thinking on the part of your subsidiary's officers [Häagen Dazs] to imagine that it can bully Ben & Jerry's, stifle its growth and cause it to roll over,' wrote Howie. 'Ben & Jerry's is a classic entrepreneurial success and its owners are aggressive. Häagen Dazs will have to learn to compete on their merits in the marketplace. That is the American way and that is what competition is all about.'

Notwithstanding the apparent 'rightness' of Ben & Jerry's case, the legal odds were clearly stacked against them. If they couldn't beat the 'bullying' Häagen Dazs through normal legal channels, then another weapon would be needed.

The 'dough boy' campaign

The key move was to make Pillsbury the target of the campaign and not Häagen Dazs – Pillsbury was bigger and had more to lose. Since the mid-1960s, the symbol of Pillsbury had been the Pillsbury 'dough boy'. The dough boy was used by Pillsbury in its advertising and other corporate communications and was a valuable symbol of the company's identity. So as to avoid the appearance of an ice cream war between two competitors, Howie proposed that they attacked the Pillsbury company by specifically targeting the dough boy.

Accordingly, the *What's the dough boy afraid of?* campaign was launched, intentionally designed to appear as a 'David versus Goliath' conflict where a small company (Ben & Jerry's) had been unfairly treated by a large 'bully' in the shape of Pillsbury.

'We didn't really know a thing about PR. We were just trying to survive,' said Ben Cohen. 'If we were going to go down, we wanted to let as many people as we could know what was going on. [We wanted to say that] the reason why you can't find Ben & Jerry's on the shelf is because this big corporation [Pillsbury] is trying to prevent you, the consumer, from having a choice about what kind of ice cream you want to buy.'

The campaign included T-shirts, bumper stickers, bill posters and other media which all bore the statement, *What's the dough boy afraid of?* Jerry launched a one-man campaign outside the Pillsbury headquarters in Minneapolis, Minnesota and it wasn't long before the local television news programmes started carrying the story on a regular basis. This proved not only to make the public sympathize with Ben & Jerry's, but also to provide a lot of free publicity for the company and its products.

From its 17-strong legal department, Pillsbury assigned Richard Wegener to 'get rid of' the 'Ben & Jerry problem'. Wegener quickly realized the size of the task facing Pillsbury. 'The publicity became bigger than the dispute itself,' said Wegener. The reputation of Pillsbury was at stake and Wegener sought to bring a rapid end to the controversy. Realizing that the campaign had grabbed the public's attention and the sympathies were predominantly with Ben & Jerry's, Wegener advised Hurley to back down.

Kevin Hurley was persuaded to sign an out-of-court settlement agreeing not to coerce any distributors. The campaign was over and Ben & Jerry's had won. The controversy not only ensured the defeat of Pillsbury, it also acted unwittingly by providing an enormous amount of publicity for the Ben & Jerry's brand.

After the victory

The success of Ben & Jerry's after the Pillsbury confrontation was marked. The distribution channels were widened still further until Ben & Jerry's ice cream was supplied through supermarkets, grocery stores, convenience stores and food service operations, as well as through licensed scoop shops, franchised scoop shops and company-owned scoop shops. By 1992, the company's turnover exceeded $130 million and it was on the verge of international development into the United Kingdom.

In the super-premium ice cream sector, a number of new and distinctive product flavours were launched including 'Milk chocolate ice cream and white fudge cows swirled with white chocolate ice cream and dark fudge cows,' 'Chocolate comfort low fat ice cream,' 'Mocha latte' and 'Triple caramel chunk ice cream'.

In addition, non-ice cream frozen sweets were introduced including a range of ice cream 'novelties', frozen yoghurts and sorbets such as 'Chunky Monkey frozen yoghurt – banana frozen yoghurt with fudge flakes and walnuts'. The Ben & Jerry's name and the company's reputation for quality meant that the new products quickly became adopted by the market.

The personality of the founders helped to frame the company's culture and its mission. Two important statements were released which described the company's approach to its approach to business.

In 1988, the company stated that, 'We are dedicated to the creation and demonstration of a new corporate concept of linked prosperity.' This was articulated via its Philanthropy Statement and its Mission Statement.

Philanthropy Statement and Mission Statement – Ben & Jerry's

Philanthropy Statement

Ben & Jerry's gives away 7.5 per cent of its pre-tax earnings in three ways: the Ben & Jerry's Foundation; employee Community Action Teams at five Vermont sites; and through corporate grants made by the Director of Social Mission Development. We support projects which are models for social change – projects which exhibit creative problem solving and hopefulness. The Foundation is managed by a nine-member employee board and considers proposals relating to children and families, disadvantaged groups, and the environment.

Mission Statement

Ben & Jerry's is dedicated to the creation and demonstration of a new corporate concept of linked prosperity. Our mission consists of three interrelated parts:
- *To make, distribute and sell the finest quality all natural ice cream and related products in a wide variety of innovative flavors made from Vermont dairy products.*
- *To operate the Company on a sound financial basis of profitable growth, increasing value for our shareholders, and creating career opportunities and financial rewards for our employees.*
- *To operate the Company in a way that actively recognizes the central role that*

business plays in the structure of society by initiating innovative ways to improve the quality of life of a broad community – local, national, and international.

Underlying the mission of Ben & Jerry's is the determination to seek new and creative ways of addressing all three parts, while holding a deep respect for the individuals, inside and outside the company, and for the communities of which they are a part.

Camelot

National and locally based lotteries had been common in many parts of the world when the UK government proposed the UK National Lottery in 1993. Whilst there was cross-party support in Parliament for the proposal, there was some disagreement in respect of who should operate it. The then opposition Labour Party argued that it should be operated by the state (via a government department) but the governing Conservative Party argued that a private sector operator would be preferable. This, it argued, would provide the opportunity for the operator to made some profit, but the main advantage of licensing a private sector business would be that the government believed that there would be a higher quality and more efficient service than a government department could provide.

Bids were invited and a number of companies and consortia applied. Each applicant was invited to forecast total ticket sales, how much would be given towards 'good causes' (a very important part of the Lottery Bill) and how much it would take in profits to shareholders. A number of operational criteria were also imposed including the importance of national coverage, the security and reliability of the IT systems and the ability of the consortia to promote and publicize the lottery. Finally, winners should be quickly identified and payments should be made without delay.

It was eventually decided to award the first lottery contract to Camelot – a consortium of five companies from the UK and the USA. The initial consortium was made up as follows:

Company	Stake	Industry
Cadbury Schweppes plc	22.5%	Food and drinks
De La Rue plc	22.5%	Security printing, banknotes, credit cards, etc.
G-Tech Inc.	22.5%	Lottery operations in other parts of the world including the USA
Racal plc	22.5%	Data communications and defence systems
ICL	10%	Computers and IT systems

In order to monitor the operation of the lottery, the Lottery Bill provided for the establishment of a Lottery Regulator who would report to the government – a quango with a similar brief to the utility regulators in the UK such as OFTEL and OFWAT. The purpose of the Regulator was to monitor the operator's behaviour, to ensure that it worked within the rules as set out by Parliament and to give the lottery players confidence in the process. A panel of independent people were invited to form a committee for the distribution of the 'good causes' money.

In 1998, it transpired that an irregularity had occurred in the bidding process on the part of G-Tech Inc. The result of this disclosure was for G-Tech to withdraw from the Camelot consortium although it was allowed to remain as one of its major suppliers. The other four partners reconfigured their shareholdings in Camelot with ICL increasing its shareholding to 20 per cent and the other three to 26.67 per cent each.

Cardiff Car Components Ltd

John Armstrong inherited South Cardiff Engineering Ltd from his father in 1958 when John was 25. Bryn Armstrong, John's father, had built the South Wales company up from nothing after the war and had made a moderate living, along with his 12 employees, carrying out general engineering fabrications. John entered the business as a time-served mechanic and, from the outset, sought to turn the small company from general engineering towards his particular expertise in motor cars. In addition to the engineering shop, John set up a small sideline servicing and repairing cars to exploit his expertise as a mechanic.

The business was located in a number of sprawling old pre-war buildings on a large tract of derelict land that had previously been a large industrial property. There was consequently plenty of room for expansion if it became appropriate. John spotted the trend in increasing car ownership as prosperity increased in the 1950s, and he was convinced that the company's engineering skills could be profitably employed in producing parts for the burgeoning motor industry.

During the late 1950s both cars and spares had been difficult to obtain, and John adapted some of his machine tools to produce automotive parts whilst other equipment was bought in and installed. By 1960, the company had attracted a reputation as a reliable supplier of a limited number of high quality and reliable 'patterned' car parts including exhausts, steering columns and suspension leaves. A customer base had been developed amongst garages and motor factories throughout South Wales and the English West Country. John's attitude to business was to 'have a go at anything' if a customer expressed a need for any given part. He took special satisfaction in successfully producing specialist parts that other car part producers found challenging. In 1961, reflecting the company's new positioning, John changed the company's name to Cardiff Car Components Limited (CCC for short).

It was at a motor suppliers' fair in the West Midlands in 1962 that John made an important business contact when he was invited to supply a range of parts acting as a subcontractor to the large Birmingham-based OEM company, E.T. Phillips (Automotive OEM) Ltd. Phillips was a major supplier of parts to the motor industry in the Midlands and had longstanding contracts with the major national dealership chains. Although the profit margins on work for Phillips were lower than for John's direct customers, CCC took the work on because it would guarantee continuous work for the factory and (in John's words), 'keep the machines running. There's no point having a machine sitting idle when it could be pressing out petrol tanks, even if the margins are lower.'

Throughout the 1960s, CCC took advantage of the growth in car ownership as it increased its product range to cater for the increasing number of car models. Distribution was widened to car dealerships throughout the country driven by the significant price differences between original manufacturers' parts and those produced by pattern manufacturers like CCC. In 1968, John sold the car servicing and repair business to finance expansion and the company focused entirely upon its car parts manufacture.

As garage labour costs increased in the 1960s and 1970s, a greater number of motorists started to do their own servicing and repairs. This created a new market for parts, sold through outlets such as DIY shops, and CCC's business increased in line with this trend. An additional opportunity arose with the increase in the number of foreign cars whose manufacturers' parts were significantly more expensive to replace than those for British-made cars. John studied the specifications of the new foreign cars and produced the most easily-replicated parts.

Throughout the 1980s, CCC continued to grow as opportunities for new products and/or markets presented themselves. John became skilful at identifying new openings and quickly developing replacement parts for cars and other motor vehicles. He was an instinctive businessman who considered himself incapable of constructing a formal business plan – a matter that came to a head when he approached his bank manager for some additional loan capital. In exchange for loan guarantees, the bank manager insisted upon seeing a five-year business plan. 'I didn't have a clue where to start,' said John. 'I just take up business opportunities as they come up. If I can make profit through a contract, I take it on. If I can't, I turn it down.'

By 1997, the company had a staff of 145, and employed a sales force of four people promoting the growing product range, which was sold under a variety of brand names. The sales force had become very overloaded with work, and did not have time to call on all potential clients. They did, however, continue to visit long established customers, however large or small they were. John dealt with the largest customers (mainly the OEM customers, including Phillips) personally, exploiting the relationship that he had forged with the customers over almost forty years in the industry.

The entire structure and culture of the business was based around the personality of John Armstrong and as he came towards the normal retirement age, many of his employees and customers started to wonder aloud about the future of CCC without him. He had plans to sell CCC upon his retirement, but he wanted to broaden its customer base still further before he did.

He visited a German trade fair in 1997. Coincidentally, there was a strike by German metalworkers at this time and this led to a substantial order from a German car manufacturer. The profit margin on the order appeared at first to be quite small, but the increase in the value of the pound sterling against the Deutschmark at the time made the order worth taking on.

By the time of the order's scheduled completion date, however, the pound had lost value against the Deutschmark by about 15 per cent and John started to express concern that, with the tight margins, the order might even turn in a loss. In the end, he was able to extract a 5 per cent price increase from the reluctant German customer to offset the losses on the shipment but the experience made John wary of any further opportunities to do business abroad.

At the same time, CCC was feeling the effects of intensified competition from other car spares companies. His key customer segments, the DIY, OEM and garage markets, were being tempted by large specialist spares companies such as Unipart, and by suppliers of cheaper components from Eastern Europe or the Far East.

The market for car parts had become much more complicated since John had entered the business some forty years earlier. In addition to the increased competition from over-seas, the number of UK-based manufacturers had increased. CCC's market share of around 15 per cent of the UK market (in 1998) had fallen from its high of 20 per cent in 1965. The legal environment also looked increasingly uncertain – there was talk of European legislation that would give car manufacturers exclusive rights to sell parts for their vehicles.

In early 1999 there was a surprise offer to take over the company from Gear-tackle Ltd, a national chain of DIY motorists shops. Gear-tackle, unlike CCC, had a reputation for formal planning and Bill Worsthorne, its CEO, was unlike John Armstrong in other ways. He held an MBA from Manchester Business School, was a career businessman and had high hopes that CCC could regain its market share with the introduction of a formal strategic planning process.

Gear-tackle offered £2.3 million to John for a controlling stake in CCC and invited him to remain on the Board as a non-executive director to see the company through its period of transition. It took less than three months for Bill and John to 'fall out' over what Bill described as 'irreconcilable differences in management style'. John finally decided to retire.

(This case is based on a real-life company, but the names and locations have been changed at the request of the companies in question.)

Appendix

Appendix: Selected profit and loss accounts (simplified) for CCC by decade

	1958	1968	1978	1988	1998
Sales (£000s)	144	987	1956	3678	5324
Costs (£000s)	136.2	840.2	1607.4	3012.2	4734.6
Profit before interest and tax (£000s)	7.8	146.8	348.6	665.8	589.4

Dansk Tyggegummi Fabrik A/S
'Dandy chewing gum – always stimulating'

Introduction
Dansk Tyggegummi Fabrik A/S (DTF, 'The Danish Chewing Gum Factory Ltd') is a family-owned company with worldwide interests. In 1996 its turnover was 1.7 billion Danish kroner (about £170 million) and 97 per cent of its output was sold overseas. It employed almost 2000 people, 1100 of whom were based at the company headquarters in the town of Vejle in Denmark. It had sales offices in 15 countries, was involved in several strategic alliances and ran a joint venture production company in Zimbabwe. It enjoyed market leadership in Eastern Europe, but its major overseas market was Russia. DTF opened a Russian chewing gum packing plant in 1996 and the success of this plant led to an increase in the company's Russian investment. A production plant employing 300 people was opened in Novgorod in 1999.

Main brands
Dandy's main international brands are:

- *Stimorol*
- *Dirol* – ('Protects your teeth from morning to evening') aimed at the 15- to 25-year-olds;
- *Fertin V6* Dental Chewing Gum for youngsters and adults and for children; *Fertin Fluorette* – with fluoride; *Fertin Vitamin C* – for adults and children; *Fertin Nicotinell*; and *Fertin* (various customers' private labels).

Company history
The company was founded in 1915 by the Danish entrepreneur Holger Sørensen, initially as a producer of quality confectionery in Denmark. The reputation of his products grew rapidly, especially in Jutland and on the nearby island of Funen, Denmark's second-largest island.

Holger Sørensen was always on the lookout for new product ideas and at an exhibition in London he spotted what was then a new item: chewing gum. He bought a chewing gum recipe and began experimenting with the new product back in Denmark. In January 1927, *Vejle Chewing Gum* was launched on the Danish market.

The new product was soon available everywhere in western Denmark and, as production grew, new and larger premises were bought in the 1930s to accommodate the new machinery needed to supply a growing national market. Sørensen began to sell his products in the capital, Copenhagen, where he gained access to a much larger retailing system. In was also in that decade, in 1939, that the English-sounding brand name

Dandy was first introduced. Dandy still identifies the company to Danish consumers.

During the Second World War, Denmark was occupied by German forces and rationing and other restrictions stopped all new product development, The factory was only just kept ticking over as demand for non-essential goods fell. After the war, the shortage of raw materials was initially a problem for Dandy, and it struggled to supply its existing domestic market. However, a joint promotional campaign with the Danish Red Cross helped. The Red Cross was given a Trade Ministry grant to finance the production of two million packets of Dandy, which were to be sold to raise funds for the aid organization, and this helped to re-establish the brand in the Danish market.

In 1946, the company opened an Export Department in Copenhagen, the only Danish city that meant anything to foreigners and also the only one with airline connections to overseas destinations. The Export Department has since moved back to the original Jutland headquarters.

By the 1990s, the company had become a modern transnational with a company structure designed to manage operations in many countries. The company is still based in Denmark.

Marketing

DTF has always tried to employ effective marketing methods. Research indicates that 90 per cent of chewing gum purchases are made on impulse, and so companies in the sector are aware of the importance of keeping the brands visible to the customer. Throughout its history, DTF has been one of the most innovative marketing companies in the chewing gum industry.

The years before the Second World War saw a growth in the popularity of vending machines and in 1929 DTF started putting up its own machines in prominent town centre locations. In the 1950s, the company commissioned strip cartoons to advertise the product. Some of these strips included a Dandy cartoon character to support the brand identity – a relatively new concept at the time.

Before mass television ownership, many FMCG producers used cinema advertising to reach their customers. DTF launched its first cinema advertising campaign in 1952 and, in an attempt to make the adverts memorable, they featured a well-known Danish comedian and a number of pretty girls.

Following the success of these early campaigns, 'pin-ups' became a constant feature in advertising and Dandy used them in print advertising, calendars and on the backs of promotional playing cards. The pin-up playing cards proved particularly successful in the United Kingdom where they were hotly debated in the press as being too daring. One Member of Parliament tried to have the product banned.

Also in 1952, Dandy launched a series of collector's picture cards to attract customers. The first series, based on the Helsinki Olympics, was followed by many others through the 1960s and 1970s, with pictures of pop stars, animals, and all the world's flags. One image which proved successful in Scandinavia met with some unexpected resistance in the UK – it was a cartoon character called Kinky Dan.

By 1996, the company was using a complete range of marketing tools including the sponsorship of sports, music and related events. Media exposure was also a major part of the publicity effort. In addition to the usual television, magazine, cinema and outdoor advertising, DTF used a number of consumer promotions and became the sponsor of the Russian weather forecast. It was one of the first Danish companies to advertise on the World Wide Web (www.stimorol.com).

In the words of the 1996 annual report, the 'marketing of the brand names *Stimorol*, *Dirol* and *V6* must continue to be given top priority. This will take place by using new, exciting initiatives in direct marketing which focus on the functionality and lifestyle of the brands and are supported by activities that give consumers action-packed and surprising experiences.'

New products and markets

In the 1950s, the Stimorol brand name was established as a throat pastille. The idea at the time was to add to the company's product portfolio in order to give it a firmer sales base. However, in 1956 the decision was taken to sell Stimorol as a throat-clearing chewing gum and one of the company's greatest successes was established. An advertising agency was commissioned to create a press advertising campaign to promote this new flagship chewing gum brand and standardized film advertising appeared in cinemas across Europe, with the sound tracks adapted to each language area.

In 1959, Klaas Kamphuis, a Dutch businessman, approached Dandy, asking if he could add Stimorol to his range of smoker's products. Kamphuis's tactics – dealing with individual outlets and ensuring that stock sales to each outlet were restricted to what could be sold – helped turn the Netherlands into a major non-Danish market for Stimorol, which in turn became the market leader there.

The company's success in the Netherlands set the tone for its later export successes. On 9 March 1966, Erik Bagger-Sørensen (the founder's son and then the CEO) signed a contract with the National Confectionery Products Co. (NCP) of Baghdad for the production and sale of Dandy's branded products (Dandy, Stimorol and Rex). This marked the establishment of Dandy's first licensed production plant.

The Iraqi development was followed in 1969 by a second licensing agreement with a Nigerian company. Later, a licensed factory opened in Turkey. With these licensing arrangements having achieved their objectives, each one was eventually discontinued. Joint venture companies were opened in Zimbabwe and Australia. Of these, the former still operates.

From 1959 to the mid-1960s, Dandy marketed a sugar-free sticks product called *Sugarfree*. It was not very successful. However, when a competitor launched a rival brand, *Caroxin*, in the mid-1960s, the 'chewing gum and dental hygiene' concept became firmly established. Consequently, Dandy launched a new sugar-free product on the back of Sugarfree in 1968. Dirol was launched as a competitor to Caroxin, but at first it failed to take much market share in the new dental hygiene market.

When it was relaunched in 1970, Dirol was packaged in larger boxes of twenty pieces. This format proved more popular and the product soon took a market share of 15 per cent. Continued interest in the dental hygiene concept led to further development of product flavours, new sweeteners and improved texture.

The eventual success of Dirol led DTF to examine other opportunities for specialized chewing gum products. To this end. the company bought the Fertin Laboratories in Sweden in 1978. This acquisition enabled DTF to explore the technical and medical aspects of including a number of clinically active ingredients in chewing gum products.

The Fertin name was used as the basis for this new range of products.

DTF's products continue to win new markets. At the Fancy Food Fair held in New York in July of 1998, the company's V6 chewing gum won contracts with the Target department store chain (900 outlets) and the Wallgreen drugstore chain (2500 outlets).

DTF in Russia

DTF had been selling to the Soviet Union through state-owned trading companies for many years when, in 1991, the old Soviet Union was disbanded. The effect of this, as far as DTF was concerned, was the loss of its traditional Russian distribution channels. It re-established its Russian presence through links set up by the Danish exporter, Jahn International A/S.

DTF's next task was to defend its Russian markets from other Western chewing gum manufacturers who were also seeking to develop the Russian market at that time. In 1991, Wrigley's began exporting its traditional flavours to Russia. DTF managed, however, to more than hold its own against Wrigley's, partly by using American-style television advertising to give its products a quality image whilst also stressing the uniqueness of the dentally active formulae.

In 1993, DTF terminated its contract with Jahn International and in 1994 a Moscow sales office was set up. The company moved from national to regional distribution in Russia and the Russian Brands Division was established as a new business unit within DTF. In 1996, the Novgorod packing plant was opened: the product was received in bulk from Denmark and then packed in the familiar Dandy packages within the Russian market.

Novgorod's progressive young Governor Mikhail Prusak pursued an aggressive strategy of attracting foreign direct investment into Novgorod in the face of stiff competition for inward investment from St Petersburg. Attracting Stimorol (and the UK company Cadbury Schweppes) was a notable victory for Prusak. DTF's success in Russia led to the plan of building a production facility in Novgorod with financial support from the Danish Investment Fund for Eastern Europe and the European Bank for Reconstruction and Development.

DTF continued to create a stir with its advertising. In Russia, it used slightly risqué American-style adverts to attract a young audience and the evidence was that this worked better than Wrigley's squeaky-clean testimonial ads. One anonymous Russian industry observer observed that Wrigley's commercials are less effective because they do not accurately reflect the lifestyle values of most Russian teenagers: 'Stimorol's ads go over well because they are more exotic and they always have a plot,' he said.

Other company activities

The Dandy Foundation was established in 1984. It distributes grants every two years, with the aim of providing general support to scientific activities related to the medical fields of oral and dental hygiene, diabetes and eye disease.

In 1992, the company achieved ISO 9001 classification, in recognition of quality management in the main company and in its associated subsidiaries in Denmark, Sweden, Germany and Switzerland.

1996 saw the opening of the Dandy Inspiratorium, the company museum. It tells the story of the company from 1915 to 1972 (the year when Denmark joined the European

Economic Community, now the European Union or the EU). In the same year, the company also introduced a new training programme for employees.

Appendices

Appendix 1: Market shares in the European chewing gum market (%)

Producer (Nationality)	Total Dragée segment	Dragée and sticks
Dandy (Denmark)	20	48
Wrigley (USA)	41	33
Warner (USA)	7	6
Perfetti	13	–
Kraft (USA)	9	–
Huhtamäki/Leaf (Finland)	5	13
Others	5	–
Total	100	100

Note: Dragée are small chewing gum capsules.

Appendix 2: Press statement
Dandy fires 120 workers
The Russians are not buying chewing gum
Vejle, Denmark, 30 September 1998
The Dandy chewing gum factory in Vejle, Denmark is laying off 120 workers because the company's sales of chewing gum to Russia are hitting crisis point. Both production and administration will suffer but the sales and marketing departments are not affected. With a turnover of 500 million Danish kroner per annum (ca. £50 million), Russia is Dandy's largest export market but the country's economic crisis is also having an effect on chewing gum sales.

For some time the Dandy Corporation's stand has been to 'wait-and-see', hoping that the situation would improve, but the crisis has now lasted for so long that employees in Denmark must suffer the consequences. At the beginning of the year the Dandy Corporation started constructing a factory in Russia, an investment of 666 million Danish kroner (ca. £65 million). If all goes according to plan, the factory in Novgorod outside Moscow will be finished in 1999. It will supply chewing gum to the Russian market and to other nations in the former Soviet Union. The factory will employ some 300 people. Dandy currently employs some 2000 people, half of them outside Denmark.

Appendix 3: Company divisional structure
(Issued by the company)
Stimorol Chewing Gum A/S
Stimorol Chewing Gum A/S is the largest of the business units within the DTF. Stimorol Chewing Gum A/S markets the Stimorol brand and customers' own brands in selected markets in Europe and the Far East, either through owned sales subsidiaries or through national distributors. For more than thirty years, Stimorol has been the preferred chewing gum brand among young people in many nations.

Quality is a key concept for Stimorol, both in the case of the product and in all aspects of its marketing. All product development involves the use of the most highly advanced technology and happens under the closest scrutiny and market analysis, to ensure that we always meet customer requirements.

Dandy Chewing Gum A/S

For Dandy Chewing Gum A/S the value of the right idea depends on correct timing. That is why we follow market developments constantly and why the organization as a whole mirrors an ambition of meeting customers' changing requirements quickly and flexibly.

Dandy Chewing Gum A/S develops, produces and sells chewing gum and bubble gum the world over. The products are marketed as our own brands, as novelties or as customers' private brands. The product portfolio includes worldwide sales of the brands Dandy, Dandy Light and Clip & Clap, as well as sales of Stimorol in selected markets inside and outside Europe. Products are marketed through our own sales subsidiaries and through a network of qualified distributors. The products are manufactured at Vejle in Denmark and the joint venture factory in Zimbabwe. Thus our activities also include the development and management of joint venture plants.

The Russian Brands Division

The Russian Brands Division is the youngest business unit in the Dandy Group of companies. The Russian Brands Division is responsible for the sale and marketing of the organization's brands in Russia, which is one of Dandy's most important markets.

Through particularly intensive marketing via national television channels, the Russian Brands Division constantly ensures that all 170 million consumers know the brands Stimorol, Dirol and V6.

Sales and marketing in the enormous country is managed via the Russian Brands Division's own office in Moscow. The office is in contact with and services the many distributors who ensure that the Dandy Group's products reach consumers across all eleven time zones.

Fertin A/S

Within Dansk Tyggegummi Fabrik A/S, Fertin A/S is the business unit, which is concerned with the successful development, production, marketing and sale of medical chewing gum. This means chewing gum which releases ethical drugs as it is being chewed. Fertin A/S produces under Good Manufacturing Practice (GMP) conditions and is recognized by the Danish State Health Authority. Fertin A/S is also a member of Mefa, the Association of Danish Drugs Manufacturers.

Fertin A/S produces brands, e.g. V6, which are marketed through our own distributors and through sales subsidiaries within Stimorol Chewing Gum A/S. Fertin A/S also produces private label products for other companies in the drugs industry.

Fertin A/S has its own product development division and is responsible for the required medical documentation. Clinical tests etc. are carried out in collaboration with selected medical doctors. dentists and hospitals, dental colleges and the Danish Pharmaceutical College. Fertin A/S has proved the advantage in administering many drugs in chewing gum, e.g. for the prevention and cure of dental and mouth diseases, ethical drugs with a high level of pre-systemic metabolization, drugs for children where fast absorption is needed and when faster distribution in the mouth is important.

Appendix 4: DTF sales and production
Main factory
The main factory is in Vejle, Denmark, capable of producing ca. 7 tonnes of gum base per day (ca. 16,500 tonnes per annum).

Sales subsidiaries
Denmark
Sweden
Holland
Belgium
Slovenia
Serbia
Belarus
Ukraine
Lithuania
Kazakhstan
Switzerland
Russia
Croatia
Latvia (including Estonia)
Georgia (including Armenia and Azerbaijan)

Strategic alliances
Kraft Jacobs Suchard (France)
Freia Marabou A/S (Sweden)
Lone Folienprint GmbH (Germany)
SmithKline Beecham (UK)
Ciba-Geigy/Novartis (Switzerland)

Joint venture production
Zimbabwe

Appendix 5: Statement on products and buyer behaviour
DTF's product can, crudely, be divided into products for children and products for adults. Research shows that 90 per cent of all chewing gum purchases are made on impulse, which is why Dandy has developed its own point of sales display stands for prominent display in shops.

Appendix 6: DTF mission statement

> *To see the consumer smile while chewing our product. The company aims at meeting people's need for having or experiencing a good taste in their mouth.*

Appendix 7: The Dandy 'strategy model'

Product quality has been a key word to Dandy right from the very beginning. As a result, quality is the basic element – the body – which holds the company strategy together.

Consumers will only buy Dandy's products if they are distributed in the right way, or in other words, if they are positioned correctly in shops. In addition, consumers must have an awareness and appreciation of the products. This is achieved by means of goal-oriented communication.

At Dandy we believe in always living up to customer requirements and expectations – these form the head of our strategy model, which controls our actions.

Derwent Valley Foods Ltd
The early years (1982–88)

Beginnings

The story of Derwent Valley Foods (DVF) began in the early 1980s when Roger McKechnie left Tudor Foods (potato crisp manufacturers) in County Durham seeking a new challenge within the crisps and snacks industry.

Roger had enjoyed a successful career in FMCGs, firstly with Proctor and Gamble and then during fourteen years at Tudor, where he had become marketing director. He was responsible for establishing Tudor as the brand leader in the crisps sector in the North East region. When he was presented with the opportunity to become the company's managing director, he decided to take his expertise out of Tudor to attempt to establish his own company.

One of Roger's longstanding friends, Ray McGhee, was a product group manager with the foods group Lyons. Ray was persuaded to join Roger in the new venture and they decided to explore the possibility of setting up the new business within the sector that Roger knew the best – in crisps and snacks.

In April 1981, Roger set out his ideas for the company:

> The company will manufacture and sell a wide range of high quality pre-packaged savoury products for purchase/consumption by children and housewives ... It will be positioned as a small, caring, totally committed manufacturer of high quality products able to give its customers remarkable service and value for money due to low overheads and the personal involvement of key managers.

As Roger and Ray developed their ideas, two of Roger's former colleagues from Tudor expressed an interest in joining the embryonic company. Keith Gill, formerly Tudor's group product manager, was energetic and good at generating ideas whilst John Pike joined with a view to overseeing production.

In January 1982, as the four were still formulating their initial strategy, Roger McKechnie went to the USA to attend the Annual Snacks and Crisps Convention. Roger noted that in contrast to packaging designs in the UK, premium crisps and snacks for the US market were often presented in high quality metallized polythene packets. This not only assured greater freshness, but also allowed for the possibility of imprinting distinctive and attractive designs on the packaging. At the same Convention, Roger identified a range of production machinery that was unavailable in the UK and which could be used to manufacture a wide range of textures and shapes of corn-based snacks.

Brand and product development

From the outset, Roger was aware of changes in the market for savoury snacks and he and his fellow founder directors began looking for ideas on products and market positioning. The traditional market for potato crisps was in maturity and offered limited opportunity for high profits, so they set about developing products that were both distinctive and which could sell at a premium price.

One product idea which was relatively new at the time was to base snack products on corn rather than potato. Corn was known to be the basis of a popular snack in South and Central America and the tortilla chip was the first of a number of ideas that formed the basis of DVF's first tranche of products. A range of exotic flavours from different parts of the world were employed and together with the unique foil packaging, the idea for distinctive brand was developed.

The name Phileas Fogg was suggested as the name of the brand after Jules Verne's character in the novel *Around the World in 80 Days*. Before long, the Phileas Fogg brand comprised a number of products including Tortilla Chips, California Corn Chips (cheese flavour) and Punjab Puri (spicy flavour). The products were packaged in 100g packs, compared with the more usual 25g packs of potato crisps. This necessitated a reconsideration of DVF's initial target segment. It was noted that the most likely target market segment for the Phileas Fogg brand would be adults as the flavours were often an 'acquired' taste and the products were typically consumed with alcoholic beverages.

Production

With the new product idea now well developed, the new company set about finding suitable premises for production and as a base for operations. Given that the four all lived in the North East of England, the most obvious option was to see what was available in the region.

A site in the former steel town of Consett, County Durham was eventually selected. John Pike explained the reasons for choosing Consett:

> There were a number of reasons [for choosing Consett]. Given that we were unprepared (nor in truth would any great advantage have been gained) to move house, we reviewed a number of locations within the North East which carried maximum grant support. Consett offered a suitable rent-free factory as well as space to expand. The support from DIDA [Derwentside Industrial Development Agency] – then run at British Steel Corporation's cost, was a significant factor. There was a council and a town happy to welcome us who could provide the labour we required.

The production facility on the Number One Industrial Estate in Consett offered 12,000 square feet of production space – an adequate area for the start-up. Employees were drawn largely from the large pool of unemployed people in the town that had suffered since the closure of the large steelworks in 1979. The machines that Roger had identified as being suitable in the USA were imported to form the basis of the plant.

Changes

It wasn't long before demand for the Phileas Fogg brand exceeded the capacity of the original factory and the company was able to secure a second factory just across the road from the first. As well as expanding production space from 12,000 to 40,000 square feet, this offered a more modern facility for both production and office accommodation. The four directors set up a large shared office in one corner of the new building to enable them to discuss strategy with each other in an open and inclusive way.

In order to consolidate its position in its market niche, DVF made a number of acquisitions in the 1980s. Anglo-Oriental Foods was a London-based Indian food specialist whilst Camsis bakery and Sisterson Foods were both based in Consett. Roger expressed his personal vision for the group as wanting, 'to become the number one upmarket snack food manufacturer in the UK. We want to be the Rolls-Royce of the snack food industry.'

By 1988, DVF had experienced four years of consistent growth and, in addition to its acquisitions, had introduced new products, some of which were based on nuts and on bread. From a standing start, turnover had grown to £14 million and the company employed 200 people. It was noted, however, that one of the most urgent needs was to appoint good managers, 'to give us [the directors] the time to do the things we are best at, such as strategic thinking and creativity in spotting new products and ideas.'

In addition to its success with the Phileas Fogg brand, DVF was able to win orders for the manufacture of supermarkets' own-brand snack products. The early customers for own-brand manufacture included Sainsbury's and Marks & Spencer.

Culture and management style

From the outset in 1982, the four directors sought to cultivate a unique corporate culture in DVF. It was described as 'informal' and was encapsulated in the maxim, 'make it fun'. Unlike other employers in the industry, DVF's directors dressed informally and encouraged their managers to do the same. The idea behind the culture was eventually articulated in the mission statement:

Mission statement – Derwent Valley Foods Limited

We will become the best UK adult snack company through dedication to quality, the bold use of new ideas, and the determination to succeed.

As we strive to achieve this goal, it is important that we maintain an environment of friendship, co-operation and respect.

The idea of friendship and co-operation was considered pivotal to the success of the company. The directors believed that through this cultural approach, an environment of creativity and innovation could be cultivated – something that would be vital if DVF was to continue its growth and success.

Honda Rover – how successful was it?

British Leyland

The history of the Rover Group goes back to the end of the nineteenth century. In the first half of the twentieth century, the West Midlands of the UK was the home of a number of independent motor companies and became one of the most important centres of motor manufacturing outside the USA. As the independents started to 'feel the heat' from foreign competitors in the 1950s and 1960s, some of the locally based producers saw the logic of merging in order to take advantage of economies of scale in purchasing and production.

Austin and Morris MG joined together in 1952 to become the British Motor Company (BMC) and were joined in 1965 by Pressed Steel Ltd – a producer of sheet steel, one of the key inputs into the car production process. The company structure changed to a divisionalized holding company in 1966 when BMC purchased Jaguar Daimler. Two years later, in 1968, BMC Holdings merged with its rival Leyland Motor Corporation (LMC) to form the British Leyland Motor Company. LMC was itself the result of several mergers in the 1960s and owned the marques Rover, Land Rover, Triumph and Leyland.

By 1975, when the Group simplified its name to British Leyland (BL), it had three major production sites: two in the West Midlands at Longbridge (the UK's largest car plant) and at Solihull, and one in Oxfordshire (the Cowley plant).

Rover in the 1970s

The 1970s was a bad decade for BL. Between 1968 and 1978, its share of the UK car market fell from 40 per cent to 23 per cent and it was overtaken for the first time by Ford motors (USA). The trade unions at the Rover plants, particularly at its main Longbridge plant near Birmingham, had a reputation for militancy, and productivity had plumbed to new depths through a series of wildcat strikes and work-to-rule measures.

The company's major products were as unsuccessful as its industrial relations. Whilst the top-of-the-range offerings held up well (the Land Rover and Range Rover), the mid-range Austin Allegro and Morris Marina fared badly against the equivalent Ford Escort, Vauxhall's Viva and Chevette, and the VW Golf. The high volume Rover products were not known for their design, their build nor their longevity. Some of Rover's products from the 1970s have entered motoring folklore as objects of ridicule such as the Austin Ambassador, the Princess and the Rover 3500. In order to set out the company's position to its staff, the then chairman of BL, Donald Stokes, said, 'Workmanship and finish of British Leyland cars must be improved. If we don't do this I think our jobs are at risk.'

The one high volume segment that showed some promise was the growing supermini market. The Ford Fiesta, launched in the mid-1970s, had demonstrated a market for this design format and by the end of the decade BL's Mini Metro was showing some promise in this sector. The traditional Mini had fared reasonably within its small niche market.

In 1977, Donald Stokes' warning finally came true. The British Labour government acquired a controlling stake in the company to prevent it from becoming bankrupt with the inevitable loss of over 60,000 jobs, with many more being threatened in the service and supply industries in the West Midlands area. It was the last nationalization of the 1974–79 Labour administration.

When the Conservatives came to power in 1979, one of Prime Minister Thatcher's first acts of industrial policy was to privatize BL. The UK defence company, British Aerospace plc (BAe), was persuaded to purchase the company as a wholly-owned subsidiary. Despite the fact that motor manufacturing didn't fit naturally into BAe's product portfolio, plans were already in hand to bring about a radical improvement in its fortunes.

The company described its situation at the end of the 1970s:

In the late 1970s, the world automotive industry was starting to stagnate after decades of consistent growth. All manufacturers were moving swiftly to find ways of adjusting to the new climate. They were looking to use research and development money more effectively, and looking to spread the risk associated with the manufacture of major components in a high volume plant.

They were also looking at new ways of gaining access to markets which were difficult, or seemingly impossible [to enter]. Increasingly, manufacturers worldwide were reaching the conclusion that a joint venture was the best way of meeting these objectives and, at the same time, remaining independent. Honda also reached that conclusion.

Worldwide joint ventures and Honda
It was import restrictions in the form of import duties and quotas that had limited transnational growth in many markets, and the automotive sector was no exception. Some producers, seeking to circumvent these restrictions, opted for the higher risk international strategy of direct investment. Most, however, decided to investigate the possibility of linking up with a local producer with a view to collaboration on research and production. By assembling cars in local factories, the cars could be sold as locally produced. Other benefits included synergies in product design, purchasing and distribution.

By 1980, most of the world's major motor manufacturers had entered into, or were considering, international joint ventures or similar collaborative arrangements. The US-based General Motors (the world's largest motor company) established collaborative relationships with Saab, Daewoo, Isuzu, Lotus and Suzuki and it was not untypical in its approach. Ford entered into similar arrangements with Jaguar, Kia, Mazda and Nissan. In some cases, international joint ventures eventually led to acquisition, such as that of Jaguar by Ford.

Honda, the Japanese motor company, had been well known in the UK for its motorcycles but less so for its cars. Like other Far Eastern manufacturers in its position, Honda had enjoyed only limited success in developing the large European market through exporting into the region since import restrictions had placed a limit on the extent to which it could develop there. Honda's cars had a good reputation for quality and many observers considered its design capability to be its key strength.

Of the three main automotive market areas (the Far East, the USA and Europe), Honda's presence was conspicuously small in Europe. It had a strong presence in its home area and had already successfully developed the North American market. Given the potential of the European market, Honda considered it a strategic priority to make some inroads into it.

The beginning of the alliance

Following meetings between Honda and BL in late 1978, a formal agreement was signed on 27 December 1979. Both parties entered into the 'partnership' warily, reluctant to expose too much to each other until a culture of mutual trust could be established. Accordingly, the initial agreement was for the joint production of a single model – the Triumph Acclaim (Triumph being a marque owned by BL). The Acclaim included parts and technology from both companies and proved to be a successful model, selling 130,000 units across Europe.

In 1981, 'Project XX' was launched to enable the two companies to develop, in tandem, an executive model under each marque. The Rover 800 series and the Honda Legend were essentially similar 'under the skin'. They shared the same body platform and both companies contributed to the design and styling.

The success of the Acclaim and Project XX persuaded both parties that they were, together, capable of producing a quality product that would enjoy success in the European market. In June 1984, two medium family cars were launched that were also essentially the same 'under the skin'. The Rover 200 and the Honda Ballade were designed mainly by Honda whilst Rover's knowledge of the European markets proved to be valuable in terms of styling and specification. Both cars were produced by Rover at its Longbridge plant.

In 1984, BL took the decision to demerge its premium marques Jaguar and Daimler. It was thought that the sale of shares in the demerged company would be useful in developing the company's core high volume products. Two years later, in order to identify the company with what it saw as its strongest marque, BL changed its name to Rover Group.

The reversal in Rover's fortunes was evidenced by the award of Car of the Year in 1989 for the Rover 200 series. Rover went on to manufacture the Honda Concerto for the European market and to launch a new mid-range car, the Rover 400 series. Despite these apparent successes (particularly its improvements in product design), Rover products continued to lose market share against its larger international competitors. In 1988, Rover's share of the UK market fell below 12 per cent and it was overtaken by Vauxhall motors – the UK subsidiary of the US-based General Motors.

The alliance in the 1990s

In the late 1980s, Honda invested in its own assembly plant in the UK. The £200 million plant at Swindon in Wiltshire was smaller than those built around the same time in the UK by Toyota and Nissan, but Rover's Longbridge and Cowley plants were able to pick up any extra volumes that Honda might require.

Following the success of the alliance in the 1980s, the two companies signed a new ten-year extension in 1989. The first fruits of the new alliance were the Rover 600 series and the Honda Accord. Like the models launched in the 1980s, these two models shared the same 'under-the-skin' components and were aimed at the upper-mid-range market. Panels for both cars were produced by Rover whilst the cars were assembled at the two companies' respective factories.

Honda assisted Rover in its international market development by distributing Rover products through its dealership network in the Far East. The Land Rover Discovery, for example, was badged as a Honda for sale in Japan.

In early 1990, the two companies made a gesture to each other as a sign of their mutual trust and 'friendship'. A 20 per cent stake in share capital was exchanged between Rover Group and Honda UK. Rover Group commented that, 'This advanced the relationship to a more formal and permanent basis and helped both companies, while preserving their separate identities, to develop long-term strategies to meet the demands of an increasingly global market.'

The two companies also formalized a joint strategy on purchasing and component supply for the expanded alliance. This was designed to take advantage of economies of scale and to ensure that quality assurance standards could be guaranteed in respect to purchased parts and other inputs.

Events in 1994

In the early 1990s, British Aerospace, Rover Group's parent company, began to review Rover's place in its portfolio of businesses. BAe is an international aircraft and armaments business and had, among other things, a strategic interest in the Eurofighter project. The fact that BAe had accepted ownership of Rover only reluctantly in the 1970s (when it was privatized by Prime Minister Thatcher) was also a key consideration at this time. Honda was not made aware of these discussions.

On 31 January 1994, a press statement was issued by BAe to the effect that it had sold the Rover Group in its entirety (apart from Honda's 20 per cent share) to the German car manufacturer BMW for £800 million. For BAe, this disposal was seen as an opportunity to refocus on its core areas. Honda found out about the sale at the same time as the press and made its anger at the move clear.

Rover's new owner, BMW, made clear that it intended to keep the manufacturing plants in the UK but that it was unlikely that it would wish to maintain the alliance with Honda in the long term. On 21 February 1994, Honda announced that it had sold its 20 per cent shareholding in the Rover Group.

Kwik Save Group plc

An introduction to the UK retail industry

The total sales through UK supermarkets in 1997 exceeded £62 billion. Of this total, the majority was food (ca. £45 billion) whilst the remainder comprised sales of household goods and clothing. The total UK food sales (from supermarkets and other outlets) in 1997 amounted to £81 billion.

The grocery sector has undergone a number of changes over recent years. Among the most important of these has been the increasing concentration of market share amongst the largest companies. The four largest companies in the sector control in excess of 60 per cent of the total market by value. Five years previously, the same companies controlled less than half of the total market.

Company	Market share
Tesco plc	20.3
J Sainsbury plc	18.1
ASDA Group plc	12.2
Safeway plc	9.9
Kwik Save Group plc	4.5
Somerfield plc	4.5
Marks & Spencer plc*	3.6
Wm Morrison Supermarkets plc	3.3
Waitrose Ltd	2.0
Iceland Group plc	1.8

Table 1 Market shares of the leading UK supermarket and superstore chains by value (%), 1996. (*Source*: Key Note)
*food sales only

The history and philosophy of Kwik Save

What later became the Kwik Save Group plc started life in 1959 in the North Wales town of Rhyl. In 1965, when the company had four stores, it changed its name from Value Foods Ltd to Kwik Save. The name change was thought appropriate to reflect the philosophy of the company: to provide foods at discounted prices. 'We do not compromise on quality,' the company says, 'but simply achieve savings on operating costs by efficiencies and adherence to our no-nonsense trading philosophy.'

The company's outlets grew steadily, both in number and in the number of products carried. Whilst pre-packaged goods remained the centre of most Kwik Save outlets, there was a steady increase in branded wines, beers, spirits, tobacco, chilled and frozen foods alongside in-store franchised departments for meats and greengrocery.

Company	Number of outlets
Kwik Save Group plc	979
Tesco plc	545
Safeway plc	500
Somerfield plc	400
J Sainsbury plc	378
Marks & Spencer plc*	285
Co-operative Wholesale Society Ltd	268
ASDA Group plc	213
Gateway (Somerfield plc)	132
Aldi Stores Ltd	130
Netto Foodstores Ltd	113
Waitrose Ltd	113
Budgens plc	108
Iceland Group plc	108
Wm Morrison Supermarkets plc	86
Food Giant Ltd	28
Savacentre Ltd	12
Lidl Ltd	10
Dales ASDA Ltd	7

Table 2 Leading UK supermarket and superstore retailers by number of outlets in the UK, 1997. (*Source*: Key Note)
*food sales only

In 1970, with the company having expanded to a total of 24 stores, it was floated on the London Stock Exchange. This provided the capital required for further expansion, and over the next decade the company increased its stores to a total of 260. Eleven years later, the company opened its 750th store and, by 1995, it owned 979 outlets in total.

In the mid-1990s, the Chief Executive, Graeme Bowler, set out Kwik Save's underlying approach as one of, 'providing shoppers with unbeatable value from conveniently located stores.' He continued, 'Outstanding value will remain the cornerstone of Kwik Save's retailing philosophy.'

The company has a succinct mission statement, and has also produced a Charter which was published in its Annual Report.

Mission Statement and Charter – Kwik Save Group plc

Mission Statement
To operate clean, bright, efficient, friendly and socially-responsible 'no nonsense' foodstores which give to the discerning shopper the best value anywhere.

*The company produced a '**Charter**' which was published in its Annual Report.*
The more efficiently we operate, the more our customers benefit from the best prices.
We sell top brands and top sellers – we never compromise on quality.

> *We always use our buying power to obtain the keenest costs and pass on the savings through everyday low prices.*
>
> *We operate smaller, efficient stores that are conveniently located and easy to shop in.*
>
> *We don't insult our customers with frills or gimmicks for which, ultimately, they pay the price.*
>
> *We believe all this adds up to the best value shopping in the United Kingdom.*

Acquisitions and concessions

Beginning in 1981, the company began a programme of expansion through mechanisms other than those which were organic in nature.

On 1 May 1981, Kwik Save completed the purchase of the Coleman Meat Company Ltd. Coleman's was an independent meat producer and butcher, and Kwik Save used Coleman's expertise to operate the meat sections in most of its larger stores thus adding to its own offerings of pre-packaged products. Eventually, Coleman's also operated the greengrocery concessions and some other 'specialist' counters in Kwik Save stores.

In 1986, Kwik Save purchased 29 Arctic freezer centres – a company which concentrated upon the growing frozen food market. Tates Ltd was purchased in August 1986 – a company which operated the Tates Lateshopper 'convenience' outlets. In the following year, Dairy Farm, a major international food retailer, purchased 25 per cent of Kwik Save's shares. The new part-owners placed two directors on the Kwik Save board. In the same year, the company purchased the first of its 43 stores in London, thus increasing the Group's presence in the South East.

In 1989, the Victor Value chain of 'limited-assortment' supermarkets was acquired. The majority of these 'conveniently-located' stores were converted into Kwik Save format shops whilst a number of others were closed because they were not deemed to have been economically viable.

The acquisitions continued into the 1990s. In 1991, 42 former Gateway properties were added to the Group in the previously under-represented North East of England. Seven Grandways stores were purchased from William Jackson & Sons Ltd and 18 stores previously operated by RT Willis (Food Distributors) Ltd. In the same year, Kwik Save bought the off-licence chain, Liquorsave, to operate the wines, beers and spirits departments in the larger Kwik Save stores. In 1992, a further 12 stores were purchased from William Jackson in the Yorkshire and Humberside region and, in 1994, 100 stores were added by the acquisition of the Shoprite chain of discount retailers – a company with a broad geographic coverage within the UK.

Whilst some of the acquisitions continued to operate under their own name, the majority were bought for their location and were refitted under the Kwik Save format. The Coleman's and Liquorsave subsidiaries operated within the larger Kwik Save stores under a semi-independent concessionary arrangement.

One of the results of this programme of expansion was a significant widening of the company's geographic base.

Shops and locations

Unlike some of its competitors, Kwik Save did not develop large out-of-town superstores.

Its focus from the outset was on smaller local town centre or suburban developments which the majority of its customers could reach on foot or by a short bus ride. The average size of its stores in 1995 was less than 10,000 square feet – very small in comparison to the major food multiples such as Tesco, Asda and Sainsbury.

By geographic area, the overwhelming majority of Kwik Save outlets were opened or acquired in areas of the country that have suffered de-industrialization over recent decades. The 990 stores are largely located in Wales, the North West, the North East and the Midlands. A number of stores were also opened in selected parts of London and the South West. There is a small presence in Scotland.

Year	Number of stores
1965	4
1970	24
1975	71
1980	260
1985	420
1990	661
1991	730
1992	780
1993	814
1994	860
1995	990

Table 3 Number of Kwik Save outlets. (*Source*: Kwik Save Group plc)

Products
Kwik Save's product range comprises both branded products from the major food manufacturers and a range of the company's own-branded products. In order to develop the market amongst the more cost-conscious customers, the 'No Frills' own brand was launched in 1993. The 'No Frills' range was packaged in simple black and white and was designed to appeal to those customers to whom value-for-money was more important than premium features. Within a year of the launch of 'No Frills', sales of the 100 products in the brand accounted for 7 per cent of total sales and was growing.

The company claims that by stocking different quality grades of products, the customer is given the maximum choice. An example of this is in its instant coffee products. Three key products are stocked. Kenco is a freeze dried premium brand and will appeal to quality-conscious shoppers, Nescafé is an everyday granule coffee whilst 'No-Frills' coffee is packaged in a plastic bag and appeals to price-sensitive shoppers. This triple-product approach is reflected in most other parts of the product range.

The focus of the product range is firmly on 'the fastest selling brands, varieties and sizes'. This emphasis means that Kwik Save aims to provide cost savings (and hence lower prices) by stocking a lower range of products than its major 'superstore' competitors, with the faster stock turn resulting in lower costs of stockholding.

Technology and systems
Kwik Save was one of the earliest adopters of scanning and EPOS (electronic point of

sale) technology in the retail industry. Investment in scanning began in 1988 and was designed to exploit the new (at the time) bar code information on product packaging. In addition to speeding up the checkout process, scanning technology facilitates rapid transfer of stock-flow information to decision-makers. The company described its technology as enabling the company to 'manage a product range tailored to customers' needs and to operate an efficient and cost-effective supply chain.'

In the mid-1990s, the computer systems were upgraded with a view to offering a number of additional advantages. In summary, the new systems were designed to 'lock in a low-cost operating base'.

The company detailed the advantages:

- *upgrading our point of sale equipment to facilitate electronic payment and special promotions;*
- *developing new systems to fit the product range and promotions to local needs;*
- *developing new stock and re-ordering systems to let us refill shelves daily – essential to our fresh and chilled food plans;*
- *extending the computerization programme within our distribution centres.*

In order to gain economies of scale in product purchasing and distribution, a new purpose-built warehousing centre was developed in central England in 1995. Located close to the M1 motorway in Wellingborough, Northants, phase 1 of the warehouse facility comprised 250,000 square feet of multi-temperature storage.

The company described the benefits of the new facility:

This centre enables us to supply chilled, frozen and dry products together, on a daily basis. We are starting to see the benefits in better availability of products on the shelves, lower stock levels, lower costs and less damage to goods through handling orders less frequently.

The retail sector at the end of the 1990s

Over the course of the 1990s, a number of changes occurred both in the retail sector's external environment and in the industry itself. A number of trends are noteworthy.

Firstly, the major 'big four' multiples (Sainsbury, Tesco, Safeway and Asda) have focused their new developments on new-build stores in edge-of-town or out-of-town locations where land is cheaper and large plots are more available compared with town centres. This trend is designed to fit the lifestyles of customers who tend to shop on a weekly or monthly basis rather than day-to-day. These stores are mainly very large in terms of floor area and they usually have equally large car parks to cater for families, parents with children and people with special needs. Whilst these superstores have undeniably proved popular with customers, local authorities are seeking to discourage growth in this type of store because of the effects they have had on the smaller town centre shops.

The second noticeable trend in the sector is the apparent reduction in purely price-based competition. The evidence would seem to suggest that consumers are concerned about other features of the store they shop at rather than just price. The provision of free parking, crèches, on-site petrol stations and a wide range of in-kind benefits (air miles, points-based loyalty cards, etc.) have all had an influence on shopping habits. The effect that these incentives will have on the economy supermarkets like Kwik Save (who have traditionally competed on a price basis) is uncertain.

Thirdly, there has been a significant expansion in the number of non-food products that the major multiples have offered. The idea of a superstore as a 'one-stop' shop has grown over the decade as the key 'cash-rich-time-poor' customers have sought to spend less time shopping. Accordingly, many of the larger retailers have added clothing, music, electrical goods, banking services, pharmacies and holiday/travel agencies to their product portfolios. The development of large stores with space for such in-store shops has been a significant factor in this trend.

The way in which the key customers shop is also expected to change over the next few years. Some stores have already increased their opening hours, in some cases to 24 hour opening, to accommodate the changing lifestyles of their customers. Home and Internet shopping is also expected to grow, and the larger retailers are making investments in their IT functions to facilitate this development.

Finally, the distinction between premium and economy supermarkets has been blurred as the 'big four' have expanded ranges to include 'basic' own brands in addition to their main own brands and other branded goods. Tesco, Asda and Safeway have all pursued this option with their ranges of such products such as Asda's 'Farm Stores' brand and Safeway's 'Savers'. By offering these ranges, the retailers in question believe that cost-conscious customers can be accommodated as well as those who wish to purchase the better-known branded and own-brand products.

Appendix 1: Consolidated profit and loss statements (1987–96)

	1996 (£m)	1995 (£m)	1994 (£m)	1993 (£m)	1992 (£m)	1991 (£m)	1990 (£m)	1989 (£m)	1988 (£m)	1987 (£m)
Sales inc. VAT	3,511.6	3,228.3	3,020.3	2,858.4	2,498.2	1,894.6	1,520.4	1,238.8	974.1	862.03
VAT	(257.5)	(236.2)	(220.3)	(207.2)	(179.2)	n/a	(74.8)	(47.4)	(42.46)	(35.92)
Sales exc. VAT	3,254.1	2,992.1	2,800.0	2,651.2	2,319.0	n/a	1,445.6	1,181.4	931.634	826.1
Cost of sales	(2,796.8)	(2,551.9)	(2,403.6)	(2,278.7)	(1,984.6)	n/a	(1,226.4)	(1,002.0)	(792.07)	(708.5)
Gross profit	457.3	440.2	396.4	372.5	334.4	n/a	219.2	179.3	139.564	117.59
Distribution costs	(349.5)	(297.4)	(249.2)	(232.9)	(206.9)	n/a	(131.8)	(106.4)	(81.45)	(69.98)
Admin. expenses	(44.8)	(36.2)	(35.4)	(33.8)	(31.2)	n/a	(19.9)	(15.5)	(13.8)	(10.45)
Trading profit	63.0	106.6	111.8	105.8	96.3	n/a	67.5	57.4	44.3	37.16
Other income (concessions and other sources)	32.2	27.5	23.7	20.5	16.8	n/a	12.9	11.2	8.69	7.75
Operating profit	95.2	134.1	135.5	126.3	113.1	n/a	80.4	68.6	53.0	44.9
Provisions	–	(6.8)	–	–	–	n/a	–	–	–	–
Profit on divestments	–	–	0.2	–	–	n/a	–	–	–	–
Interest payable/receivable	(4.9)	(1.8)	(0.1)	(0.2)	(2.5)	n/a	4.86	4.6	2.186	1.701
Profit before tax	90.3	125.5	135.6	126.1	110.6	101.7	85.3	73.2	55.176	46.6
Tax	(31.6)	(45.5)	(47.1)	(40.5)	(36.4)	n/a	(29.9)	(25.0)	(19.755)	(16.408)
Profit after interest and tax	58.7	80.0	88.5	85.6	74.2	n/a	55.4	48.2	35.421	30.2

Appendix 2: Consolidated balance sheets (1987–96)

	1996 (£m)	1995 (£m)	1994 (£m)	1993 (£m)	1992 (£m)	1991 (£m)	1990 (£m)	1989 (£m)	1988 (£m)	1987 (£m)
Fixed assets										
Tangible assets	635.4	626.2	517.4	465.3	405.3	n/a	253.72	217.48	183.13	168.12
Investments	–	–	–	–	–	n/a	3.721	3.721	–	–
Current assets										
Stocks	179.0	180.2	148.4	154.9	116.5	n/a	70.751	61.277	43.9	37.86
Debtors	51.7	36.6	7.9	16.2	15.9	n/a	13.913	10.683	6.5	6.05
Short term investments	9.5	9.7	41.6	–	3.6	n/a	11.833	22.217	37.5	18.3
Cash at bank and in hand	11.4	19.5	14.7	31.2	14.7	n/a	7.536	6.651	6.3	5.9
	251.6	246.0	212.6	202.3	150.7	n/a	104.033	100.828	94.24	68.16
Creditors: amounts falling due within one year	(460.6)	(431.4)	(285.4)	(318.5)	(260.3)	n/a	(153.46)	(148.8)	(104.5)	(91.2)
Net current liabilities	(209.0)	(431.4)	(72.8)	(116.2)	(109.6)	n/a	(49.428)	(47.97)	(10.24)	(23.06)
Total assets less current liabilities	426.4	440.8	444.6	349.1	295.7	n/a	208.013	173.227	172.9	145.06
Creditors: amount falling due after more than one year	–	–	(0.1)	(0.2)	(0.3)	n/a	(3.441)	(3.441)	(14.9)	(12.1)
Provisions for liabilities and charges	(44.2)	(5.3)	(34.3)	(1.1)	(1.0)	n/a	(0.7)	(0.5)	(0.5)	(0.5)
Net assets	**382.2**	**435.5**	**410.2**	**347.8**	**294.4**	**244.3**	**203.9**	**169.3**	**157.5**	**132.4**
Capital and reserves										
Called up share capital	15.6	15.6	15.5	15.4	15.4	n/a	15.33	15.26	15.2	15.15
Share premium account	19.0	18.4	14.9	14.1	12.6	n/a	10.6	9.25	8.9	7.5
Profit and loss account	347.6	401.5	379.8	318.3	266.4	n/a	177.9	144.8	133.3	109.8
Shareholders' funds	**382.2**	**435.5**	**410.2**	**347.8**	**294.4**	**244.3**	**203.89**	**169.3**	**157.5**	**132.4**

Appendix 3: Selected operational statistics

	1996	1995	1994	1993	1992	1991	1990	1989
Number of Kwik Save stores at year end	979	979	861	814	768	745	661	643
Average store size (square feet)	7,442	7,282	6.950	6,620	6,440	6,240	6,050	5,910
Total sales area, including concessions (million sq feet)	7.3	7.1	7.2	7.3	6.5	6.1	5.3	5.0
Total number of concessions	1,849	1,864	1,664	1,560	1,507	1,472	1,113	1,062

Case Study

Sainsbury Homebase

The parent company

Sainsbury is best known in the UK for its food retailing interests. The grocery business began in 1870 and for most of its history focused entirely on the grocery area. In 1995, the Sainsbury Group comprised five operating divisions:

- *J. Sainsbury supermarkets* – one of the UK's leading retailers accounting for 18 per cent of the food retail market. It is the largest division in the J. Sainsbury Group, accounting for ca. 80 per cent of Group sales and almost 90 per cent of profits. A typical store stocks over 19,000 product lines.
- *Savacentre hypermarkets* – adopting the Sainsbury approach to the hypermarket format of superstore. The hypermarkets stock a different range of consumer goods from the food-based Sainsbury supermarkets, including houseware, Babyshop, Cookshop, Lifestyle clothing and swimwear, patisserie and similar products. The company also has partnerships with overseas hypermarket chains including Mammoth in France.
- *Shaw's supermarkets Inc.* – Sainsbury Group's major overseas business. Shaw's is a chain of 87 stores in the North Eastern United States – Massachusetts, New Hampshire, Maine and Rhode Island. Shaw's carries a limited range of 2,500 products with a focus on value-for-money.
- *Giant Food Inc.* – also a US based retailer. Sainsbury purchased 50 per cent of the voting shares in Giant Food Inc. in 1994. It operates over 160 stores in Maryland, DC, Virginia and Delaware.
- *Homebase house and garden centres* – a chain of 83 UK based do-it-yourself stores and garden centres.

The Homebase division

The DIY sector underwent an important change in the late 1970s as supply became concentrated in fewer but larger DIY 'sheds'. Prior to this, DIY enthusiasts tended to have to buy from smaller specialist shops such as paint shops, tool shops, etc. The 'shed' concept brought everything for home improvement under one roof whilst, at the same time, the retailers were able to extract keener prices from their suppliers due to the much-increased economies of scale.

Wishing to benefit from this trend, Sainsbury launched its Homebase concept in 1981. Homebase gained market share throughout the 1980s along with the growth in the DIY market in general. The parent company allowed Homebase to operate within the Group as a division with its own structure and management expertise. By 1995, Homebase was the fourth largest business in the sector and operated 83 outlets, selling a wide range of products for all types of home improvement and gardening.

In 1995, Ladbroke Group plc offered Sainsbury its Texas chain of DIY stores. For Sainsbury, this deal would mean that it could increase its number of DIY outlets to 300, making it second in the sector to the market leader, B&Q. In addition to the extra market share, the acquisition of the Texas stores was described as having 'an excellent geographical fit with Homebase'.

Sainsbury's plan for Texas was to convert each outlet to the Homebase format, thus losing the Texas name altogether. It was envisioned that the process of integrating the Texas and Homebase operations together would take two years – a process that would have a number of implications for human resources.

Human resource strategy 1995–98
The acquisition of the Texas chain brought an extra 17,000 employees to the Homebase operation. Whilst this would eventually become subject to review, the first priority was to agree upon the senior management team to bring the two businesses together. At the time of the integration, Homebase's head office was in Croydon, South London whilst Texas was based in Northampton, about fifty miles north of the capital.

The decision was made to keep the operation based at Croydon and this caused the majority of the Texas senior management team to leave the company. Homebase management regretted the loss of these key people as they would be unable to bring their undoubted expertise to the integration process and the conversion of the Texas stores.

At the staff level, Homebase imposed new terms and conditions upon its new employees that were previously covered by the Ladbroke contract. In order to standardize approach and practice, 177 training sessions took place across Texas stores covering till training and customer care. 'Conversion' teams from Homebase stores were developed to convert Texas stores to the Homebase way, whilst the existing Texas staff were dispersed to other Homebase stores in order to 'soak up' the organizational culture and the ways of 'doing things the Homebase way'.

These HR measures represented a significant drain on Homebase resources, but were considered essential if the integration was to be successful. Homebase store managers were placed in Texas stores and vice versa and this highlighted a number of potential problems.

The reaction from Texas employees was that 'they [Homebase] don't understand us'; and from the Homebase staff, 'What on earth has happened – why have we done this?' In order to address these problems, Homebase adopted a policy of 'mixing staff up' where convenient in order to spread the Homebase culture, values and behaviours amongst the Texas employees.

Running parallel to these measures, Homebase felt the need to restructure the unprofitable Texas kitchen business and this resulted in 70 redundancies.

Strategic issues at the end of the 1990s
In the late 1990s, a number of changes occurred in the UK DIY sector. The market leader, B&Q, moved away from the 'shed' concept to the DIY 'warehouse'. Another competitor, Wickes, increased its market share by increasing the differentiation of some of its products.

In order to address these and other threats, Homebase (which by now had fully absorbed the Texas chain) began a fundamental review of its operations.

The previous Homebase strategies which stressed choice, customer service and site acquisition had not included any human resource input in the decision-making process. The problems of integrating Texas changed the attitude of some staff and the store managers lobbied the main board to have the human resource people involved in the next phase of the development strategy. Accordingly, the board of Homebase appointed a director of human resources in March 1998.

This appointment led to a number of senior management focus groups to consider the 'people' issues in the organization. In order to establish a coherent human resource strategy, Homebase wanted to ascertain the customer's view of the organization. It transpired from this research that what customers wanted was to be able to find staff in the stores and then to have the staff help them in their product choices in a helpful and friendly manner.

Whilst the customer views were accepted and welcomed, the problem that was immediately encountered was that of high staff turnover which acted against the development of product expertise. In order to establish the reasons for the staff turnover, an employee attitude survey was carried out to ask staff what they wanted from their jobs and what motivated them to work. In addition, Homebase made an examination of its competitors and some other retailers to identify what they envied in the staff of their competitors and in their human resource practices. The best practice in the industry was identified and a number of measures were introduced to varying degrees of success including staff associations. A vision was developed that, 'In Homebase, every person is a priority.'

This new approach was backed up by a new commitment to employee communication. One such innovation was the introduction of news and views staff councils whilst a staff satisfaction index is monitored by the human resources department on an ongoing basis. The agreement by the main board of Homebase that human resources should be involved in any major business strategy development decision is seen as a major achievement.

Appendix 1: Sainsbury Group UK statistics at the time of the Texas integration

	Sales (inc. taxes) (£m)	Operating profit (£m)	Number of stores	Sales area (000s of square feet)	Full time employees	Part time employees
Homebase 1995	376.9	30.8	83	3,082	1,957	3,390
Homebase 1994	328.1	22.6	76	2,810	1,764	3,248
Sainsbury supermarkets 1995	9,597.2	784.3	355	9,338	33,568	67,911
Sainsbury supermarkets 1994	8,864.6	697.0	341	8,827	34,225	60,788
Savacentre 1995	697.7	40.9	10	864	2,458	5,698
Savacentre 1994	658.7	38.4	10	864	2,571	5,650

The Gulf War (1990–91)

The invasion

The BBC World at One news on 1 August 1990 was among the first bulletins to break the news that Iraq had invaded Kuwait, its southern neighbour in the Middle East. It was reported that after a military build-up by the Iraqi army on the Kuwaiti border, President Saddam Hussein, the allegedly despotic Iraqi leader, had finally ordered his troops into the Emirate of Kuwait – an oil-rich but relatively defenceless state situated between Iraq and Saudi Arabia. The evening television news carried pictures of Iraqi tanks and armoured personnel carriers establishing themselves in the capital, Kuwait City.

Political leaders across the world were quick to condemn the invasion. Prime Minister Thatcher in the UK and President Bush in the USA were among the first to record their disapproval of the Iraqi 'aggression'. An emergency session was called at the United Nations headquarters in New York where resolutions were quickly passed not only condemning the invasion but also demanding an immediate and unconditional Iraqi withdrawal. It was agreed by the UN that a peaceful or diplomatic resolution to the conflict would be preferable to a military confrontation.

Formulating a response

When the full picture of the invasion was emerging, United States President George Bush assembled a 'war cabinet' in the White House to consider the USA's possible responses to the Iraqi actions. The key players in the early days of President Bush's deliberations included Vice President Dan Quayle, Secretary of State James Baker, Defence Secretary Dick Cheney, National Security Advisor Brent Scowcroft and the Chairman of the Joint Chiefs of Staff, General Colin Powell. At the early meetings, the possibility of military actions was considered in the event that diplomatic efforts failed.

The political complexity of the Middle East, with its numerous tensions and potential flashpoints, meant that the objectives of any military campaign would have to be very carefully formulated. President Bush proposed that any military exercise in the Gulf should be mounted by a coalition of nations, each of whom had strategic interests in the relative stability of the *status quo* in the Gulf (as a key supplier of oil to the West). This would offer the advantage of avoiding an image of the USA and the West 'policing' the region with its military superiority. The disadvantage (to the USA) of a coalition would be that any military action would necessarily have more limited objectives than otherwise it might. It was well understood by media observers, for example, that President Bush and other Western leaders would probably have wanted to bring Saddam Hussein to trial, but this outcome would be unlikely if a coalition including Iraq's Arabic neighbours was to remain intact.

The allied coalition took shape through intense top level diplomatic negotiations until a total of 30 nations either agreed to take part in a military campaign or offered its full support. It was then agreed, by the coalition participants, that any military campaign should have very specific and immediately measurable aims – to eject Iraqi militia from Kuwait and no more.

Once the overall 'grand plan' objectives had finally been established, the US 'war cabinet' appointed its key military personnel to oversee the military part of the campaign should it became necessary. The allied powers agreed that the US should lead the campaign and the US government appointed General Norman Schwarzkopf as the commander of forces in the theatre of war.

Over the next few days, Schwarzkopf entered into intense discussions with Dick Cheney and Colin Powell to put plans in place that would work towards the achievement of the coalition's limited overall objectives. The plans had to include the inputs from the other countries that had offered military assistance to the campaign – Britain, France, Syria, Egypt, Saudi Arabia and others. Countries who offered financial support but no military personnel were also offered the chance to put in their ideas.

In November 1990, political upheaval in the governing British Conservative party led to the replacement of Margaret Thatcher by John Major as Prime Minister and he immediately made clear that there would be no change at all in Britain's policy in respect to the Iraqi 'crisis'. Mr Major, in consultation with the Americans, appointed General Peter de la Billière as the Commander of the British forces in the proposed Gulf campaign. General de la Billière joined Schwarzkopf in the Gulf to contribute to the planning of the military campaign.

As the year turned it became clear that the diplomatic efforts were unlikely to bring about the Iraqi withdrawal. Saddam Hussein had invested much in the Kuwaiti invasion and he had succeeded in uniting most of the Iraqi people in support of his actions. Diplomatic activity by Javier Perez de Cuellier, the United Nations General Secretary, had come to nothing and, as a last resort, President Bush dispatched his Secretary of State, James Baker, to engage in face-to-face meetings with the Iraqi Deputy Prime Minister, Tariq Aziz. Secretary of State Baker carried a letter to the Iraqi leadership from President Bush in which the President stated bluntly, 'There can be no reward for aggression. Nor will there be any negotiation ... You and your country will pay a terrible price.'

This 'last gasp' meeting predictably failed to change the Iraqi leadership's mind and Mr Baker returned to Washington empty-handed. With this news, President Bush consulted the allies and the decision to finalize preparations for a military solution was made.

Operation Desert Storm

From the earliest meetings in the White House, the possibility that the situation would need to be resolved through a military campaign was openly acknowledged. Accordingly, throughout the intervening months, military planning had been taking place in parallel with the diplomatic efforts.

In consultation with the allies, President Bush negotiated access to bases in countries neighbouring Iraq. Iran and Jordan decided to remain neutral in the campaign, but Iraq's neighbours, Syria, Saudi Arabia and Turkey all agreed to allow their military bases to be used for Operation Desert Storm. Israel was encouraged to remain neutral in the campaign because of the sensitivity of its relationships with its Islamic neighbours, particularly with the Palestinians and the Egyptians.

Generals Powell, Schwarzkopf and de la Billière formulated a military strategy that would meet the allies' strategic objectives for the war. The overall aims of bringing about and 'rapid and decisive' victory were tempered with the need to keep Israel out of the conflict and the political need to reduce collateral damage to Iraqi civilians or civilian property.

Accordingly, it was decided to place an emphasis upon gaining an immediate superiority in the air. The US moved 48 bombers and 1000 strike aircraft into the theatre whilst 200 other aircraft were provided by the UK, Saudi Arabia, France and Kuwait. In support of the air capability, six aircraft carriers and over 100 warships were positioned in the waters in and around the Mediterranean, the Red Sea and in the Gulf itself. These were armed with a range of high-technology sea-launched weapons including the satellite-navigated Tomahawk Cruise missile.

Ground-based troops were mobilized into the area based just behind the Iraqi borders of the collaborating countries of Turkey, Syria and Saudi Arabia. The US army assigned 350,000 troops to the campaign whilst the UK assigned 20,000; Saudi Arabia, 20,000; Egypt, 30,000; Syria, 20,000; and other countries a total of 20,000 between them.

The balance of power in the area was overwhelmingly biased towards the allies. Although the Iraqi army boasted 350,000 troops, Western intelligence experts estimated that their state of readiness would not be as high as that of the allies. Iraqi had an estimated 500 military jets and a small number of ground-based Scud missiles.

On 16 January 1991, President Bush ordered the allied forces to prosecute the operation. Saddam Hussein defiantly declared, 'The devil Bush and his treacherous gang have begun the great showdown – the mother of all battles between triumphant good and doomed evil.' The Soviet leader, President Gorbachev, was one of the few world leaders to openly express regret over the beginning of the conflict. 'I want once again to underline,' he said, 'that we did everything feasible to solve the conflict by peaceful means.' France's President Mitterand spoke for the majority of leaders when he admitted that diplomacy had failed and said, 'It is now time for the guns to speak.'

Within the first few hours of the military campaign, allied forces had launched hundreds of bombing air raids to take out the Iraqi communications systems. The priorities also included the destruction of Iraq's air capability and raids were made over known Iraqi air force sites.

Saddam Hussein's main weapons became his adroit news management and his secreted land-based Scud missiles. In an attempt to appeal to the sympathy of the West, he released film footage of a basement in which many Iraqis had been killed which he claimed had been struck by an American Cruise missile. Meanwhile, on 18 January, he attempted to destabilize the allied coalition by launching a series of Scud missile attacks on Israel in the hope that Israel would be tempted to retaliate. Whilst Israeli tolerance was tested, its government was persuaded to maintain its neutrality in the interests of the cohesion of the allied forces. More Scud attacks on Tel Aviv followed on 25 and 31 January, resulting in several fatalities.

The ending
As it became clear that the allied forces were winning the campaign, it was reported that

the Iraqi air force was flying its remaining military jets into neighbouring Iran for safe keeping. Meanwhile, the Iraqi command ordered the spillage of large quantities of crude oil into the waters of the Gulf – a move that caused concern in the West that it could cause a sizeable environmental disaster.

On 22 February, with Iraq's air defences knocked out by allied missiles and air attacks, President Bush set an immediate deadline for Iraq's withdrawal from Kuwait. Failure to comply would, according to Mr Bush, bring about, 'an instant and sharp response.' Prime Minister Major added, 'We are not prepared to be strung along any longer.' The Iraqi army in Kuwait and southern Iraq had had their supply lines cut off by the allied air strikes and morale in their ranks was reported to be very low. Saddam Hussein, determined to the end, dismissed Bush's 'high noon' deadline and condemned the US president as, 'God's enemy and the Devil's friend.'

As the allied troops entered Kuwait to finally evict the Iraqi army, Saddam ordered the withdrawing troops to set fire to Kuwait's oil wells. The first explosion on the night of 22 February was seen from HMS Brave, 40 miles away. The officer of the watch, Lt Paul Hanson, said, 'A massive sheet of flame suddenly leapt into the sky. It was a huge orange fireball which lit up the sea for miles.' In the Saudi capital, Riyadh, the US military spokesman, Brig.-Gen. Richard Neal said, 'This is orchestrated, systematic destruction ... he [Saddam] intends to destroy Kuwait.'

Within 100 hours of the ground war starting, the Iraqis had completely surrendered Kuwait and agreed to the allied terms of surrender. Advancing allied troops found the Iraqi army demoralised and unable to put up a defence. Many of them had abandoned their hardware in their haste to get home and the allied forces entered as far as Southern Iraq without experiencing any resistance.

On 27 February, with the key objective of liberating Kuwait accomplished, President Bush ordered the end of the campaign. Saddam Hussein, in negotiation with the allied high command, agreed to a programme of weapons inspections by the United Nations to ensure that Iraq's stock of weapons of mass destruction could be monitored and destroyed. Meanwhile, the allied forces faced the task of extinguishing the burning oil wells and clearing up the oil spill in the Gulf. The British forces lost a total of 16 people in the conflict whilst the Americans lost 35. The Iraqi casualties were estimated at over 150,000, of whom a third were killed.

In financial terms, the cost of the war was considerable. Within the first two weeks of Operation Desert Storm, the cost had reached £1.25 billion and was increasing at the rate of £30 million a day. In addition to the allied powers' expenditure, Saudi Arabia made £8 billion available and Japan gave £5 billion. The total allied cost of the war was estimated at over £40 billion.

The UK decorative paint industry

A paint can be defined as *any compound capable of application to a substrate* [surface] *which will provide the benefit of decorating, obscuring, preserving or providing resistance to external chemical or environmental attack*. Given such a broad definition, it will not come as a surprise to learn that many categories of the general product type can be found. In addition to the familiar brush-applied decorative paints, several other specialist products exist. The majority of paint production in the UK falls into four main user categories: decorative, industrial, automotive (including OEM) and 'specialist' coatings products. Within each category, several distinct chemical technologies exist. Whilst the majority of paints in each category retain the traditional form of organic solvent-borne compounds that dry naturally in air, novel formulations over the past two decades or so have concentrated upon water-based paints and those that form by chemical reaction rather than air-drying. Among the most innovative technologies over recent years are powder coatings (used in such applications as consumer white goods), water-based, high performance automotive coatings and the relatively new water-borne and 'odourless' decorative paints.

The UK has one of the longest-established paint industries in the world with a history that can be traced back well over a century. Since the mid-1980s, the UK has been able to boast the largest paint producer in the world (ICI Paints Division), whilst some of the most significant research in paint and associated technology has been undertaken by companies in the UK. The UK industry has total annual sales in excess of £1.5 billion, which makes it (in terms of aggregate turnover) about the same size as the crisps and snacks industry or the UK-based film industry.

The number of competitors within the industry varies according to the general buoyancy of the economy as a whole. As a mature product, sales of paint closely reflect the overall rate of national economic growth. In the mid-1980s, the number of UK producers peaked at over 330 but this number reduced to around 250 during the recession between 1991 and 1993 due to falling demand from industry, local authorities, the DIY sector and construction companies. Between 1993 and 1997, the number of paint companies increased again as the general demand in the economy increased.

Paint supply is concentrated in the hands of a relatively small number of relatively large producers. The top ten manufacturers collectively account for over half of the total volume. The two largest companies, Kalon Group plc and ICI Paints Division, both hold in excess of 10 per cent of the total UK market. Most of the larger producers have pursued external growth strategies over the past decade, including a number of key acquisitions in the EU and North America. At the other end of the size continuum, some paint producers employ fewer than five people with their products being distributed to a handful of local independent contractors and DIY outlets. One such producer is Culloden

Paints Ltd in Glasgow where the proprietor both produces and distributes the product using a small production facility and a van which has been equipped to carry cans of paint to a limited number of local buyers.

The technology contained in the majority of paint products is relatively straightforward. Most conventional paints (including all decorative gloss and emulsion paints) are manufactured by a process called *high speed dispersion* (HSD) which involves stirring the 'ingredients' together at very high rotational speed until the requisite level of consistency is achieved. HSD machines are rather like large kitchen mixers and can be purchased, reconditioned, for as little as £5,000. The formulations ('recipes') for most simple paints can be readily obtained from suppliers of raw materials who have a vested interest in ensuring that paint manufacturers have ready-to-use formulations for successful paint production.

As a product, paint is considered to be a part of the broader chemical industry. As such, producers are subject to health, safety and emissions legislation in the same way as for other parts of the chemicals sector such as petrochemicals. This has presented a number of challenges to paint companies over recent years. Two such hurdles have been the COSHH Regulations 1989, which significantly tightened materials handling rules in the workplace, and the Environmental Protection Act 1990, which increased restrictions on environmental malpractices including emissions of harmful substances into the environment. In common with other companies in the chemical industry, many competitors have seen the apparent advantage of pursuing international standards accreditation and these (ISO 9000 quality standard and ISO 14000 environmental standard) have consumed significant amounts of management time. Some of the larger paint buyers have made it a condition of supply that all paint suppliers should be accredited with ISO 9000.

In terms of market demand, the largest volumes reside in the relatively undifferentiated products that are used in the major decorative and industrial markets. These include the familiar gloss and emulsion products for decoration (both retail and trade) and the high volume industrial finishes used in automotive OEM and refinishing, marine and steel fabrications. Other products are more differentiated and occupy small-volume niche markets and these, predictably, gain higher profit margins. This category includes specialist coatings such as anti-graffiti, self-cleaning and powder coatings, and the high performance temperature-stable finishes used in applications like aircraft construction. The largest companies that operate in the UK are largely dependent upon the decorative and industrial sectors. ICI's key brand, Dulux, constitutes a large proportion of its output and the same is true for others. Kalon's output is largely own-branded by the large DIY retailers (sometimes called 'sheds') whilst another competitor owns two high-volume products – the Crown and Berger brands of decorative paint.

In the decorative paint sector, the industry structure has changed over recent years. Concentration has significantly increased among the key volume buyers. Whereas in the early 1970s, decorative paint was retailed largely through small independent DIY stores, the expansion of the DIY 'sheds' has meant that buyers are now able to purchase in much higher volumes whilst competition among manufacturers has intensified for shelf space at the expense of competitors' products. Concentration has also increased, although to a lesser extent among the trade buyers such as painting contractors and construction companies.

The basic ingredients in paint fall into three chemical categories. Resins (also called *binders* or *vehicles*) are typically synthetic polymers that bind together other components whilst also providing the mechanism by which the paint sticks to a substrate and provides weatherability. Because most binders are derived from oil products, the costs to paint manufacturers are, in part, dependent upon the market rate for crude oil.

The second category, pigments and extenders, are typically dry powders that are dispersed into the vehicle and provide colour, opacity and some chemical properties such as anti-corrosiveness. These compounds are also subject to variable market prices according to the relative volumes of market supply. The most-used pigment is titanium dioxide, the white pigment that adds colour to almost all white and light-coloured paints (into which additional tints are added). Titanium dioxide results from the processing of a titanium ore which, like all ores, is subject to price variations according to the abundance (or scarcity) of the availability of the ore. Whilst the supply of such ores to the titanium dioxide producers is normally relatively plentiful, deficits can arise from time to time as mines are exhausted prior to new sources of ore becoming developed. In such circumstances of deficit, the market price of the pigment rises, thus putting cost pressures upon paint producers.

Thirdly, most paints contain a solvent (usually an organic oil-derived compound) that makes the paint 'wet' and which evaporates when the paint is applied. Most of these components require production on a large scale and are consequently made by large chemical intermediate manufacturers, many of which are chemical multinationals (such as Exxon, Bayer, Total Oil, Shell, Sandoz) for whom paint components comprise a relatively small proportion of their output. Like binders, much of the content of solvents is oil-derived. Accordingly, the prices charged to paint companies for solvents are largely a function of the price of oil (which, in turn, depends upon the production volumes of oil on the world market).

Who owns Newcastle United?

Newcastle United's league season had not been a good one. The 1997–98 season had started with much promise, with a recently appointed new manager (Kenny Dalglish), new player signings and a place in the European Cup. In addition, the recent flotation of over a third of the company's stock on the Stock Exchange had provided the club with capital with which to improve the ground and invest in new players.

Despite beating Barcelona in the opening rounds, the team did not get through to the second phase of the European Cup and the league season went from bad to worse. By March 1998, a run of bad results saw the team slip to a league position which was perilously close to the relegation zone. The intensely loyal but increasingly frustrated Newcastle fans began to openly vent their disquiet.

The new transfers had made disappointing contributions to the club's efforts on the pitch and the faith that had been placed in Kenny Dalglish was beginning to show signs of breaking. Concerns also crept in that the financial pressures being exerted on the club from its new 'masters' in the City may have had a detrimental effect on the club's ability to bring in the new players that the fans thought might help the team's performance.

Frustrations came to a head in mid-March, 1998. The *News of the World* newspaper published a story reporting some alleged behaviour by the club's most senior two directors, Freddie Shepherd (club chairman) and Douglas Hall (club deputy chairman and whose family owned 58 per cent of the company's shares). It was reported that the two men had, on a trip abroad, frequented brothels and had made some indiscreet comments regarding the club, some of the players and the fans. In discussions with a reporter posing as a Middle-Eastern businessman, the two directors reportedly ridiculed the Newcastle fans for paying £50 for a replica shirt that only cost £5 to buy in. Star player Alan Shearer was compared to Mary Poppins and the directors allegedly described the women of Tyneside as 'dogs.' The two directors also allegedly boasted that they had sacked Kevin Keegan, the former manager.

The report went down very badly amongst the fans on Tyneside. A local television poll asked whether the two directors should resign and 97 per cent of callers voted that they should. The former Newcastle striker Malcolm MacDonald weighed in to the controversy by insisting on local television news that Shepherd and Hall should go.

In the days following the disclosure, the company's share price started to slip as investors registered their discomfort with the internal controversies at the strategic level in the company.

Shepherd and Hall remained silent for a few days, but eventually decided to issue a public apology in an attempt to defuse the row that had taken hold among the fans and in the City. It was issued to local newsrooms on the morning of a crucial relegation match against Crystal Palace. The lunchtime news bulletins carried the statement and then cut to street interviews where fans were asked if they accepted the apology. All of them said that they would not accept it and the insistence that they should resign was repeated.

The home game against bottom-of-the-table Crystal Palace was a disaster – the team lost 2–1. It was a dreadful end to a bad week. After the game, some of the vocal and frustrated fans congregated outside the offices section of the ground and chanted, 'Sack the board, sack the board, sack the board' – scenes that were recorded and broadcast on national television.

Malcolm MacDonald repeated his demand that Shepherd and Hall should resign and Kevin Keegan added his weight to the calls to resign by commenting that 'the fans own the club'.

As the weekend of 21 March approached, the directors still refused to resign. After all, Douglas Hall (via his holding company) was the majority shareholder and was thus technically in control of the club. The *News of the World* published another batch of damaging allegations against the two directors on Sunday 22 March. They were alleged to have said that they liked the fans to get drunk because they owned the bars in which the fans drank and hence were able to extract more profit from the same fans.

On Monday 23 March, the non-executive directors of Newcastle United plc met in an all-day meeting. It was later announced that Shepherd and Hall had resigned. Local television news carried more interviews with fans in the town centre, all of whom said that they were pleased to see the two directors go. The following day, Sir John Hall, Douglas's father and the former club chairman, was re-appointed club chairman until the end of the current season.

Sir John held a press conference on the Tuesday in which he expressed anger at the way that the two directors had been treated by the press and by the fans. It was pointed out that both Douglas and Freddie had made a massive contribution to the development of the club including much of the behind-the-scenes work involved in bringing both Alan Shearer and Kenny Dalglish to the club. Sir John conceded that the two directors had acted foolishly but he deeply resented their hounding from office by 'mob power'.

As the league season progressed, the team's performance showed little sign of improvement. The one high point was the FA Cup semi-final defeat of Barnsley which guaranteed Newcastle a place in the 1998 FA Cup Final. At the conclusion of the game, team manager Kenny Dalglish defiantly dedicated the win to 'Douglas and Freddie'.

During the summer of 1998, the fans' attention was drawn away from Newcastle United and towards the World Cup in France. Then there was a development in the week following the end of the World Cup. On 15 July, the Board of the plc met at a secret location and speculation grew among the fans that the secrecy may be because Hall and Shepherd were about to be reinstated as directors.

A press release was issued on 24 July that the two directors had indeed been reinstated. The two men issued a statement to the fans. Freddie Shepherd said that he and Douglas had been 'very stupid' but qualified their statement by saying that with them sharing 65 per cent of the company's stock, 'it was always going to be difficult with us on the outside.'

The news was reported in the national as well as on local television, and cameras focused on their reserved parking spaces outside the office section of St James Park, the company's home ground. The point was made that even although they had technically resigned in the spring, in reality the two had never really left.

When the fans were interviewed for the television news, opinion was somewhat more divided than it had been when they had previously called for their resignations. Some maintained their defiance whilst others seemed to accept that the club needed good management and that Hall and Shepherd had proved to be competent in the past.

Glossary

Acquisition The purchase of the entirety of one business's shares by another. The acquired business becomes a subsidiary of the acquirer.

Added value The difference between the full cost of a product and its financial value to the market. High added value is one of the objectives of strategy. It tends to be measured in terms of profit.

Annual report and accounts Audited annual communication between a limited company and its shareholders. In the UK, it has five compulsory statements by law (the chairman's statement, the auditors' statement, the profit and loss statement, the balance sheet and the cash-flow statement).

Augmented benefits Benefits added to core (or basic) benefits that are intended to differentiate a product.

Backward vertical integration Acquisition of or merger with a supplier.

BCG matrix (Boston Consulting Group matrix) Framework used to rationalize and understand a business's product portfolio. It divides products according to their market share and the rate of market growth. Four categories are identified: *stars* (high market share in high growth market); *cash cows* (high market share in low growth market); *question marks* (low market share in high growth market) and *dogs* (low market share in low growth market).

Benchmarking A collection of techniques used to compare certain aspects of business practice and the transfer of good practice procedures from benchmark companies to 'followers'.

Business ethics An area of research in which the nature of the relationship between business organizations and their role as moral agents is explored. It also describes research into the interface between business organizations and their social constituencies.

Capital The finance used to invest in a business with a view of making a return from it in future years. It is used to purchase the other resource inputs that enable an organization to carry out business activity.

Change agent One of the models of change management wherein the change process is overseen and managed by a single individual (the change agent). Offers the advantages of specialist management of a change process and the personification of the need for change.

Collaboration Businesses are said to collaborate when, instead of (or perhaps as well as) competing, they choose to work together in pursuit of both parties' strategic objectives.

Competences The abilities that an organization possesses that enable it to compete and survive in an industry. It includes an element that is tangible (its physical resource base) and another which is intangible (know-how, networks, etc.).

Competitive advantage The ability of an organization to out-perform its competitors. It can be measured in terms of superior profitability, increase in market share or other similar performance measures.

Competitive positioning (school of thought) The approach to business strategy that argues that an organization's success in strategy rests upon how it positions itself in respect to its environment. This is in contrast to the resource-based approach.

Core competences Competences are core when they become the cause of the business's competitive advantage. Also called distinctive capabilities.

Corporate reports Same as annual report and accounts (*see above*).

Cost benefit analysis One of the non-financial tools sometimes used in evaluating strategic options. It involves weighing up the benefits that will arise from a course of action against its costs.

Cost leadership (in generic strategy framework) The approach to business that seeks to achieve higher than industry-average performance by keeping unit costs lower than those of competitors. It is characterized by an emphasis upon the high volume production of standard products.

Critical success factors (CSFs) Those features owned by an organization that are the cause of its superior performance. Management approach to CSFs is to lock them in as far as possible.

Culture The character or personality of an organization. A culture can be understood by examining its manifestations under the categories of the cultural web.

Deliberate strategy Strategy that is planned in advance and which follows a rational process through each stage from analysis through to implementation.

Demerger The disposal of a business (usually a subsidiary) by making it into a stand-alone business and selling it off, usually via a flotation.

Differentiation (in generic strategy framework) The approach to business that seeks to achieve higher than industry-average performance by being distinctive rather than cheap (more distinctive than competitors). It presupposes that markets will pay more for extra product features.

Distinctive capability *See* Core competence.

Diversification Business growth that involves developing new products for new markets.

Economies of scale The benefits gained in unit costs (cost per item) of increases in size, and hence, the dilution of fixed costs.

Emergent strategy Strategy that is not planned in advance and that arises from a consistent pattern of behaviour.

Entry barriers The obstacles that a new entrant to an industry needs to negotiate in order to gain market entry. Examples include the cost of capital, the legal and regulatory obstacles, access to supply and distribution channels, the costs of competing (especially lack of scale economies), etc.

Environmental analysis Essentially the same as strategic analysis – an analysis of an organization's internal environment and its external macroenvironment and microenvironment.

External analysis The analysis of the external environments in which an organization exists (micro and macro) with a view to identifying opportunities and threats.

External growth Growth of a business by merger or acquisition (in contrast to organic or internal growth).

Factors of production Inputs into an organizational process that make normal operation possible (otherwise called resources).

Fiscal policy Regulation of a national economy by the use of government revenues and expenditure.

Five forces analysis A conceptual framework for understanding an organization's position in respect to the forces in its microenvironment. Can be used to explain the structure of the industry and the performance of competitors within it.

Focus strategy (in generic strategy framework) Competitive advantage gained through serving one (or few) market segments.

Forward vertical integration Merger with or acquisition of a customer.

Franchising An arrangement for business growth where the idea or format is rented out (from a franchiser to a franchisee) rather than directly developed by the originator of the idea.

Generic strategy A distinctive posture that an organization adopts with regard to its strategy. It is suggested that superior performance arises from adopting a cost leadership or differentiation strategy with either a narrow or broad product and market scope.

Globalization The most extensive stage of business development in which an organization's interests are spread throughout the world and are configured so as to compete and respond to differing customer requirements in many different national and local cultures.

Horizontal integration Merger with or acquisition of a competitor.

Hostile takeover An acquisition attempt that is not supported by the board of the target company.

Human resource One of four resource inputs that can be deployed to help create competitive advantage. Comprises the employees and any other people's skills that are used by the organization (such as consultancy skills that it has access to).

Hybrid strategy An approach to generic strategy that adopts elements of both cost leadership and differentiation.

Implementation The part of the strategic process that involves carrying out the selected strategy. It involves making the requisite internal changes and reconfiguring the organization's resource base to make it possible.

Incremental change Organizational change that is carried out in many small steps rather than fewer large steps.

Industry A group of producers of close substitute products. The players in an industry compete against each other for resource inputs and in product markets.

Industry analysis Part of strategic analysis. The analysis of an industry, usually using the five forces framework, with a view to gaining a greater understanding of the microenvironment.

Intangible resources Sometimes called intellectual resources – resource inputs that are not physical but which can be amongst the most important at causing competitive advantage. Examples include patents, legal permissions, licences, registered logos, designs, brand names, etc.

Integration The collective name given to mergers and acquisitions.

Intellectual resources *See* Intangible resources.

Internal analysis Part of strategic analysis (along with external analysis) wherein the internal parts are examined for strengths and weaknesses. The value chain framework is often used to assist the process.

Internal growth Growth in the size of a business without the use of mergers and acquisition. It involves the reinvestment of previous years' retained profits in the same business venture.

Internationalization Business growth involving development across national borders. Can be achieved by using market entry strategies such as exporting, direct investment, international joint ventures, alliances or franchising.

Joint ventures A collaborative arrangement between two or more companies. JVs tend to be for limited time periods, usually for a project or similar. Can also take the form of multi-partner consortia.

Just in time An operational philosophy which aims to carry out (usually) production without any waste. Sometimes called stockless production.

Key issues The issues that 'fall out of' the SWOT analysis which is, in turn, the summary of the strategic analysis. In practice, key issues are those issues that are the most pressing, the most important and the most critical.

Licensing The renting-out of a piece of intellectual property so that the licensee enjoys the benefits of the licensor's innovation upon the agreement of a royalty payment. Most commonly applied to recipes, formulations, brands (such as lager brands), etc. Not to be confused with franchising.

Macroenvironment The outer 'layer' of environmental influence – that which can influence the microenvironment. It comprises four categories of influence – political, economic, sociodemographic and technological.

Market The group of customers that a business or industry can sell its outputs to. Can also mean the specific part of a total market that an individual business sells to. In economics, market is taken to mean the 'place' or arena in which buyers and sellers come together.

Market segmentation The practice of subdividing a total market up into smaller units, each of which shares a commonality of preference with regard to a buying motivation. Markets are segmented by applying segmentation bases – ways of dividing customers in a market from each other.

Market share The proportion (usually expressed as a percentage) of the market for a product type held by a supplier to the market. Can be defined in terms of value or volume.

Mergers A form of external growth involving the 'marriage' of two partners of (usually) approximately equal size. The identities of both former companies are submerged into the new company.

Microenvironment The near or immediate business environment that contains factors that affect the business often and over which, individual businesses may have some influence. Usually comprises competitors, suppliers and customers.

Mission statements A formalized statement of the overall strategic purpose of an organization.

Near environment *See* Microenvironment.

Objectives The state of being to which an organization aims or purposes. It is the end to which strategy aims.

Operational objectives To be distinguished from strategic objectives. The level of objective which tends to be short- to medium-term in timescale and which have the sole purpose of helping to achieve the higher level strategic objective.

Organic growth *See* Internal growth.

Paradigm The worldview or way of looking at the world held by an individual or organization. It is a very powerful determinant of the culture and behaviour (and hence performance) of a business.

PEST analysis The key stage in macroenvironmental analysis. It involves auditing the macroenvironment for political, environmental, sociodemographic factors and technological influences.

Planned strategies *See* Deliberate strategy.

Portfolio Can refer to either the spread of interests in respect to products and markets. The principle behind any portfolio is to spread opportunity and risk with a view to making the organization less vulnerable to trauma in any one product or market segment and to enable it to be in the position to quickly exploit any opportunities.

Prescriptive strategy *See* Deliberate strategy.

Price elasticity of demand The relationship between the price of a product and the quantity of the product sold. Price elastic products are those whose quantity sold is relatively price responsive. Price inelastic products are those where a change in price would be expected to bring about a proportionately lower change in quantity sold.

Product The output of an organization intended for consumption by its markets. The result of the adding value process.

Profit and loss account One of the three compulsory financial statements in a company annual report. The P&L statement reports on the total sales, the costs incurred in creating those sales and hence (by subtraction), the profit made over a reporting period.

Quality Usually defined as 'fitness for the purpose'. It is not to be defined in terms of luxury or premium.

Related diversification External growth by developing new products for new markets. Related diversification suggests that the new products or markets have something in common with existing products or markets such that the risk of the diversification is lessened. Related diversification is in contrast to unrelated diversification.

Resource-based approach A way of understanding the source of competitive advantage as arising from the way in which an organization obtains and deploys its resources to build and develop core competences.

Resources The key inputs into an organization that enable normal functioning to take place. There are four categories of resource – physical (e.g. stock, land, buildings, etc.), financial, human and intangible (or intellectual).

Selection of strategy The second stage in the overall strategic process which takes the information gained in the strategic analysis and uses it to evaluate options and to decide upon the most appropriate option.

Stakeholders Any person or party that can affect or be affected by the activities or policies of an organization.

Stakeholder theory The belief that the objectives of an organization are determined by the relative strengths of the various stakeholders.

STEP analysis *See* PEST analysis.

Stockholder position The belief that business objectives should be determined predominantly for the financial benefit of the owners (shareholders). In practice, this position is taken to mean that the objectives of a business should be to maximize its profits.

Strategic alliances A collaborative arrangement between (usually) two businesses where part of all of the two companies' value chains are shared for mutually-beneficial strategic purpose.

Strategic analysis The first part of the strategic process. Its purpose is to gather information about a business's internal and external environments so that sufficient information is available to make possible the informed evaluation of options.

Strategic groups The subgroups within an industry that compete head on with each other for the same types of customers or for similar resource inputs. The members of a strategic group will normally consider an ongoing monitoring of each other's activities to be an essential part of their strategic analysis.

Strategic implementation *See* Implementation.

Strategic objectives In contrast to operational objectives, strategic objectives are those pursued at the highest level of an organization. They concern the whole organization, are concerned with the overall product and market scope, and tend to concern longer time scales than operational objectives.

Strategic options Generated as part of the second stage of the strategic process (evaluation and selection). The options that are considered as possible courses of action for the future.

Strategic process One way of looking at strategy is to conceptualize it as an iterative process. According to this view, the process has three distinct stages – strategic analysis, strategic evaluation and selection and then finally, strategic implementation.

Strategic selection *See* Selection.

Strategy There are a number of definitions of strategy, perhaps best understood in terms of Mintzberg's five Ps – *plan, ploy, pattern, perspective* and *position*. A strategy is usually taken to mean the process that is performed in order to close the gap between where an organization is now and where it aims to be in the future.

Strengths Those internal features of an organization that can be considered to add to its ability to compete in its strategic group (or industry) and to increase its competitive advantage. Strengths are positive attributes that an organization owns.

Structure The term used to describe the shape of an organization. In strategy, a consideration of structure usually refers to its height, width, complexity and the extent to which it is decentralized.

Stuck in the middle A phrase used to describe the position of an organization that, in respect to the generic strategy framework, is neither purely cost leadership nor differentiation. It has been argued that to be stuck in the middle is to expose an organization to the probability or returning below-average profits although this view has been challenged.

Substitute products Products that provide identical or comparable benefits to those of the organization's products. Substitutes can be either direct (being of the same substance and providing the same benefits) or indirect (being of different substance but providing the same benefits).

Supply chain Not to be confused with the value chain. Usually refers to the entire path that a product and its component parts takes from the primary industry stage to when it is sold to the final consumer on the chain.

Synergy The effect that is observed after two or more parties (e.g. businesses in a merger) come together and the whole becomes greater than the sum of the parts. Sometimes expressed as 2 + 2 = 5.

Unrelated diversification External growth by developing new products for new markets. Unrelated diversification suggests that the new products or markets have little or nothing in common with existing products or markets such that the risk of the diversification is increased, but that portfolio benefits are maximized. Unrelated diversification is in contrast to related diversification.

Value adding *See* Added value.

Value chain analysis A conceptualization of the internal activities of an organization. The framework divides the internal activities of an organization into two categories – those that directly add value (primary activities) and those that support the primary activities (support or secondary activities). The analysis of an organization's value chain is intended to show up the strategic importance of any key linkages or any blockages – points where value is added less efficiently than it might be.

Vertical integration Merger with, or acquisition of a supplier (backward vertical integration) or a customer (forward vertical integration).

Waste Anything that does not add value in an organizational process (such as machine inefficiencies, tooling up and tooling down, bad quality, stock, etc.)

Weaknesses Those internal features of an organization that can be considered to detract from its ability to compete in its strategic group (or industry) and to reduce its competitive advantage. Weaknesses are negative attributes that an organization owns.

Index

Tutor Support material is available....

A free lecturer's supplement containing:

- *Guidelines*
- *Model answers*
- *Solutions to activities*
- *Ideas for development of case studies*

is also vailable either as **hard copy** or is **downloadable from the BH website (password protected)** from Autumn 1999.

To order a **Tutor Resource Pack for Business Strategy**, please contact our Management Marketing Department, quoting **ISBN 07506 4515 6**, on:

Tel: 01865 314477
Fax: 01865 314455
E-mail: bhmarketing@repp.co.uk